Thrive in the Coming Dark Age

How to Build the Ultimate Survival Homestead

By Former Army Ranger Instructor and Engineer
Joshua Morris, M.S.

Copyright©2023 by Joshua Morris
All Rights Reserved.
No Part of this book may be reproduced in any form or by any electronic or mechanical means, including information storage and retrieval systems, without written permission from the author, except for brief quotations in a book review.

Illustration 1: Author on the Far Left, Faces of Others Obscured to Protect Privacy

For Our Fallen:
It appears Futile to Fight the Darkness...
When Standing in the Light it Seems
That Darkness Indeed Covers all Things
So Against the Darkness we Break our Bodies Young and Old
And Bring back Stories of the Heroic and the Bold
Who Fought with Courage and Died Well
But to Save us Died at the Gates of Hell
Though Perished not these Intrepid Beings
But Instead were Carried on Angel's Wings
And not Forgotten, not for a Single Day
As we Earn Their Sacrifice Each in our Own Way

                                                         -Joshua Morris

Table of Contents

Chapter 1: The Descent into Chaos **8**

Chapter 2: The Coming Dark Age **18**
    The Obvious Decline of Western Civilization 18
    Effects of Resource Scarcity 23
        The Syrian Example 23
        The Ukrainian Example 24
        The African Example 26
    Four Scenarios for the Future of World Civilization 28

Chapter 3: What is the Earth's Carrying Capacity? **32**
    Carrying Capacity Chart 32
    What Should Humans do to Survive this Dilemma? 36
    How will you survive the Descent into Chaos? 38
    Understanding the Coming Situation 40

Chapter 4: Choosing a Retreat Location **44**

Chapter 5: Water **48**
    Rainwater Catchment 50
    Gravity Flow 53
    Groundwater 54
    Windmills and Hand-Pumps 57
        Equipment and Erection 60
        Hand Pump installation (attachable to windmill) 63
    Solar Pumps 65
    Ponds 70

Chapter 6: Introducing the Homebunker: **75**
    The Basics of Masonry Construction 78
        Planning Considerations for building a Bunker 78
        Foundations 83
        Bunker Walls 86
        Bunker Roof 90
        Concealment considerations 97
        Passive Solar Heating and Cooling 98

    Active Heating of your Home 105

    Vertical air exchange 109

Chapter 7: Agriculture and Sources of Protein 110

    Livestock 111

        Grazers 112

        Rabbits 123

        Chickens 125

        Livestock Guardian Dogs 128

    Hunting for Protein 129

        Hunting Big Game, post-collapse considerations 130

        Small Game and Trapping 137

Chapter 8: Sources of Carbohydrates 140

    Nut Trees as Carbohydrates 141

        Making Flour from Nuts 144

    Cattails as a Major Food Source 144

    Planting Grain Without Machinery 145

    Survival Vegetable Plot 146

Chapter 9: The Homestead Dairy 155

    Nutrition for Dairy Animals 158

    Caring for the health of your dairy animals 162

    Harvesting and Processing Milk 165

        Butter 165

        Making Cheese 167

Chapter 10: Preserving Food 170

    Building the Root Cellar.. 170

    Stocking and Caring for a Root Cellar 175

    Canning Food 177

    Dry Curing Food 179

        Dry Curing a Ham 179

        Jerky 180

        Curing Fish 181

    Smoking Meat 181

Hot Smoking 181

Cold Smoking 182

Chapter 11: Electricity **184**

Determining your Energy Needs 184

Efficiency..186

Appliances...186

Designing your Off-grid Power System 188

Batteries..188

Solar..191

Wind Power 196

Hydro-Electricity and Micro-Hydro 202

Charge Controllers 207

Inverters..209

Solar Hot Water Heating 211

Chapter 12: Transportation **214**

Pack Animals 215

Solar-Powered Utility Vehicles..217

Chapter 13: Security...**220**

Rules of Engagement and When to Shoot 221

A Few Scenarios 221

Escalation of Force Starts with Discreet Behavior 223

Shaping Your Homestead Location 223

The Double Line in the Sand Technique 224

Obstacles...228

Key Terrain 229

Chapter 14: The Gear Locker **231**

Firearms 232

Zeroing your rifle..236

Optics and Lasers 238

Night Vision and Thermals 241

IR lasers...245

Radios 247

5

- Body Armor 249
- Drones 255
- Cameras and Early warning Devices 258

Chapter 15: Making the Leap, How to afford your Rock n' Roll Survival Lifestyle!!! 260
- About the Author: 263

Chapter 1: The Descent into Chaos

There's a modern human psychological fallacy that infects most people. It's the idea that somehow giant problems like political corruption, nuclear proliferation, corporate greed, and environmental degradation are somehow impacted by our individual voting habits, our personal political arguments, and our social media posts that "spread awareness." But the truth is that we are like a bunch of fleas pretending to be in control of the dog that we are merely riding on. Most people could all use a dose of stoicism, and perhaps read some Marcus Aurelius. Instead of deluding ourselves, we need to evaluate the hazards that are in the road ahead, recognize the potential disasters that are bearing down on the future of civilization, and prepare now to deal with the implication of societal collapse, resource depletion, and human conflict.

Why is this important? Imagine and think deeply about what it feels like to be caught unprepared, to be swept up by chaos and events that are out of your control. Let me give you a glimpse of what it's like to witness a society in freefall, where everyone is suddenly a victim, either prey or predator. I'll take you there.

Illustration 2: The author (right) in Iraq in March of 2003, the dictator was on the run, total chaos was about to ensue. It's a story of the dark side of human nature and societal collapse.

It's strange sleeping in a dead man's sheets, resting your head on his pillow, with his family's belongings strewn about the floor... Childrens toys on the carpet, a woman's slipper in the doorway, a shattered family photo frame fallen from the nightstand, and putrid, rotting food in the powerless refrigerator in the next room. But when you have just invaded his country, routed his nation's armies, and been trying to sleep on his dirt, concrete, and shattered glass for weeks, then you sleep like a baby in his bed, even if he was there the night before. Germs and bed bugs are the last thing that you are worried about. It was April of 2003, and I was a scout-sniper squad leader. We had parachuted into the Republic of Iraq earlier in March. After weeks of action and little to no sleep, we were posted in the house of a of a dead Iraqi Baath party official and his family who had left behind everything. Of all the paths that fate can take us on, how does one man end up a victor and another a victim in the storm of chaos?

There are many scenarios that can bring chaos into our lives; pandemic, conflict, famine, and natural disaster. What does it feel like to watch this descent into chaos, the breakdown of law and order, the beginning of a New Dark Age? I have seen first-hand the consequences of this downward spiral in the Middle East, the Balkans, Latin America, and Africa. It can happen anywhere to anyone. This book is designed to help you survive and even thrive during difficult times using lessons from what I have practiced and observed in the dark corners of the world. Now back to the story...

It was early morning, and I was in the middle of a vivid mefloquine dream about being with my new wife in our apartment back in Italy, when I was rudely awoken by Specialist Butler. He was shaking my shoulder and whispering tensely "Sergeant, your turn. There has been some shooting." The sky outside the window was just beginning to lighten from black to purple and the stars had nearly faded. I had been sleeping in full gear, body armor on, with ammo pouches overflowing, frag grenades carefully taped, and my M-4 Carbine at my side. I jerked my weary body up off of the most comfortable bed I had slept in for 3 weeks. Strapping on my night vision, I stumbled towards the stairwell, stepping over a broken table lamp and a pile of clothes. I climbed the stairs to man the sniper rifle that we had placed on the rooftop balcony. As the sky turned from black to purplish blue, the dogs howled and the Islamic "Adhan" call to prayer echoed across the city towards the nearby airfield. "Damn, I hate it when I wake up in this place," I thought to myself. Dreams can take you anywhere in the world, but you will always wake up to the choices that you have made. Smoke billowed from a burned-out vehicle on the road below my perch, and I could just make out the silhouette of a lifeless body on the pavement. We were at the edge of the city of Kirkuk, close enough to see people walking in the dark to defecate in the bushes and fetch water from a nearby irrigation ditch. The airfield sat next to the city, and beyond that flat, bare farm fields. It was April of 2003 and the Iraqi Army had just fled from our sector, leaving a trail of burnt personnel carriers and smoking tank hulks. The morning was eerily quiet.

But then, just as the sun began to peak above the horizon, shots rang out at the far edge of the city. I could see a few tracers, but we were far from the action. "Come on and bring it," I mumbled under my breath. When in combat it is not uncommon to thirst for the action, the adrenaline, the power. It started as three or four bursts of automatic weapons fire, then there were three or four volleys. Periodically, the gunfire would continue, then stop, and then continue again later. Vehicle engines could be heard racing up the street several blocks over, light pickup trucks. I awoke my five-man team, and everyone joined me on the roof as the sky turned to light. The entrances downstairs were blocked and we placed a claymore remote-detonation mine facing the stairwell leading to the roof, just in case anyone tried to break in.

We made our report over the radio, but were ordered to hold our positions, do not engage. The Kurdish militias had entered the city, and revenge was theirs. They were in communication with the higher ups. Our orders were to treat them like an allied military force. The only problem was, on this day, they were not behaving like a real military, they were an armed group of marauders and looters. Law and order, and civilization in Babylon had broken down on that day and chaos ensued. The grim reaper was afoot. All day long, we saw pickups, taxis, and even motorcycles, speeding by with looted goods, household items, and weapons. One truck would speed by with AC window units, the next might have 3 sinks and a toilet in the back. One taxi had an anti-aircraft gun barrel hanging out a busted back window. Towards the afternoon, teenagers began pulling down electrical wires with plans to sell later as scrap metal. They were destroying their nation's infrastructure right in front of our eyes. All the while random gunfire would ring out, occasional screams could be heard, but not seen from our position. It was hard to just be an observer, but we obeyed our orders to hold our position in the house near the edge of the airfield; "Do not enter the city," we were told.

By the end of the day, the air was heavy with the acrid smell of gun smoke and burning tires from the city. Just then, across a large field from us in one of the three story apartments at the edge of the city, several shots rang out, we could hear shouting from inside the building, more gunfire, then screams. Four figures emerged from the ground floor, a woman and three children plus one baby that she carried. She rushed away from the building toward the irrigation ditch, with the children following like a row of frightened ducklings. A dark silhouette appeared in the second story window of the apartment building, and then emerged onto the apartment terrace. I looked through the team spotting scope and watched as a skinny militia man with a Kalashnikov shouted and gestured excitedly, as the woman put distance between herself and the building. How could we understand? Years of conflict and cultural divide had made these two ethnic groups into mortal enemies, waiting for the right moment to take revenge on the other. To us, it was a woman and her children, to them a subhuman enemy. Specialist Butler was on the sniper rifle now. "Take aim at the second story terrace of the southwest corner apartment building, in front of the third window from the left," I instructed him. Shots rang out from across the field, I scanned to the woman and her children, they were not hit. Were the militia men shooting at them? It wasn't clear, screw it, "Butler, engage!" "But our orders..." he whined in protest. Maybe after weeks in this country, he had lost his appetite for violence, but I was amped up, feeling the adrenaline in my veins. "I'll handle it, move aside," I told him as I took up his spot behind the rifle. Another burst of wild gunfire rang out from the Kalashnikov, followed by one decisive shot from my bolt action Remington 700 sniper rifle. The woman and her children disappeared safely down the long irrigation canal towards the Tigris River... Even now, exhilarating chills run from the tips of my fingers to the very top of my skull just thinking about the moment. The chemicals produced by the human body and brain during combat are more powerful and real than any drug, but the terror and reality of death surrounding battle will haunt the back of your mind like a silent demon for the rest of your life. For some people, and for myself, it provides motivation to fight back against the darkness and to work hard towards real goals like safety, stability, and protecting your loved ones.

When I remember the survivors like the woman and her children in the canal, I realize that they had become refugees in a shattered country. Who would help them? Would they make it past the next armed group of marauders? Would the children be sold like slaves or forced to fight as child soldiers for a terrorist army? I have no idea what happened to them. This is what happens when law and order break down. The storm of chaos is out there for everyone; it doesn't care about your creed, your skin color, your mother's love or your father's occupation. It only cares if you are at the wrong place on Earth and the wrong time in history.

A few days later, my platoon sergeant showed up in our sector to bring a resupply of food, water, ammunition, and something new; a satellite phone! "Call your wife," he said as he tossed me the phone. My wife and I had been married for just 9 months. We had met two years earlier as I was stationed in Northern Italy, and she waited for me there. I found a quiet spot and dialed her number. "Ciao Amore, come va?" I asked her (How is it going). "Ciao, mi manchi tanto!," (I miss you a lot) she responded, and she began to tell me about her day. I had to cut her off and explained that I didn't have a lot of time but that that I missed her and I was fine. "Stiamo avendo un bambino," she said hurriedly, which means, "we are expecting a baby!" I was overjoyed and filled with emotion; our first child was coming! I told her how excited I was and how much I missed her again and then our time was up. It was time to say goodbye all too quickly. I had to wipe away the tears and compose myself quickly before taking the satellite phone back to my boss.

I was lost in my own thoughts for the rest of the day, everything had changed. I would soon have a child of my own, and I had just witnessed someone else's wife and children lose their own father and be forced to become refugees. Most people don't come face to face with many of the world's 100+ million refugees, but for me, it was becoming all too real. These were people, just like me, and it could happen to any of us, and to any of our loved ones. I had just witnessed the results of a breakdown of law and order, due to a brutal conflict. But conflict is not the only threat on the horizon. Global warfare, pandemics, resource depletion, famine, nuclear conflict, natural disasters, and other crises are all capable of crushing societies, even ending civilization, and causing a New Dark Age. When this happens regionally, or God help us, globally, then it leads to chaos and the suffering of millions, or someday billions of refugees. Seeing someone else's family become refugees was painful enough. The thought of something like this ever happening to my own young family was something that I was unwilling to accept, and I am sure that you feel the same way. This concept has motivated me to always strive for better preparedness and to understand what it takes to survive and even thrive under the most perilous circumstances. This book is a guide for those who take nothing for granted. It is for those who have their eyes wide open about the numerous threats to our civilization and our species. If you want to survive as the New Dark Age approaches, then pay close attention!

My fascination with humanity's descent into chaos began in the late 1990's and it has been the focus of my lifelong thirst for knowledge on the subject. Earlier in life, my education as a child growing up in the Midwestern United States had taught me that our society was constantly progressing to bigger and better things. Global progress meant that science and technology could solve our problems and feed a rapidly growing world population. After joining the Army at the age of 18, my travels would teach me that my education was largely wrong. Serving as an Army Ranger and a paratrooper, my first deployments included Central America, Africa, Bosnia and Kosovo. In the Balkans, burned out apartment buildings and factories dominated the skyline, and the residents had retreated to their more humble beginnings. Families had created safe havens by living in walled-in brick compounds, ringed by rusty wire and cinder block walls, topped with broken, mortared-in shards of glass. Luxury meant that there was a hand-pumped well in the center of the compound where you might see one of the skinny occupants taking a quick sponge bath or washing clothes by hand. Had these people not heard of our global march towards progress? Had we failed them? Surely, they represented humanity's past and not our future.

Fast forward to September 11, 2001. I was at a training area in Germany, preparing to go into "the box." That was what we called our maneuver training area where we were at the time preparing to parachute into a training exercise. I remember just prior to that exercise, discussing whether or not mass parachute assaults would ever be used again in combat. It seemed to me that we had moved beyond the need for such tactics and that humanity had progressed negating the need for the U.S. military to come to the rescue. Really, it was time to tackle bigger problems; climate change, habitat loss, social justice issues.... Then, late in the cool, crisp, sunny Bavarian afternoon, as we received our training "threat brief," the world suddenly changed. First there were just whispers, then our briefer, interrupted the training exercise to inform us that not one, but two planes had been flown into the world trade center. News of the third and fourth hijacked planes came later. There was little time for those in my unit to think about it, and news was not easily accessible (no smart phones). That night, our training went forward as scheduled, and I found myself on the breach team of a night raid, cutting through fences and kicking down doors. We had renewed vigor in every step, every shot fired seemed more important. After a few more days of vigorous training, we finally came back to catch up on news reports and soak in the magnitude of the disaster that was September 11th, 2001.

I think that the world changed for everyone on that day. Priorities shifted; world views were turned on their heads. Maybe global progress would not materialize after all. Perhaps science and technology would not be able to save us from ourselves. Feeding an increasingly hungry and over-populated world had seemed a daunting task before, but could we still hope to accomplish it while zealots dedicated themselves to bringing about the apocalypse? Further, were all of these issues, population growth, hunger, environmental destruction, social decay, zealotry, and terrorism, somehow related to each other and part of a grim future that humanity was creating for itself? Was this a future that did not fit into the paradigm of "global progress"?

I had little time to ponder the question. Fast-forward: March, 2003, was another turning point in my way of thinking. I found myself parachuting into Northern Iraq as the Iraqi Army was being pounded ferociously by B-52 bombers and AC-130 gunships. I remember thanking God that I was on the right side, as the ground shook during one of the hundreds of air strikes that we called in during that invasion. It is a humbling sight to watch as a government ceases to exist and a 500,000 man army abandons their weapons, tanks, and vehicles in the wake of their fearful retreat. It was as if the Ark of the Covenant had been opened to melt away the regime of Saddam Hussein.

Just after the fall of the regime, I remember escorting our commander to visit a hospital that needed our assistance. Next to the hospital was a dusty, run-down café with some plastic tables out front. There were three Iraqi soldiers, still in uniform, drinking Assam tea. Most other soldiers had shed their uniforms, so these three caught my attention. One of them kept staring at us confrontationally as if to say, "okay, now what, now where is my job, my paycheck?" I think that's what all Iraqi men were thinking. It wasn't long after that that Paul Bremer gave the answer, they were all fired! What I expected to see was a 21st century version of the Marshall Plan for the Middle East. I expected to see strict law and order, employment of Iraqis rebuilding their country, and an international effort to put things back in order. Instead, I witnessed the limitations of a mighty armada, human governments, bureaucrats, and leadership. I witnessed ineptitude at all levels, stagnation of action, 500,000 newly unemployed military-aged males on the street, followed by chaos and extremism filling the vacuum. A brutal regime was indeed toppled, but what followed was chaos, looting, petty vengeance, and convoys of stolen goods, pickups filled with air conditioners and flush toilets, Russian-made heavy machine guns, etc. No, we would not overcome humanity's flaws, or our brute instincts. In the real world, little has changed since the times of the Old Testament; humans are rarely noble, but much more often, they are savage. All you can do is prepare to deal with and protect yourselves from the savagery and chaos. The good shepherd values the sheepdog.

Still, in my mind, I did not blame our leaders, or the Iraqi people. I came to see the situation as something inevitable. The Iraqis never had much sense of hope to begin with, at least not hope based on reality. They had already lived for years with scarcity, hunger, oppression, and environmental degradation. Humans had been trashing Mesopotamia since Hammurabi was an infant. I think some of them were hoping for some kind of a miracle, maybe something like what they had seen in Hollywood movies; the "Top Gun" ending followed by fancy American cars, spacious homes, green fields, and high tech farming equipment. I remember driving through crowded Iraqi streets with teenage boys shouting, "Hello how are you!" "I love Amereekee!" and "Good Bush!" (referring to our president) It was surreal. Were they naïve? Are we naïve?

Global progress would suggest that the Iraqis might at least be able to move in the direction of such prosperity, and the United States certainly threw plenty of money at the problem. I began to ask myself, "Why do such places still languish when global progress promises a brighter future, innovative solutions, and stability?" After seeing the Balkans destroy itself and then the Middle East descend into chaos, I was on a mission to search for answers. What is it about human civilization that leads us to collapse? Is this something that is inevitable? Is the idea of modern "global progress" realistic or is it a way that we try to make ourselves feel better? Did past civilizations tell themselves the same thing? Babylon, Greece, Easter Island, the Maya and the Anasazi; did they also see themselves as part of some march towards never-ending human progress? Are we different? If our predicament is so dire, so predictable, then how should an individual deal with it, and keep one's family safe when the descent into chaos begins? After Iraq, finding the answers to these questions became my obsession. I had already seen the destruction, the death, the chaos. I had learned much about how to survive, to protect one's self, to fight, and destroy the enemy. But why is there a need for these primitive skills? Had we not progressed beyond the basic survival instincts of beasts?

To find these answers, I hit the books hard. With my Army tuition assistance, I studied History, with a minor in Anthropology, graduating Summa Cum Laude from Columbus State

University in 2010. This taught me about the cycles of human civilization, innovation, growth, resource depletion, collapse, chaos, survival, societal rebirth, etc. I found that there are many confusing variables in human civilizations, but there are also certain constant patterns. These patterns are based almost entirely on natural resource consumption. Innovation in the utilization of these natural resources is what allows society to flourish. When society flourishes, it depletes the very resources that it depends on, and then it collapses. The Anasazi innovated to use water and nutrients in the desert, until the resource was depleted. The Easter Islanders innovated to use the trees and fertility of their island to flourish, until they cut down every last tree. We have innovated beyond primitive human imaginations, using petroleum, chemical fertilizers, and rare minerals to flourish globally, but to what end? I knew that history would not give me the entire picture; I needed to know more about the resource and innovation piece of the puzzle.

I decided to study Engineering, earning a Master's degree in 2012 from Missouri University of Science and Technology. It was a drastic shift in area of study, but to me, a logical one. History tells us where we have been in the past, and how we got there. My engineering studies focused on where we are in terms of resources, and how we can move forward with or change the utilization of those resources. These studies taught me about the innovation that built civilizations, including our own. It also taught me that the resources we depend on are surprisingly measurable and finite. My studies have taught me that, without a doubt, these resources will not last another 100 years. It's a simple math problem. Children born into this century, children that are learning to walk today, will run out of things like petroleum, phosphorous (critical fertilizer), and lithium in their lifetimes. They will also have to confront diminishing vital resources such as fertile soil, potable water, and forests. Think about that for a moment; take away all of the plastic in your home, take away the food produced with fertilizer, take away the gas in your car, and everything delivered by gasoline. You would have to make major adaptations in technology, or live like a hunter-gatherer, or you would die. But what if I told you that there was precious time for you to adapt; would you use that time wisely?

Humans have overcome similar adversity in the past, first by expanding into virgin lands, and later through the green (agricultural) revolution, leveraging improved crops, fertilizers, and mechanization. Our situation today is different, in that there is no more suitable virgin land to expand into. While innovation has saved us in the past, I believe that there are limits to what human innovation can do, in the face of extreme scarcity of resources and growing populations. When such scarcity begins to cause poverty, hunger, and sickness, it then leads to conflict, chaos, and collapse.

In the end, my quest brought me back to where I started. While the causes and nature of the conflicts that I witnessed around the globe are complex, there is no denying that resource scarcity and competition played a huge role, the biggest role, in these conflicts and those that have followed. With an ever-increasing human population and continued depletion of the resources that our civilization is built on, it seems that human conflict will likely not decrease, and that the idea of continued "global progress" will not keep our families safe and prosperous. Instead, basic survival and creative innovation are the traits required to thrive in an increasingly resource-deprived and chaotic world.

Having come full circle on my studies, I decided to focus my efforts on teaching my family those skills and traits that I have identified as being critical to thrive, despite the coming adversity. We have lived an off-grid, self-reliant lifestyle for over a decade. Our success can be credited largely to a combination of the best modern innovations, such as solar power, and greenhouse agriculture, combined with the best traditions from our past, including windmill water-pumping and passive solar heating, just to name a few. Our creed is self-reliance, developed from the knowledge that all past civilizations have flourished, centralized their efforts, depleted their resources, and failed. To counter this, we think that human survival depends on de-centralization, self-sufficiency, and good stewardship of the land. Any interruption to the long supply chains that keep our cities fed and happy is a disaster that will affect millions. On the contrary, an independent homestead or community producing all of its own necessities may fail, but it affects far fewer individuals, and becomes easier to resolve with a little outside assistance from neighboring communities or homesteads. In addition, inhabitants of a large city will waste and deplete resources without even knowing it. On a country homestead, we have found that we are much less likely to throw away food when we grew it ourselves, or leave an un-needed light on when we know that we might drain our battery bank. Leaving the water running when you have just a 1000 gallon tank for the entire family is unthinkable. Extending this idea a little further, I know that I cannot afford to lose any topsoil when I know that my children's children will need it someday, and that every drop out of our aquifer is a blessing.

This is just a taste of the type of knowledge that I hope to share in this book. At the same time, I know that this type of lifestyle, and this type of change will not be easy. Human change in the past has never been easy; the Renaissance came only after the Dark Ages took their toll. With this in mind, I have provided for you, a full range of survival and thrival tools in this book. In a way, they tell the story of my own experiences. They include a detailed description of what to expect. I will elaborate on what it is like when a country descends into chaos, based on my own wartime experiences and observations. I will share what I know about resource scarcity and promising innovations that may help you and your family. There are many detailed descriptions on how you and your family, loved ones, and community, can be more self-reliant. This is a lifestyle that is both critical for human survival, and that can be fulfilling at the same time.

Finally, I will share what I know about survival and security implementation that I learned from my training as an Army Ranger, Ranger Instructor, Infantry Officer, and Engineer Officer. I have spent years in the third world and understand how it works. My degree in history was focused on how past civilizations fell into chaos and how certain individuals survived. I studied Geo-Engineering for my Master's degree and have spent the past decade and a half engineering homes, farms, and essential services to be self-sufficient and sustainable. I want to share with you the expertise that I have gained during a lifetime of experience in the field of survival, high-level self-sufficiency, and informed preparedness. This is designed to first, avoid conflict in the face of resource scarcity and societal chaos. Second, should conflict become unavoidable, this security advice may provide you with some of the tools and concepts that will keep you and your loved ones safe.

We are at a time in human history unlike any that has ever been seen. A careful examination of history, and society's relationship with resources and our natural environment, gives important clues about what our future holds. As we witness nation after nation descend into chaos, how will you prepare for the future? I have spent my life studying this exact scenario. This book is designed to give you the tools to achieve self-sufficiency and survive in an uncertain and chaotic world. This book is for survivors; this book is for you!

Chapter 2: The Coming Dark Age

    We have all been there; you catch something on the news in a far away country. It sounds frightening, but your life is busy, and what are the chances that it will affect your life? You are busy working towards your dreams in a first world country. But then the bad news continues, the problem worsens and then spreads from one country to the next. You begin to realize that you are not so insulated; after all, you are living in a global economy and a global society. Soon, the crisis is all that you hear about on the news. It may start as a virus in one country, violence in another, a shortage of materials in yet another, and a shortage of labor somewhere else. It is like watching a global train wreck in slow motion, and no one can stop it. You witness the crash of the stock market, see the fear in the eyes of your neighbors as they empty supermarket shelves, and you try to reassure your children that this will pass and good times will return. But will they truly ever return for good? Or are diseases, global conflict, and increasing resource scarcity the true hallmarks of the 21st century? The answer is yes, we are unfortunately entering a new dark age, where third world problems will come to America and to all first world nations.

    How will you survive as the third world comes to your neighborhood? We witnessed what happened to city dwellers during the Covid-19 pandemic. They were by far the most affected. Instead of being in the middle of the rich abundance of the city, they were in the middle of the danger, and at the end of long supply chains, far from natural resources. To survive this "Neo-Dark Age", you need a new paradigm, a new way of thinking. You need to create an island of self-sufficiency and abundance for yourself and your loved ones.

    This book is a guidebook that takes you along that journey of self-sufficiency to lead you to your own life of self-sustainment, independence, and thrival, even in the midst of economic hardship, chaos , and even societal collapse. Together we will examine the changing conditions in our society, and what changes you can expect to see in your lifetime. The third world has existed all around us for as long as anyone can remember, and it should be no surprise that in hard times, it will encroach on our own communities, no matter how remote or prosperous we think ourselves to be. This book describes how security is achieved in those conditions and how prosperity can be attained and protected. I have already seen this achieved by people in many desperate countries and will describe how it is accomplished in this book. We will also look at examples from history of those who survived the collapse of their civilization, adapting and thriving in a rapidly changing world. Finally, this book will guide you on how to create your own environment of abundance, shaping your surroundings to provide ample water, food, shelter, security, and basic comforts.

The Obvious Decline of Western Civilization

    For most of us, the course of human civilization is unalterable. While we should continue to do what we believe is morally right, the reality is that our influence on our 8 billion roommates on this planet is severely limited. So, like any problem that cannot be avoided, we deal with it best by facing it head on. What is the real source of the vast multitude problems faced by our species today? Many politicians and pundits point to the ailing economy, political and religious extremism, or climate change. In reality these issues are all serious, but they don't get at the root of the human predicament. They are symptoms of a much bigger, yet obvious problem. The Human population has skyrocketed in the past 100 years in a completely unprecedented way. We have adapted and used technology and imagination to push our natural resources to the limits of production capacity. As a result, we now see a precarious situation in which pandemics and other vectors will flourish and resource scarcity has begun to place an increasing strain on human communities and nations whose populations and birthrates are bursting at the seams.

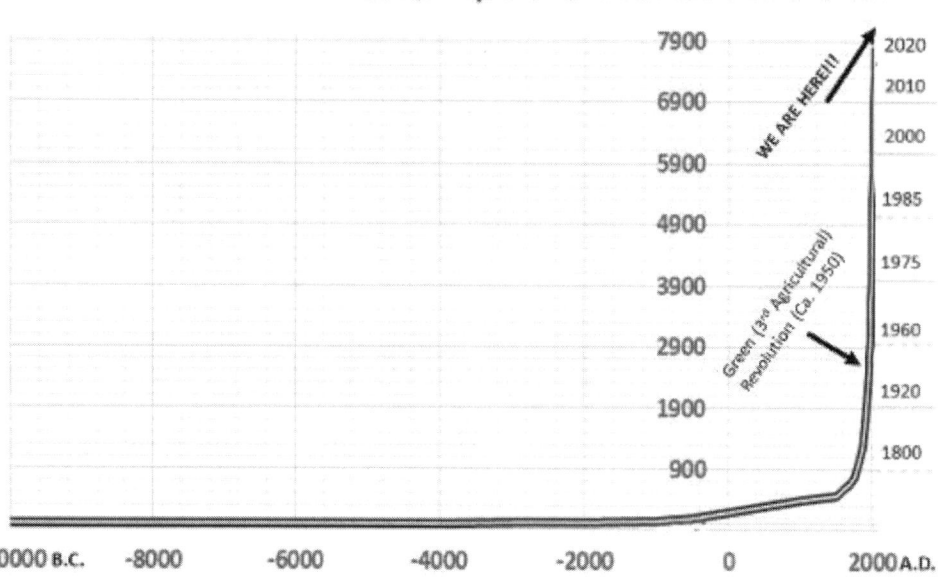

Figure 1: When any Biological Population, Human or Animal, Grows at this Rate, then a Population Correction is Imminent, Like Jumping off of a Cliff means that a Fall is Imminent

If any wild population of animal species were to show a population growth rate such as the one above, then wildlife biologists would know immediately that they were in for a crash. In the case of humans, we are able to innovate and modify our world in a way that we can raise the planet's carrying capacity for humans. Nonetheless, there is a limit to this carrying capacity, even for a thinking, innovating, and reasoning species. But when you turn on the news, and you see significant portions of the world behaving in ways that defy reason and destroy innovation, then realize that we can be put right back into the category of a species that is once again subjected to the cruel laws of nature, natural selection, and the kind of death and suffering which kept our population below 1 billion souls for approximately 200,000 years of Homo Sapiens existence.

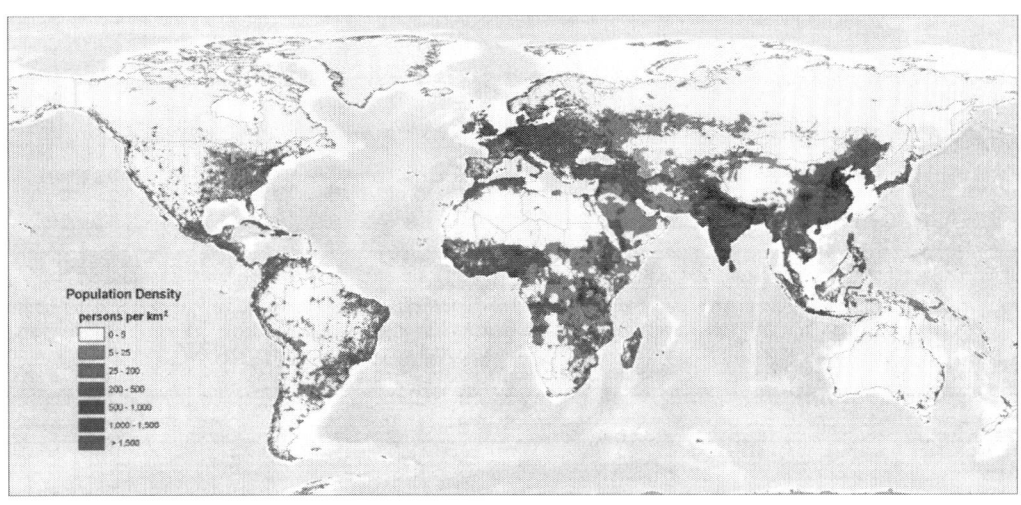

Figure 2: World Population Density Map, Population Density Exacerbates Resource Shortages and Societal Disruptions. -From the National Geographic Mapmaker "MapMaker: Population Density (nationalgeographic.org)" : July 27, 2023

This has become apparent first in parts of the globe where birthrates are highest and resources are most limited. China and India are by far the most densely populated areas on the planet. It is no surprise that they are often the source of new diseases. This isn't about race or culture but more about the science of population density in relation to the spread of disease. Parasites and vectors thrive where the host population is most abundant. Unfortunately, the rest of the world is becoming more densely populated with each passing year. The Middle East and much of Africa have witnessed growth rates as high as 3 to 5 percent annually for years. At these rates, the doubling time for populations is about 15 to 20 years. When a population doubles this quickly in an area such as the desert or on top of already exhausted cropland, then basic resources become scarce, and just as demand for basics like food and water is growing, availability declines due to environmental degradation. This situation is often exacerbated by drought or climatic events. Disease will follow. Whether or not these catastrophes are attributed to anthropogenic climate change is not the fundamental question, because the real issue is overpopulation, coupled with resource scarcity, with or without drought. It is a very simple equation where the demand for resources begins to outpace the supply so quickly that the natural environment is simply consumed. This has been witnessed most blatantly in recent decades in places like Zimbabwe, Somalia, Afghanistan, Yemen, Libya, the Sudan, and Syria. Many other areas are on the brink of such scarcity; think of Egypt, Nigeria, Greece, Eastern Europe, and the Balkans.

Some of these warning signs from across the globe seem strikingly familiar to what has occurred prior to the downfall of ancient civilizations. In one example, Easter islanders depended on the trees and natural vegetation on their island for food, yet they cut down every last tree and cleared every forest until the island was barren and they had to resort to cannibalism and eating rats. In another instance, prior to the downfall of Rome, crime was rampant, and marauders from all across the ancient world traveled to Italy to plunder and pillage. Nevertheless, circuses, the modern-day equivalent of sports, attracted the full attention of citizens, right up to the last day of the empire. Finally, we can point to the Bronze Age collapse in ancient Greece, when Mycenean elites had spent centuries centralizing wealth and power, using their riches to build opulent palace complexes right next to shanty towns of more common people. By investing solely in their own comfort and not the prosperity of society as a whole, they created resentment and also an irresistible target for internal and external thieves and marauders. These are just a few brief examples of times when human nature leads to the inevitable downfall of a civilization. But it is frightening that our society is guilty of all of the above tragic flaws; overconsumption of finite resources, use of wealth only to elevate the elite class rather than society as a whole, and an unhealthy fixation on entertainment despite impending collapse.

    While civilizations have risen and fallen for millennia, a real threat to permanently end global civilization as we know it has only become apparent with the last several decades. What has changed? The answer is two-fold. First, technology has allowed one human to accomplish things quickly that would once require vast amounts of manpower. For example, one individual with a drone can monitor livestock miles away, or also with a drone, launch a hellfire missile and kill dozens. It takes just a few individuals to run a drill rig to bring ground water to the desert, or the same amount of people can also drop a nuclear weapon to kill millions in just seconds. With modern technology, the Earth can be very rapidly shaped and engineered to support more life, but it can also be destroyed even faster.

    In other words, what humans could once only imagine can now be made a reality because of technology. Technology today is like water, meaning that it will always find a way to trickle down and reach the lowest levels. Drones were once a tool for governments and wealthy nations. They are now on their way to ubiquity; even primitive terrorist organizations use them, and children play with them. We once believed that we could limit access to nuclear weapons and even thermal weapons technology, but these too are gradually finding a way into more and more hands. Because of this, the impact that humans have on one other and the planet is magnified. Some would say that we are simply more aware of our problems because of the internet and social media. In truth, most of the problems of western civilization have been magnified thanks to technology and the human population explosion.

    Unfortunately, human nature has not changed since the collapse of the Roman empire or the last pharaoh. This means that greed, hatred, jealousy, and blind ambition are still with us. There are certain social or even spiritual movements that would argue that we can permanently end these tendencies. New Age followers argue that we can all empathize to the point of gaining a single collective consciousness. Certain new-testament-only Christians might argue that we merely must turn the other cheek. But alas, pictures of ISIS beheading Christian children show us that the Old Testament is still applicable today when dealing with human nature. The Russian military and mercenaries have been turned loose on a modern western nation to rape and pillage and torture prisoners of war with sledgehammers or through castration. It is estimated that 9 million children are held in slavery worldwide. This all means that we have unfortunately not advanced as far as we sometimes think. Yes, the news, the video, and the pictures are out there; they are real, and people, it is time to get serious, and it is time to get tough. A frog thrown in boiling water will absolutely flip out, jumping and thrashing. Many of us today are instead like frogs placed in gradually heated water, who could even boil to death without perceiving the slow heating of our surroundings. Don't fool yourself, but instead pay close attention, and you will see that a boiling point is coming.

    This boiling point is largely due to our current human population explosion, which is truly alarming if you take a close look at the numbers. The collapse of ancient civilizations were merely micro examples of our current situation because modern civilization is so much larger due to the modern population explosion. It took from the dawn of modern humans 180,000 years ago until the year 1800 A.D., for the human population to reach 1 billion. This then took only 100 years to double, reaching 2 billion by the year 1900. Then it only took 50 years to double again to 4 billion just after World War II. Today we are double that number again at 8 billion at the time of this writing. Even though it took 180,000 years for our population to reach 1 billion souls, we now add another 1 billion about every 12 years.

    Now let's do a little math. It takes about 1 hectare (2.2 acres) of the Earth's arable land to feed, clothe, and shelter a human being. Granted some of us consume more than others, but this is the average. There are only 15 billion hectares of land on the planet, but 6 billion of those are wastelands; some are desert and still others are covered in ice or rocks. This leaves about 9 billion hectares of productive land on the planet. At our current rate of population growth, we should reach 9 billion souls by 2035. This means that the threshold of 1 productive hectare of arable land per person will be met and quickly surpassed by the year 2035 and 10 billion by 2050. Obviously, with population growth rates and resources being unequally distributed throughout the globe, many countries will exceed this threshold early, and this is already starting to happen.

Effects of Resource Scarcity
The Syrian Example

Nowhere are the effects unsustainable population growth more apparent than in the developing world. In the country of Syria, in 1980, the population stood at about 8 million individuals. In 2010, it had tripled to 24 million individuals. In order to feed such an explosion of added humanity, the Assad government successfully ventured into industrialized farming, or at least it seemed to be successful, at first. Rural electrification paved the way for electric water well pumps to remove water from the country's aquifer and irrigate the fields. Yields were extremely high through the 1990's and the rapidly growing population was fed and relatively content. The largely rural Sunni east fed the more urban coastal Shiites of the western part of the country. It seemed that technology again had raised the Earth's carrying capacity to support more humans. Believers in infinite human progress grinned from ear to ear as old cultural conflicts seemed to fade.

But then, at the dawn of the 21'st century, reality set in in Syria. All at once, farmers began calling pump installers across Syria. "Come fix my pump!" they would plead, but the pumps were not broken. Instead, the myth of unlimited resources was shattered when the aquifer proved all too shallow, and wells with new electrical pumps ran dry. In many places, it was dropping rapidly, by as much as 6 meters annually! The drop was so sudden and drastic that NASA's GRACE satellite, which detects gravity anomalies on the planet, detected a rapid decrease in the mass of the Earth's crust under the Syrian breadbasket due to the irreparable consumption of water from the aquifer. Small farmers with shallow wells were the first to fail. Deeper, more expensive wells would also succumb to the law of limited resources. By 2009, droughts began without the assistance that irrigation had previously provided. Many Sunni farmers fled their lands in the northeast for Damascus and the Alawite-ruled coast.

They found little welcome and no abundance of resources in urban areas. Failed farms means a failed economy, and the new refugees only put a greater strain on already limited resources. With no hope, no future, and help from the countries ruling class, they began the Syrian civil war. Many were also easy prey for violent Islamic extremists seeking recruits. By 2011, the uprising was in full swing.

In 2015, following the announcement by German Chancellor Angela Merkel that Germany was ready to host refugees, the exodus began. Not only Syrians, but also Afghans, Pakistanis, Yemenis, and a host of Africans began to flood Europe by the millions. Merkel somehow thought that Germany could provide relief from the war, and the situation would improve. I'm not criticizing the refugees at all. In fact, I would also flee to a more stable country if I were faced with that situation. What I criticize is the idea that we humans can go and ruin one country at a time, destroy one patch of this beautiful blue-green paradise, and then we can shuffle our people to another country where we will certainly ruin another country and another, until what? I'll let you decide how this ends.

While the terror threat is a factor, let us set this aside for a moment and examine the wisdom of Merkel's logic. We must first recognize that the problem in Syria was initially environmental, not social. In addition, this environmental predicament was a result of human overpopulation, and the use of technology and cheap electricity was a short term fix. However, regardless of technology, any biological population which has overshot its carrying capacity is certain to degrade its environment until that population is lowered by environmental resistance. This resistance may take the form of disease, starvation, war, etc. Once the carrying capacity of an area is lowered, it has been ruined or at least degraded to the point where the land and resources will not recover for decades or centuries. This is a biological phenomenon that applies to all species, and among humans of all nationalities.

As mentioned earlier, Earth's human population has skyrocketed at such an alarming rate that we are destined to rise above the carrying capacity of our terrestrial environment at some point, if we have not done so already. With this in mind, it is clear that the German Chancellor and her associates brought her country and in fact all of Europe one step closer to the brink of disaster, where exceeding the carrying capacity will undoubtedly lead first to environmental degradation and then human suffering, just like what is occurring in Syria. Any country that elects leaders with a similar mentality, in today's world of constrained resources, surely invites similar disaster. Many people here will cry for compassion or attempt to call out racism or xenophobia, but I can assure you that hard realities such as the Earth's limited carrying capacity, a failed harvest, or a hungry belly care as much about your race or cultural identity as does a starving lion. Scarcity, like the lion, is after us all, and we should plan accordingly. With relatively greater resources, lower population density, and an Ocean on both sides of the United States, you may wonder what we really have to worry about from these far-off abstract threats, but as I mentioned, overpopulation is a global phenomenon in a globalized society. When the dominoes really start to fall, they will not be stopped, not even by vast oceans.

The Ukrainian Example

Many readers might wonder what the Ukraine-Russia conflict has to do with scarcity. After all, Russia is swimming in natural gas and petroleum, and their population is less than half that of the United States. What has occurred is that world energy resources have become so valuable that those who control them, control the world. They may use this power to blast off into space, like Jeff Bezos, or vaccinate entire continents like Bill gates, or even fill outer space with trains of satellites like Elon Musk. But, in the case of Vladimir Putin, his aspiration was to turn back the hands of time, and forcibly reunite the Soviet Union, starting with the subjugation of Ukraine, subjugating the latter. In a world of plentiful resources, Putin's petrol could be shut off and he could easily be dethroned. But in a world where every drop of oil and gas is needed to produce food for 8 billion people and where every Chinese and Indian family aspires to drive their own family car, and where Americans demand to have any item delivered conveniently to their doorstep, we also cannot afford to turn off Vladimir's petrol pump. Yes, the U.S., U.K., and other countries may boycott, but the petrol will flow anyways to Germany, India, China, etc.

While we all know that oil and gas are finite fossil fuels, this situation does not mean that we are almost out of geological petrol now but we are nonetheless reaching peak oil. The concept of peak oil does not mean that one day you have fuel and the next day you do not. Instead, it means that supply slowly has a hard time meeting demand. You start to see supply interruptions, price spikes, government attempts to buffer prices, and you start to see conflict. Part of this conflict is caused by the warlord mentality. "I have a resource and you do not, therefore I can do as I please, rape, pillage, and destroy, and you, my neighbors, will comply and you have no choice but to continue to purchase my product."

Up to the invasion of Ukraine, we were subjected to speeches by Vladimir Putin justifying the invasion based on historical and cultural reasons, and still more speeches by Joe Biden about the moral importance of protecting Ukraine's border. Nonetheless, the true reason for the conflict is that until recently, Russia has supplied nearly 60% of the European Union's natural gas needs and 50% of their energy needs. Much of this fuel flowed through pipelines in the Ukraine, and Russia paid Ukraine around 2 billion dollars annually for using the pipelines. In recent years, the EU has shifted away from using their own fossil fuels and has even shuttered many of their nuclear plants. Once again, Germany, the largest among others, made a critical error in reducing their domestic supply of fossil fuels and depending on Russia for their fuel. Germans and others inadvertently financed the war and the atrocities that Putin has unleashed upon Ukraine.

The follies don't stop there. In December of 2021, just before the Russian invasion, Germany shut down half of its nuclear plants. They had planned to shut down the rest of their nuclear power by the end of 2022, just as Europe voiced the need to stop using Russian petrol. At the same time, France suspended operations at almost 1/3 of their nuclear plants at the end of 2021, because of technical issues. At best, this is poor timing by the leaders of these countries, which can be disastrous in a world of scarce resources. At worst, the warlords are in control of the game, and sinister forces set up a scenario where the warlord Putin could consolidate his control of European energy sources and put the E.U. and NATO in a stranglehold. Notably, Russia took control of Europe's largest Nuclear energy plant during the opening days of the war, in Zaporizhzhia, Ukraine. Now that Zaporizhzhia is on the front line of the war, it can be used as a bargaining chip, or it could be blown up to create the largest nuclear catastrophe that the world has ever seen. Clearly, this war is about energy, controlling ever-scarcer resources, and the rise of warlords.

If this were not bad enough, consider that the Ukraine also produces about 1/6th of the world's grain supply and 40% of the wheat for the World Food Program. Much of Ukraine's grain is earmarked for Africa and the Middle East, because of the high demand in those countries and the geographic proximity. Unfortunately, the Russian Navy controls the Black Sea, and it can use this to choke off this part of the world's grain supply. And why would it not, considering that Russia is also a huge exporter of grain. While this means that millions may starve as a result, Russia will profit because of higher grain prices. Not only has Russia held the world hostage by holding up this vital food supply, but they have even directly bombed Ukrainian grain storage and transport infrastructure in order drive up the price of their own exports and put pressure on the world to withdraw support for Ukraine. This kind of destructive hostage taking and the use of food as a weapon is a typical warlord tactic which is further enabled by fast-growing populations and strained resources.

The African Example

In African countries such as Somalia, the Central African Republic, The Congo, and Liberia, between 35 and 40 percent of all children are stunted both physically and mentally, because of malnourishment. Nowhere is the rise of warlords more apparent than in these countries, but what we have seen so far from African warlords thus far is only a preview. Scarcity in Africa manifests itself primarily in a lack of food, nutrition, and means of producing food. Africa holds by far the fastest growing population in the world and despite optimistic predictions, the population growth rate is actually not slowing. Chaos that is caused by scarcity is not due simply to a lack of food and other resources, but instead it is caused and exacerbated by the fight for control of these increasingly scarce and therefore increasingly valuable resources. In other words, a starving population is seen by a warlord as an opportunity to control food resources and wield power in the same way that controlling scarce natural gas supplies is a way of wielding power. They will often point to religious, tribal, and ethnic differences as an excuse to take from one group and give to another. But the root cause of this problem is not religious or tribal or ethnic. It is instead a math problem involving resources and how the rich and powerful, or the ruthless and cunning choose to allocate those resources.

In 2007 and 2008, more than one quarter of all governments on the African continent suffered from food riots, government instability, and political chaos caused by hunger and grain shortages. Was the cause drought, pestilence, or crop failure. No, instead the primary culprit was the RFS-2, or the American Renewable Fuel Standard, which was part of the Energy Independence and Security Act of 2007. Faced with increasing fuel prices, the U.S. congress began mandating 10% ethanol be added to most gasoline blends. This all sounds great but what it translates to is "we are going to start burning food in our gas tanks instead of using it to feed people." In fact, let me explain to you why this is exactly the worst thing you can do when faced with high fuel prices. Again, if growing resource scarcity was not a concern, and populations were not bursting at the seams, then this would be fine. But in a world where we are just one bad decision away from chaos, burning 6 billion bushels of corn annually is really playing with fire.

So let's get back to that math problem and how it affects current global events. The United States currently dedicates 40% of our corn crop, which is approximately 30 million acres of corn annually, to the production of ethanol. Grain is about 20% of the human diet on average, meaning that one acre of corn is enough grain to feed 60 people each year. This means that the United States, the largest producer of the world's corn, is burning enough of the grain annually to feed 1.8 billion people, nearly 20% of the world population. When we first started to do this, food prices in Africa and the Middle East skyrocketed, causing political chaos and civil unrest. President Obama, like all national politicians, supported the ethanol mandate because of course, the state of Iowa is crucial to political victories in the U.S. election system. So, when the Arab Spring led to the toppling of 5 governments and social violence in 10 countries, Obama cheered on the protesters' enthusiasm for democracy. This was not so much about democracy but instead, this was caused primarily by a shortage of grain and bread and the people simply could not afford to buy food.

You may ask, "what does this have to do with African resource scarcity today?" While the world has adapted to U.S. ethanol production, the human race is still just one mistake away from mass starvation and chaos. Because of population growth, there is no end in sight to food scarcity. In Africa, this predicament is most acute because population growth rates are higher by far than any other continent or region. In fact, Africa is on track to increase from 1.4 billion inhabitants to 2 billion inhabitants in less than 15 years, by about the year 2037.

Of course, the solution seems simple, just stop producing ethanol. Instead, we are doing the opposite. Within the past several years, U.S. Presidents of both parties have proposed raising the amount of ethanol consumed by American vehicles and in the summer of 2022, the EPA even lifted the summertime ban on E15 under emergency authorization. This was done to deal with higher-than-normal gas prices, but it only increased food prices, which are also at record highs. Not only are fuel prices and fertilizer prices on track to make food unaffordable for the poor, but grain shortages from the Ukraine conflict and now the increased use of ethanol will likely deliver a knockout punch to poor countries in the next few years.

We will likely see a repeat of events that occurred in Africa starting with the Renewable Fuel Standards of 2007, except now populations are higher and resource scarcity is more acute. Expect to see large areas of Africa become destabilized as warlords use food resources as a weapon, dividing one ethnicity or religious group against another, rationing food to supporters while starving their opponents. Expect also to see European and American politicians grapple with and allow large migrations from this chaotic situation in Africa to come to American and European cities, putting a strain on their own systems of healthcare, food distribution, and welfare. You heard that right, the politicians mandate the burning of grain in our fuel tanks for political reasons, and then they are puzzled about a starvation induced migration crisis.

The problem is that this downward spiral does not stop in countries where resource scarcity is most acute. And problems that cropped up 10 and 20 years ago were never solved, meaning that with each wave of disaster and shortage, the toll on human population is more dire. We can see that one war may cause a fuel shortage, and the fuel shortage then causes a fertilizer shortage and a food shortage. This leads to hunger, mass migration, and then more conflict, right back to where we started. Unfortunately, the only thing that could stop this chain of events is benevolent and wise leadership which is perhaps the most scarce resource of all.

In summary, modern conflict is not about culture or history or morals; it is about the control of resources. Global corporate and multinational forces have begun to fight for the limited resources on our crowded planet, and the powerless masses and even the middle class will pay the consequences. What will the future look like? While the future may be impossible to predict, there are a few likely scenarios, and the most likely is perhaps not the one that we would choose, but rather it is the one that is chosen for us by gluttony for power, general ignorance, and mass desperation.

Four Scenarios for the Future of World Civilization

1. Chaos World: This scenario looks something like a cross between *Mad Max* and a country like Somalia or Syria. In this case, humans spend their energy fighting over resources that grow ever scarcer. Law and Order breaks down as warlords, dysfunctional governments, and starving mobs fight for limited and disappearing resources. In this scenario, whatever group is able to inflict the most violence on others will be the group whose members are fed and get to live another day. It is a scenario in which humans become something very similar to animals. When you see governments fail and countries devolve into chaos, you are seeing a glimpse into the future Chaos World. You can see this in much of Yemen, Somalia, Afghanistan, and Syria. These are, not coincidentally, also the countries with some of the highest birth rates in the world. Where will this occur next? Keep an eye on the Sudan, Niger, Myanmar, Ukraine, Venezuela, South Africa, then possibly even Greece. This is a world where survival and especially happiness becomes difficult, but not impossible. The main obstacles to survival in this world are violence at all levels, hunger, and lack of medical care.
2. Orwellian world: Just as in the dystopian novels of George Orwell, this scenario features authoritarian governments that wield power over all of their people for the benefit of the ruling class and the survival of the poor masses. In this case, scarce resources are both rationed and hoarded by all-powerful governments and oligarchs.

Often the danger of Chaos world convinces the masses to allow and even demand that governments impose Orwellian world. In Orwellian world, governments can regulate how law-abiding citizens live their lives, what they read, what they say, how they dress, where they shop, and even what they teach their children. When you see countries like China, North Korea, Iran, and Russia, this is a glimpse of Orwellian world. The state survives and order is maintained but where there is no freedom, there is no pursuit of happiness. Leaders of these authoritarian countries may appear nationalistic and pragmatic, but their self-interest always shines through. The leader of North Korea, for example, is a fat man in a starving country. Or take, for example, Vladimir Putin who was revealed to have a 700-million-dollar yacht with a submersible dance floor in Italy while sending 100's of thousands to their deaths in human wave attacks and urban warfare hellscapes. In Orwellian world, injustice does not matter because the individual does not matter. Only the state matters and the state exists only for the benefit of the dictator, oligarch, or whatever party happens to be in power.

3. Sustainable World: In this world, innovative technologies and careful resource utilization and reutilization are used to perpetuate human survival into the future. Scarce resources are preserved and regenerated through human effort and intelligence. In this scenario, government power is used not to enrich the elite class but instead to improve the lives of the masses. Renewable and clean energy sources, sustainable agriculture, population control through education, and respect for human rights helps civilization create a future where scarcity and violence are overcome. European nations have made some strides in this direction, such as Iceland with their 100% reliance on renewable energy, or Finland, where 70% of the land is covered by forest and they maintain the highest score on the world's happiness index. The problem with sustainable world is that it is a lone lifeboat on the titanic, and it will be sunk as everyone piles in. What has the western world's solution been to the third world sinking into chaos? Did we make a good effort to help those countries a better place, or did we profit off of their turmoil? Aid, refugee programs, and peacekeepers have not been effective. Prime examples are the Arab spring and the War in Syria, which set off an immigration to the European Union that consistently exceeds 2 million per year. In Afghanistan, after 20 years of war and investment, 15 percent of Afghans are homeless, and in the first month of war in the Ukraine, 10% of Ukrainians left their country, the largest country by mass in Europe. While efforts to create sustainable world are admirable, currently that lifeboat is on track to be sunk by a violent, hungry, and homeless world. I'm not criticizing the refugees, because I would do the same if you took away my food and home and above all the future of my children. A hungry mob is always an angry mob, and no amount of empathy will change how destructive a mob is. What are our leaders doing to create a more sustainable world? Well at the time of this writing, it is

difficult to order an electric vehicle because of supply shortages, but members of congress grow rich overnight because of their clairvoyant trading on the stock market. Grain is being intentionally bombed instead of feeding the poor, and more fuel is being burned in tank engines than ever before. Our leaders, left, right, and center are using their power to enrich themselves and their overprivileged children, and not to create a more sustainable world. For this reason, while I would certainly choose a sustainable future, I find it highly unlikely. The best you can hope for is to create a sustainable island around yourself and perhaps teach others to do the same, but you have to be pragmatic and tough to protect a thing that is beautiful.

4. Hybrid World: A hybrid world with a combination of the above scenarios is the most likely future in the near term, and it is already unfolding today. In a hybrid world, one community in Sweden will achieve carbon neutrality while the next community down the rail will become a violent no go zone for police, fire, and essential services. One country in Europe will achieve 80% renewable energy while a neighboring country will be on the receiving end of 10 billion dollars of exploding ordinance per year. One Latin American country will be a prosperous tourist paradise while the neighboring country will demand that the government redistribute all land and wealth equally by force, causing mass migration and panic, ushering in a new era of warlord rule and unspeakable violence. But the most important point to remember about hybrid world is that the poverty and violence in the neighboring community, country, or continent cannot be contained or isolated. Instead, it spills over and spreads like the clouds of Mordor because of population growth and globalism. For this reason, I have laid out in this book many planning considerations, practices, and skills for keeping safe during this coming Dark Age. As time moves forward, this hybrid world will demonstrate larger extremes and disparities between violence and peace, richness and poverty, brutal chaos and Orwellian order. It will be a Dark Age of technological miracles alongside surreal levels of mass pain and suffering. Excess will be on full display by our leaders and influencers while hunger and scarcity will be inescapable for the majority of the world.

To understand what is happening as well as the implications for you and your family, you must first understand something about the Earth's carrying capacity. Carrying capacity and numbers are forcing human civilization into the dilemmas that we are beginning to face. After teaching university level environmental science courses for several years, I feel that I have a very accurate reading of the pulse of our constantly declining resource situation as well as the increasing demands of our human population. I always tried to show my students that societal collapse is not a problem related to compassion or political views, but rather it is really more of a math problem, directly tied to finite resource availability and impending scarcity. After a quick discussion of the carrying capacity and resource situation of modern society, we can move on to what action to take to prepare yourself for a turbulent future.

Chapter 3: What is the Earth's Carrying Capacity?

Carrying Capacity Chart

After witnessing the Covid-19 pandemic, it is logical to ask ourselves not only why this happened, but also how often will it happen again in the future. Vectors, environmental depletion, and conflict will continue to happen because the human species has exceeded the Earth's carrying capacity. We will have a century of pandemics, violence, and resource shortage until we get below the proper carrying capacity. Let's take a look at carrying capacity, because it is a critical consideration when attempting to understand the relationship between living things and their environment; in this case the relationship between the human population and our planet. The planet and all of our resources are of course finite; even renewable resources will run out when they are consumed faster than they can be produced, especially when overconsumption damages the renewal process.

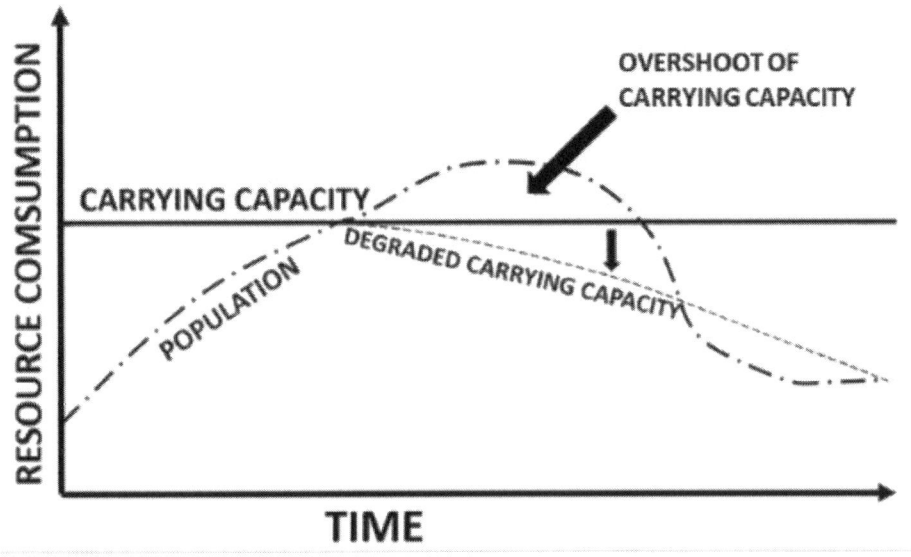

Figure 3: All Species are subject to a Carrying Capacity Limit that Limits the Size of the Population, to the amount that the Ecosystem can Support and Feed

Given a finite amount of resources, many of which are renewed annually through natural processes, we can support a finite number of organisms living on those resources. For example, an island that produces 10,000 lbs. of grass can support 100 rabbits that eat 100 lbs. per year. When the rabbit population of that island grows past 100 rabbits, this is called "overshoot", but the rabbits don't all suddenly die. In fact, the rabbits may surge to a population of 200 individuals, twice their **sustainable carrying capacity**. In the absence of a sudden declaration of open rabbit hunting season, two things will occur. First, they begin to encounter greater forms of **environmental resistance**, which are things such as disease, hunger, and predators. Environmental resistance is anything that puts downward pressure on the population of a species. It normally means a great amount of death.

In humans, you can include war on the list of types of environmental resistance. While war has existed since before the dawn of civilization, competition for resources clearly increases the likelihood of conflict among any species, and in humans, this means war.

Returning to the case of the rabbits, the second thing that happens is that they begin to degrade their environment. In this example, **environmental degradation** means that they will overgraze and damage the vegetation, causing it to produce less food the next year. As the grazing becomes more intense, plant life is unable to sustain leaf growth, roots die back, and the plants eventually die. Now, remember, the carrying capacity consists of the number of individuals of a species that an ecosystem can support. So, by going above that carrying capacity, these rabbits have clearly caused environmental degradation. This is also referred to as **overshoot** of the carrying capacity. The problem of environmental degradation is that while the rabbits once had enough forage and vegetation to feed 100 individuals, the population still surged to 200 rabbits. As a result, they have caused so much damage to the vegetation, eating it down to the roots, that they can now barely feed 25 individuals. This means that many rabbits will inevitably die through some type of environmental resistance such as starvation, disease, predators, or by scratching and clawing each other to death. Only then will they be able to have enough food for all, meaning they are at or below carrying capacity. This is a fixed law of nature. When this type of environmental resistance happens in nature, we simply call it natural law, but examined closely it does involve massive amounts of suffering, death, and what is referred to in the bible as "wailing and gnashing of teeth."

Humans are, of course, subject to the same laws of nature as other organisms. Our population was kept in check for 2.5 million years by the laws of nature, and a now-forgotten meager existence of hunger, struggle, and death. However, we modern humans now have the ability to first imagine and then to geo-engineer the Earth to create greater abundance, creating projects such as irrigation, terracing, mulching, mining, fertilization, redistribution of surplus, etc. Nonetheless, even after using our extensive Earth-shaping abilities, we find that we still have limits, and areas such as the Syrian Desert or the plains of Niger tend to find that out rather more quickly than other areas.

As you know, inhabitants of places like Syria or the South Sudan are left to kill each other for the scarce resources that remain. Others have fled their local environment, only to hasten the consumption and depletion of resources in other countries. If we were to examine two neighboring countries with equal resources, equal population, and equal carrying capacity, we might find country "A" with a growth rate of 5% and country "B" with a growth rate of 0%. If both countries start with a population of 15 million and a carrying capacity of 20 million, it would seem that they would be in great shape for many years. But with the given growth rates, country "A" will double in population in just 15 years (Rule of 70: Doubling time = 70/growth rate). This means that with a population of 30 million, country "A" has just overshot their carrying capacity by 10 million. Country "B," with a growth rate of zero, can only accept 5 million refugees without exceeding her carrying capacity, but wanting to be virtuously humanitarian, country "A" accepts 7.5 million refugees. Now both countries stand with 22.5 million inhabitants each, over 10 percent above the sustainable carrying capacity. And so, begins the degradation of the environments of both countries, lowering their carrying capacity even further, so that they can no longer sustainably support even the original carrying capacity of 20 million. Within a few years, environmental resistance hits hard with hunger, diseases, and social struggle bringing death and suffering to all. The moral is that once carrying capacity is overshot, a transfer of refugees is generally not going to fix the situation, it is just a temporary band aid.

The above example is known as **Human Osmotic Pressure**, because humans will pass through borders to seek areas of lower concentration in the same way that fluids pass through cell membranes. This pressure leads to more famine, because the growing populations invariably exceed carrying capacity, degrade the environment and farmland, and lead to food shortage. The uprooting of populations combined with the growing areas of famine then lead to conflict. Finally, the stress of conflict and migration combines with poor nutrition from famine to weaken even individual immune systems, leading to terrible pandemics.

This type of chain reaction is just like a positive feedback loop in the human body, where a symptom exacerbates the underlying problem, which worsens the symptom, until the problem leads to further complications or even death. For example, I may have high blood pressure, which gives me anxiety. The anxiety makes my heart beat faster, and I feel this so I get more anxious which raises my blood pressure even more until I have a heart attack. In the case of human societies, overpopulation causes a shortage and hunger. People get angry and start stealing from farmers, the government sets price limits. Farmers get screwed financially and stop producing. The famine gets worse, and full blown war and famine breaks out.

This law of carrying capacity and limited resources does much to explain what happened in Syria. In more prosperous areas, such as Saudi Arabia, things have taken shape much differently. While the population of Saudi Arabia is clearly beyond the carrying capacity of its sand ecosystem, wealthy inhabitants have begun to import resources on a massive scale, especially food, that they have already depleted in their own country. Recent reports have revealed that Saudis have begun to buy up vast areas of farmland in the United States, including thousands of acres in places like Arizona's oasis, the Imperial Valley. They have even purchased some areas where water laws allow them to pump aquifers at unlimited and unsustainable rates, so that they can export commodities such as alfalfa back to Saudi Arabia. In this situation, while a refugee crisis is temporarily averted, vast resources are expended to transport these commodities across the globe. Obviously, depleting aquifers in one country to feed another, has the effect of lowering the carrying capacity in the producing country. So, in some situations, resources are moved around because of scarcity, and in other situations, the people themselves are moved to where there are still resources to be extracted. The cause and the effect is the same; too many people with fewer and fewer remaining resources.

With such globalization, the human ecosystem is now the entire planet. We now have the ability to redistribute food and other necessities across the globe. In this way, as resources are consumed, the carrying capacity of the entire Earth is lowered all at the same time. This is evident today because of the severe environmental degradation that surrounds us. Bread baskets such as the plains of the United States and the Ukraine are slowly eroding away, and the lack of organic material in the soil is masked by heavy chemical fertilizer applications. Thin-soiled regions such as Amazonia are deforested and depleted of nutrients year after year. Eighty-five percent of all global fisheries are considered depleted, and seventy-five percent of industrial wastes are dumped into waterways.

Areas such as the American Midwest have enough resources that they may appear to be infinite, but this is not the case. Many of our aquifers, such as the Oglala aquifer, beneath several Midwestern states, is being pumped at a rate much faster than it can be replenished. Vast areas in Texas and Oklahoma that used to rely on this aquifer are already without water. This aquifer, like many others, is considered fossil water, as it contains water that fell as rain as far back as 10,000 years ago. Due to the high pumping rates of modern irrigation, some areas are depleting more than 100 years of water accumulation in just one year.

As we use corn and even turn it into ethanol, we unwittingly are depleting finite resources such as topsoil and critical mineral fertilizers such as phosphorous, which are projected to be mined out within this century. It is estimated that it takes at least 100 years of natural processes to create just one inch of topsoil. After 100,000+ years of ice age processes, grazing by herd animals, and deposition of rich manures and organic sediments, many areas of the Midwest United States have accumulated often between 2 and 12 feet of topsoil over the millennia. However, about half of that original topsoil has been lost since the time of the dustbowl, just 80 years ago. In many of these areas, such as the cornfields of Iowa, Missouri, Nebraska, and Kansas, topsoil is still being lost at a rate as high as 7 inches every 20 years on certain highly erodible soils. This means that within the next 20 to 40 years, many of these areas will cease to produce the grain that currently feeds much of the world. I remind you that we just hit a global population of 8 billion and are on track to reach a population of 9 billion hungry souls by the year 2035.

Globalization and technological innovation at times seem to raise the carrying capacity of the Earth. But in fact, we are only kicking the can down the road and enabling ourselves to overharvest already depleted resources all the way to the most remote corners of the globe. Norman Borlaug, who received the Nobel Peace prize for agriculture in 1970 was a realist when it came to the limitations of modern science. In the 1950's and 1960's, many scientists had believed that humans were nearing our carrying capacity limit on the

Earth. But, just in time, Borlaug had helped double and triple yields of the world's grain crops, such as wheat, rice, and corn, in an event known as the "Green Revolution" or the third agricultural revolution. This was done by developing better genetic varieties and using new chemical fertilizers. Even so, upon accepting the Nobel prize, he stated that if populations continued to rise, it would take a second "Green Revolution" in agriculture to prevent mass starvation. The world population has more than doubled since he spoke those words. He understood the limits of what nature and technology together can provide, and it seems that today we are up against those limits.

But it gets worse; here is the real dumpster fire in the story: In the natural world, as an animal population overshoots its resources, there is a lag time between the boom and the bust. In our previous example, the rabbits had a carrying capacity of 100, but their population hit 200 before they began to die off. This is a reflection of what truly occurs in nature because populations can be carried to this higher-than-sustainable level by consuming and thus degrading their own environment. A starving rabbit will scratch and claw the ground and pull up the roots of the grass for one last meal even though it means that the grass will never come back. It is the same as a hungry farmer consuming his seed corn, to live just one more day. He can have a heck of a Thanksgiving eating that seed corn and his winter stockpiles, but then what? This delay tactic only makes the impending drop in population even more catastrophic. As countries with high birth rates, but low amounts of resources rely more heavily on countries of greater abundance, the environmental degradation will accelerate, even with our best efforts at agricultural innovations. Topsoil and irreplaceable minerals and nutrients will be consumed and depleted, aquifers will be drained, and still there will be even more mouths to feed. Globalization, refugee resettlement, and shortsighted technological solutions are just such a delay tactic. These uniquely human abilities only allow us to raise our population that much further above our global carrying capacity. Unfortunately, it only means that we will have that much further to fall when the environmental degradation and lack of resources catches up to us.

By understanding the laws of nature, and concepts such as finite resources and carrying capacity, we also come to see that environmental degradation is a sure sign of a carrying capacity that is being lowered right before our eyes. And what then comes after the lowering of carrying capacity? The answer is of course a New Dark Age and a descent into chaos, caused by environmental resistance in the form of disease, famine, and bloodshed. THE TIME TO PREPARE IS NOW!

What Should Humans do to Survive this Dilemma?

There are two types of people in the world and each type will have a different reaction to the seemingly insurmountable problems on the global horizon. The first type of person will give way to despair. This type will not give this book a second look, so we will focus on the second type, you.

The second type of person is a survivor, committed to outlasting others when the shit hits the fan, and even thrive given the opportunity. This book is dedicated to you, one of the survivors. The first thing a survivor must do to deal with a challenge is to find out what it is all about and gather all the facts and information possible to take destiny into their own hands.

Your first reaction may be to work towards a solution for everyone, and this is admirable. After all, family planning can lower global birth rates, agriculture can be practiced sustainably, and diets can be made more sustainable. But the truth is that we have already surpassed the carrying capacity of the planet's resources, and when this happens, there is only one way that population levels can go. Once they begin to drop, the descent will soon become rapid. The pandemics, hunger, and refugee crises have only just begun, and government solutions are rapidly becoming impossible in the midst of such a crisis.

Government solutions have been attempted in the past and they come up short. For example, locking down the entire world for a pandemic seemed viable in the short term. But thinking that we can accomplish multiple global emergency response efforts over an extended period without generating an economic and political collapse is wishful thinking. With supply chains interrupted and 8 billion mouths to feed, chaos and conflict will eventually prevail. This descent into chaos will lead to a new Dark Age, and not only disease but also refugees will be the sign of the coming collapse.

Refugees are forced to concern themselves with the next meal, the next bottle of water, and not freezing to death. There is no time for education, for learning to live sustainably, or for thinking about the next generation. Humans will stop at nothing to feed their hungry children, stealing, looting, even murder. Other groups such as ISIS turn to religious extremism, often prompted by fanatical leaders bent on seizing resources and territory for themselves and their followers.

Human refugees will flee from one country to the next, surpassing the carrying capacity of each region along the way. Years ago, it was Zimbabwe, Somalia, and Ethiopia. Now we struggle to find a solution as Yemen, Libya, Syria, Iraq, Afghanistan, and Ukraine become failed states without the necessary resources to support the masses. Tomorrow, we may ask ourselves if it will ever end as Nigeria, Morocco, Turkey, Italy, and Greece collapse beneath the pressure of refugees coupled with scarcer and scarcer resources. India, Bangladesh, and even China will become unmanageable as any interruption to their food supply would mean starvation for millions and the chaos and war that goes along with it.

Some would point to history and say that immigration and refugees are a part of an ongoing cycle. But the fact is that there is no precedent for the current situation because the world population has never spiraled out of control the way that it did in the 20th century, and the way that it continues to do.

Governments will not collapse outright as a result of resource shortages and massive suffering. They will, however, circle the wagons and begin serving their most prominent constituents first, and everyone else will come last. This means that the ultra-rich, corporations, and even wealthy crime cartels will begin to wield the power and authority of the state. We are already beginning to see this as national debts soar due to strained resources, waste, and increasing corruption. The debt must be serviced to line the pockets of the rich and influential, whose influence grows while the influence of average citizens diminishes. Justifiable fear and national emergencies will be used to further centralize power into the hands of governments. Governments with more unchecked powers will then become even more corrupted by that power. The power of the voters will disappear and those who control increasingly scarce resources will control society.

In the meantime, populations will continue to grow while refugees and desperate people find that they can no longer look to the government to help them survive. In such a situation, it is reasonable to expect shortages of food, clean water, medicines, heating fuel such as firewood, and other necessities. It is one thing to miss a meal or three, but it is quite another to watch your children go hungry. Desperation will be followed by crime and brutality, as life for ordinary citizens descends into chaos. Only through preparedness and resilience will some individuals emerge unscathed. This is where you, the survivor, will play your part. Where all seems lost, the survivor finds hope, even opportunity.

As one of the survivors, you will need versatility, resilience, and a multitude of self-reliance skills. This book will help you gain those skills to include building your retreat or homestead, supplying yourself with water, producing food from crops and livestock, creating your own energy, and providing security for yourself and loved ones. As a former Army Ranger with a Masters in Engineering and many years of off-grid living experience, I am here to share what I have learned about survival and self-reliance with others who want to continue to thrive in a world that is descending into chaos.

How will you survive the Descent into Chaos?

I have had visitors from the city who visit my homestead and tell me that they **want** to have a self-sufficient farm like mine someday. That's when I like to share some wisdom that my grandfather passed on to me. In his Scottish Brogue he would say, "Why don't you **want** in one hand and try **crapping** in the other and see which one fills up first?" I'm only teasing, and my grandpa was always too busy to explain, but I think that the point of this old highland proverb is that wanting something is not enough, and good things in life require incredible amounts of work, planning, negotiation, and persistence. Know that true prepping is probably the hardest job that you will ever have, though it is extremely rewarding if you keep a positive attitude. I graduated from Ranger and Sniper schools among others, but taking my family off-grid was much harder, and there were many times when I wanted to quit. If my wife had not been so tough, we would have rung the bell and quit long ago. It takes not just desire but also a lot of planning and hard work to build a self-sufficient homestead. The fact that you are reading this book is a good start and an indication that you have a desire to save yourself and your loved ones, maybe even your community. There is a point during the sinking of a ship when you realize that baling water has become futile and that the titanic is going down. I am surprised at the number of Americans that I have met who seem to believe that the ship is going down sometime soon, but they seem content playing in the band, dancing, partying, or stuffing their faces. This might be because after so many have grown up unaccustomed to hard work, they cannot bear the thought of rolling up their sleeves, even to save themselves.

I have some neighbors that moved to our remote area from the city, largely to prepare for the coming disaster. They seemed to understand that there was a need to prepare, and they took that first step. Unfortunately, hard work was not on the agenda. Country neighbors watched, dumbfounded, as they built a cookie-cutter suburban house in the middle of the forest, totally dependent on grid power and equipped with excellent Wi-Fi. Every child had multiple electronic devices for their constant entertainment. They did manage a few chickens, which were promptly consumed by the local forest mammals, within about a week. Everyone loves chicken, especially opossums and raccoons. The unsightly chicken house had to be burned to the ground. They started a food and ammunition storage, but it took up too much space so had to be replaced with an entertainment room. Rain barrels and other preps were purchased but just sat in the garage. The family took weekly trips to the city and quarterly flights to Disney to get away from their "primitive" country lifestyle. It was almost like rewarding themselves for the hard farmwork that they never did. Soon the neighbors returned to the city and all the conveniences that they had so sorely missed. Please, if you are reading this book, don't follow that example. Instead use this book like a guide and like a list that will keep you on track. The table of contents from the following chapters can be used almost exactly like a list, picking out those that seem most pertinent to you.

When I say, "Save Yourselves!", I don't mean run around like a chicken with its head cut off, trying to find the fire exit. What I mean is, start preparing as early as possible because there is too much work today to put it all off until the last minute. At a minimum, you will need time at least need to find a decent homestead, create a livable shelter, find a steady source of water, start producing your own food, be able meet your basic mental, medical, and health needs, and develop a solid self-defense plan for yourself. This is the head-start that I attempt to give you in this book.

So, from the former Ranger instructor in me, "The first thing that you need to do is get your f***ing game face on." Next, get your loved ones on board. You may be a loner, but chances are, that you have other people that you care about and do not wish to live without. Be patient with them; most people don't like to be dragged around by the horns like a goat, digging their heels in and fighting you the whole way. Instead, point out real issues, such as the limitations on vital resources such as fossil fuels, phosphorous fertilizer, topsoil, and potable water. You might also appeal to history, and the fact that all civilizations eventually meet their demise, usually when they are partying the hardest. In doing so, you are not selling an idea, you are just revealing the truth that people don't like to acknowledge.

This is exactly how my wife and I made our decision to move off-grid and become self-reliant. We looked at all of the evidence, and we came to the decision together. Later, we talked to my parents about it, and they had basically come to the same conclusions independently of us. We made the move to our remote wilderness first, hacking out a shelter and a living, then bringing in the elders later. We have three generations of preppers on one piece of land, with all ranges of ability and personality types. Everyone has something to contribute, and that is key.

I think my wife has always been the hardest worker. She has worked beside me the entire time while also watching the children and has cooked most of the meals. (I don't refuse to cook, but my family generally refuses to eat what I cook.) She does most of the gardening and has kept our finances straight even before we had a real desk. I have taken the lead on construction and infrastructure projects like water, fences, and field clearing, but my wife has normally been right by my side with these projects, at least when she wasn't 8 or 9 months pregnant. Our children have grown up tending livestock, feeding them, and keeping track of their needs and issues. The children can also pull weeds in the garden, milk the goats, hunt, fish, and trap under my supervision. My parents have provided immense financial backing for land, critical water infrastructure, livestock, and more. They have also helped resource bonus items like the internet and hired farm hands. Amazingly, they were willing to uproot themselves while in their sixties, after my father largely lost his ability to walk, and follow us to build their own homestead which complements ours in many ways. If you are older and doubt your own ability to prepare for the coming disaster, know that other senior citizens have already done it successfully, and that with a little help from this book, you can too. It has been a team effort and everyone has contribute wholeheartedly. It takes hard work, perseverance, ingenuity, financial resources, and a little luck. The fact that you are here today proves that you have these traits in your genes. Many of your ancestors likely used these traits to survive the Great Depression, a civil war or two, the Dark Ages, the fall of Rome, and probably the Ice Age. You too can survive and consider what I used to tell my students in Ranger School: "You need to get it in your head that you would rather die than quit." That is how you decide to survive!

Understanding the Coming Situation

Most Americans have been lucky enough to not have witnessed the social chaos that ensues after the fall of a government, the failure of infrastructure, and the breakdown of the social safety net. While being deployed repeatedly to third world countries and failed states during my time in the military, I witnessed the mayhem and surreal scenes that develop as human beings scratch and claw at each other to feed their children and jockey for power to fill the vacuum left by a collapsed government. This type of situation does not necessarily mean all-out violence, and it does not mean desperation for everyone. Instead, what occurs are pockets of extreme violence and suffering as well as safe enclaves where small communities pull together and thrive. In the middle and throughout, there is thievery, sexual violence, dark religious fervor, and a healthy black market.

Such a situation is confusing for all present as friend and foe become indistinguishable and alliances shift from day to day. On one occasion, my small five-man team was conducting a reconnaissance of a neighborhood that had been the site of fierce battles between U.S. Forces and insurgents. A still-functional Soviet-Era loaded, but unmanned anti-aircraft gun was parked on a hill just beside the twenty-house enclave. After setting up an initial observation post, we began to clear what we thought were empty homes as our sniper team provided overwatch.

After peaking around a tall stone wall, I noticed a scruffy militia fighter out of uniform rummaging through debris in front of a home. We quietly readied our grenades from behind the wall and waited to see if more fighters would emerge. After a few tense moments, it appeared he was alone, and perhaps not such a threat. After all, there were probably half a dozen different armed groups in our area, some friendly and some not-so-friendly. With two guns covering the fighter, I stepped from behind the wall. "My Friend!" I confidently exclaimed. He reacted with a nervous but big smile saying, "My Friend, Good Bush!" "Aww shucks, thank you," I replied. With his comment, I was to understand that he was a fan of the American president. I asked what he was doing but alas, his English capabilities were almost exhausted. "No Ali Baba," he said. "Okay, well let me know if you see Ali Baba," I responded, pointing at my eyes with two fingers. He grinned nervously with his dirty jagged teeth. From the pile of loot in the yard, it was clear that he was just on a mission to consolidate captured booty; kitchen appliances, A/C units, a pair of shoes for the wife, etc. "Go right ahead it's your country, have a fan-F***ing-tastic day" I told him, getting back to my mission. Miraculously seeming to understand me now, his smile quickly faded. He was more like a jackal with a pile of carcasses than a human, but this is what happens in times of chaos. I got tired of seeing that attitude, but hey, it's a good lesson in human nature in difficult times, times like the Dark Ages.

At that point in time, our command couldn't have cared less that a group of barbarians was ransacking the neighborhood, as long as they were friendly barbarians. We used demolitions to blow the anti-aircraft gun and watched as the original fighter's friends returned to pick up another load of home-improvement items. It turns out they were, in some murky indirect way, on our side. "What about law and order?" you ask. Well, when a society has just collapsed and chaos ensues, your bubble of safety no longer encompasses an entire country. Instead, you must pick your battles, and try to create a little bubble or enclaves of security where it is most feasible and create alliances when and where you need them, even if it is with barbarians.

Now using Iraq as the example, this was clearly an intentionally collapsed society, but the result will be the same, time and again, as social institutions break down and chaos seems to reign. During those early days after the fall of the Iraqi government, my team and I were sent to many neighborhoods, villages, and towns on various information gathering missions. We witnessed the entire spectrum of coping mechanisms in these communities. Some communities were deeply divided, invariably on ethnic or religious lines, leading to bloodshed. Others were more homogeneous and seemed to thrive with their newfound independence and lack of interference by government officials. The communities which thrived all had the following characteristics:

1. Good source of clean water
2. Agricultural production capability
3. Shelters with heating and cooking capability
4. Remote and away from heavily used transportation routes
5. Natural barriers to potential intruders
6. Cohesive population with similar beliefs and values
7. Established community hierarchy, council of elders, community strongmen, etc.
8. Some self-defense capability (young men with guns that know how to use them)

The point is that even in a situation of total chaos where suffering, looting, rape, and murder are rampant, it is still possible for life to go on and people to thrive given the right location, resources, and community. It is significant to note certain so-called necessities that are not on this list. These are things that you might think you need but you don't. Electricity is not on the list, and with a little innovation, you don't need it. Vehicular transportation is not on the list, and most humans on the planet don't own a vehicle. Such a community may not have a market, but barter, gifting, and charity will exist anyway. The size of these communities will vary. Some large neighborhoods within cities and population centers were surprisingly calm bubbles of self-sufficiency and order. These were invariably ethnically and religiously homogeneous. Cooperation was based on a rigorously uniform belief system.

At the other end of the spectrum, even single-family units could be found surviving and even thriving, but only in extremely remote areas. The rule is: the smaller the survival enclave, the more remote the location must be. The reason for this is that a survival enclave provides a juicy target for looters, such as the ones that we encountered stealing appliances. Because of this "juicy target factor" it requires a large enclave with robust security to survive in areas where looters can easily find and travel to a new juicy target. Therefore, a small, one family enclave that is only reachable by a half day journey on a mule, will likely not be seen as worth the effort.

With this knowledge, and considering the criteria laid out above, let us turn our attention to creating your enclave. It is important because you are a survivor, you care about your family and friends, and you know that we live in times of distress, volatility, and that chaos may be just around the corner.

Chapter 4: Choosing a Retreat Location

    The moment has arrived; You have made the decision to prepare, and to lead your loved ones on a path of resilience, survival, and a prosperous future despite the coming turmoil. What kind of place will you choose as your survival retreat, your homestead? This is perhaps the most critical, life and death choice you will ever make, and it will determine much about how the rest of your preparations and post collapse experiences will play out. I remember when my wife and I made this decision. We could see the writing on the wall: growing populations, shrinking resources, the history of human conflict, etc. We scoured geographical information, researched the resources of various locations, considered the people that lived there, and reviewed our budget and goals repeatedly. Once you take that first step, understand that there is no going back. If you are not yet at your survival location, then I would strongly advise against making that decision until you have read this entire book. If you are already there, that's alright but you might skip this chapter. Security and many other details about your homestead location will be discussed later in this book, but in this section, let us examine desirable geographic regions, types of terrain, resources, and finally favorable social surroundings that will help tip the odds in your favor when desperation begins to grip our society.

    Geography is a broad topic, but let us focus on climate and resources that allow for survival during trying times. Too often, I read stories of greenhorn preppers that move to the high elevations of the Rocky Mountains, only to rely on hauled water and fossil fuel heat and electricity to survive at their rugged location. If this is you, congratulations you have bought yourself an isolated location to starve and freeze to death after society fails you and your outside supply chain is unexpectedly cut off. Such a location is likely to require 8 cords of wood annually just to heat 1000 square feet, gardens will grow only intermittently with maximum effort and skill, and outdoor labor becomes nearly impossible for weeks at a time due to the cold. In addition, if water sources are available, pipes will freeze and burst without careful planning and consistent heating. This type of situation is right for some, but ask yourself, are you in the physical and mental condition to endure such hardship for years at a time? What have you done in the past that convinces you that you will thrive under such austere conditions? Is your family equally tough? Are you really as hard as woodpecker lips?

    If the answer to any of these questions is no, then let's picture another location. Population density is still fairly low, but the place is survivable. There is some rough terrain and thick vegetation that makes it easy to tuck in a modest shelter within a concealed holler or on the edge of a shady meadow. Pockets of rich soil are just big enough for a family garden, and winters are fairly mild, with abundant firewood everywhere. Rainfall is adequate, more than 20 inches per year, and a variety of wild game and maybe even fish can be found as well. This description fits many places within the United States, and abroad as well. It could be the Catskill Mountains, the Ozark Highlands, the Southern Appalachians, or the foothills of the Cascades. There are many choices, but remember, your goal is long term survival, not just isolation. If you buy a place on a barren mountain next to a glacier, then you might as well be in Antarctica, so choose carefully. Remember these five characteristics: **rainfall, temperature, soil, resources, and population.**

Narrowing down your location from a broad geographic area to specific terrain and layout of a property is also critical to your survival. While the geography of my family's homestead fits the above description, we have some relatives with prepper tendencies that have chosen the most inhospitable spot, simply due to lack of knowledge or forethought. First, let me say that these are what you would call, "city folk." They started with excellent intentions, but their only knowledge of survival comes from watching the latest episodes of survival genre TV. So, this particular family, with a very high budget, decides to buy 20 acres with access on the corner to a beautiful spring-fed river. They then proceeded to build a fancy home about 100 meters above the river, away from all water sources, on a rocky ridge dotted with the most stunted, water-starved trees that exist in that area. Keep in mind that their initial intention was indeed to prepare for societal collapse. A year into their adventure, and after the construction of their home, I asked the father if any of them had yet been down to the river. He replied that it was way too steep to risk climbing down, but they did see it from the porch during a flood and it is a beautiful view. On-grid electricity pumped water up from a 600 foot well and unfortunately the only thing they had grown or produced were rocks. After living in the country for 2 years, this particular family began missing the city so much, that they made weekly trips to visit urban relatives, and eventually decided to move back. Sorry guys, I should have written this book for you earlier. Location, location, location! At a minimum, you need drinking water, some decent soil, firewood, and a favorable microclimate also doesn't hurt.

What is a favorable microclimate you ask? Well, back before air conditioning and forced-air furnaces, people had figured out how to situate their homes and farms in relation to terrain to keep it just a little cooler in the summer and a little warmer in the winter. In the northern hemisphere, a gentle, south-facing slope is angled toward the low trajectory of the winter sun, providing amazing added heat in the winter. This not only makes a home easier to heat, but also makes it easier to keep animals warm in the barn, and to get soil up to a good growing temperature in the early spring. Our family's home is on just such a slope, and in the winter, it is often up to 10 degrees Fahrenheit warmer than the other side of the valley where there is a north-facing slope. From our ridgetop, you can spot a neighbor's cabin on the north-facing slope across the valley. After a good snow, we have noticed that the neighbor's hillside and roof will often take 2 to 3 days longer to melt off than our own. This is especially important after an ice storm where you need to get out and tend to your animals and maintain your homestead. In mountainous areas, depending on your latitude, north-facing slopes can sometimes never see the sun all winter. Don't ignore this tip!

I have seen misleading homesteading articles and books that have suggested that a south facing slope is hotter, even in the summer, and that you might even plant trees to shade the southern side of your house. This is absolute hogwash! In the North America, and the entire northern hemisphere north of the tropics, the sun takes a higher path in the summer than the winter, making it go almost straight overhead in the middle of the summer. This means that shading on the east and west side of your home or barns is very important in the summer. In the winter, you want a wide-open south side in order to soak up the sun's heat while it is on a low, winter trajectory.

Other people may be tempted to build on an east or west-facing slope to catch that beautiful sunrise or sunset. This is very tempting indeed, but keep in mind that an east facing slope will heat up quickly in the summer and cool down early in the winter. West facing slopes will make for a hot evening in the summer and in the winter and it may seem like the sun will never come over the horizon to warm you up. I remember my time as a Ranger instructor in the mountains of North Georgia. With hundreds of mountain patrols under our belts, we instructors knew the cold spots and warm spots in those blue ridge mountains through hard years of experience. Students were leading the patrols, so on cold winter days it was very tempting to drop hints about where to set up the nightly patrol base. On a south or east facing slope, BOB would rise and warm up the entire patrol first thing in the morning. BOB was an endearing military acronym for the sun, meaning "Big Orange Ball." Set your patrol base up on a north slope or west slope and you will freeze without BOB to warm you up in the morning. Years of patrolling in the mountains will teach you about the importance of microclimate, the hard way, or you can just take my word for it!

Elevation and terrain features are perhaps more critical considerations than slope direction. It is tempting to put a home on a mountain top. What is not to love about a mountain top; great views, commanding position, your land all laid out before you… Unfortunately, a mountain top can be extremely cold and windy. If you would burn 2 cords of wood per winter on the slope, plan on burning 4 cords on the very top of the mountain. If you are determined to build on a mountain top in cold climates, please put twice the normal amount of insulation in your walls and seal them up tight. Mountain passes, or saddles, are even worse than mountain tops. Air will constantly be flowing through the mountain passes and wind chill will have a huge effect. On one particular night while teaching Ranger school, we were ordered by a commanding officer to halt and set up camp near a road in a mountain pass, due to cold weather. It was about 5 degrees below zero in the Blue Ridge Mountains, which would normally not be a big deal. In those temps, you could normally just drop down on the south side of the mountain, shelter from the cold north wind, and ride it out until BOB (big orange ball, aka, the sun) arrived. But, under orders, we sheltered near the road in the pass, where gusty winds brought windchill temps down to 35 degrees below zero. Emaciated and half-starved Ranger students spooned in groups of three and four, getting up every 45 minutes for calisthenics. Despite our efforts, we had 3 cases of hypothermia that night. Microclimate can mean life or death, as well as a prospering or failing homestead.

While mountain tops and passes can be windy, valleys and areas near streams can be even colder. From our house on a south-facing slope, winter morning temps are generally 5 to 10 degrees warmer than the valley, just 100 feet below. The reason is that cold air sinks, and pools up in the bottom of valleys. In the summer, the bottom of the valley can be problematic as well, due to mosquitoes and other insects that thrive in wetter areas. Never forget, a gentle south-facing slope is a great place to build a homestead.

These are just a few guidelines that may help you find the perfect location for your homestead, but the most important guideline is your own observation. When considering a major undertaking such as building or purchasing a homestead, it is well worth your time to observe that homestead in all conditions. Try to visit your homestead during a cold spell or even an ice storm. Does the ice melt off or does it hang around in the shade long after everything else has melted? Observe how prevailing winds affect the temperature. Keeping the north wind off in the winter is priceless, but a little breeze in the summer is not too bad either. Your observations will be the key, don't ignore them or be blinded by a beautiful view. Many more considerations for choosing an ideal homestead location will be discussed in the following chapters. Security considerations and self-defense of your homestead are so important that I am saving these items for their own chapter, later in the book. Location is everything when it comes to survival, so pay close attention. Remember, this is your homestead, your shot at survival, and your opportunity to thrive.

Illustration 3: An Ozark Spring Developed by the Author to deliver Water straight out of the Mountain and into a Holding Tank

Chapter 5: Water

Experienced homesteaders will confidently tell you that water will make you or break you. I remember the last midnight storm that came through our area, ripping up oak trees and knocking out grid power for almost two days. For us, we woke up to just another morning, happy to have the rain for our fields and experiencing no shortage of electricity from our battery bank. Later in the afternoon, I ran into a couple of sets of neighbors on the county road. They had that look in their eyes that said, "Where is the rescue crew!?" At the top of the list of their problems was a lack of water. You see, most wells in our area are from 100 to 400 feet deep. The water is abundant and pure but if your only way to get it to your home is a grid-tied electric pump, then you are at the end of a long electric supply line that could be cut off at any moment. These electric pumps are normally connected to a pressure tank that often holds between 20 and 80 gallons. After our last big storm and grid power outage, neighbors were talking for weeks about their plans for rain catchment, solar pumps, and windmills. Then they fell back into the comfort of relying on the utility companies, and preparations for self-reliance were forgotten.

We do have some Amish that live off-grid several miles away and they spend around $20,000 to install a well and windmill at each of their farms. The driller is hired, and they do the pump installation and windmill erection themselves. With this in mind, a clean gravity fed spring or similar reliable water source above your living area adds at least $20,000 to the value of that land in terms of off-grid improvements. A system that has no mechanical or electrical parts that can break down is truly priceless. A gravity-fed spring on the surface would be ideal, but whatever the water source is, the simpler, the better.

Let us take a look at water needs and do some math. Before you consider whether or not a water supply is adequate or not, think about how much you might use at your homestead. The average American in the U.S. uses between 80 and 100 gallons per day. The U.N. recommends 35 gallons per person daily, and many residents of undeveloped countries without running water use around 10 gallons or less per person per day. When my family first moved off grid, we used about 15 gallons per person per day. We now have more water resources and so now use closer to 35 gallons per person per day without being inconvenienced at all.

If you would like to lower your average daily consumption of water from the U.S. national average of about 90 gallons daily to a reasonable off-grid usage of 35 gallons per day, there are many ways that you can save. About 1/3 of typical water usage is for flushing toilets. This can be eliminated completely by using graywater to flush toilets. On our homestead, handwashing and laundry water goes into a gray water tank, which vents outside to prevent odors. This graywater tank feeds into toilets via gravity flow, eliminating the typically 30 gallons of water usage daily. New toilets use about 1/3 of the water of old toilets, so this is one item that should be purchased new. If this sounds like too much trouble and you don't mind a cold toilet seat, an outhouse will also solve this problem. Our Amish neighbors have plexi-glass windows on their outhouse to let in light during the day. At night, they bring the lantern, and hopefully don't lose too many down the hole! In any case, these techniques can bring your water usage from 90 down to 60 gallons per day, just by not flushing any fresh water.

If you would like to get from 60 gallons down to 35, consider the second largest use of water in the U.S., a shower. When I think of wasteful showers, I think of my sister in South Florida, who has two shower heads that leave you feeling not just clean but even just a little raw from the high pressure. According to water.usgs.gov, old shower heads use around 5 gallons per minute with new, water-saving shower heads using just about 2 gallons per minute. With a 10-minute average daily shower time, this means that you will save nearly 30 gallons daily with a low flow shower head. Just setting up a proper toilet and shower system can bring you down from a usage of 90 gallons for the average U.S. American household to 35 gallons for a conserving household, making your off-grid dreams that much more achievable. I do not stress to my family or anyone else the need to save water on handwashing, dishwashing, or drinking because I do not want anyone to get sick. I will say that it is best to have two basins to wash dishes, one full of hot soapy water and then one to rinse with cold water, which should be turned off when not in use. This all might sound nit-picky, but when you have lived off grid as long as my family and I, you realize that there are real limits to resources, and you are actually saving yourself when you attempt to conserve. A child only has to see their family run out of water once to realize just how precious it really is. Discomfort is a great teacher, which explains why so many idiots are running around in our very comfortable suburban neighborhoods today.

Have you ever seen a magazine article about someone or known someone who claims to be living off-grid but still has to haul water? I am sorry to say, but hauled water is on-grid water! The future of our civilization is not one in which you will be able to rely on complex public infrastructure for a dependable water source. Fortunately, there are many options for providing water for your homestead, including rainwater catchment, aquifers, solar pumps, windmills, springs, and ponds.

Rainwater Catchment

Watering livestock and gardens can easily be accomplished with rainwater catchment, especially when abundant springs or other reservoirs are not available. For homesteaders on a budget or in areas without other water resources, rainwater catchment is also a great option for human consumption as well. It may be all that you can afford and so all that you need to know. It is the most cost-effective and least reliant on technology. Rainwater catchment should be practiced by everyone at least as a backup for your main water supply. The main drawback for rainwater catchment is that you need to store the water in a large cistern for droughts and it is also difficult to keep the water in excellent, pure condition in a cistern. You will have to be vigilant to keep your cistern free of insects, rodents, leaves, and bird poop, especially if you want to drink it.

Illustration 4: Constructing a very deep, 10,000-gallon, concrete, rainwater cistern. The walls will be coated with a potable water safe cement-based water proofer and then a concrete lid will be constructed.

For rainwater catchment, you will need at a minimum a safe and clean roof, a gutter, and water storage. If you want to have pressurized water, you will need to either pump the water uphill, upstairs, or into a pressure tank. Ideally, you will have a collection surface, such as a barn, on top of a hill, along with your tanks. This means that no pump will be required. Our family has collected water since 2009 from our barn roof on top of the hill, with no issue and no repairs whatsoever. Our home could be abandoned for 100 years, someone could come turn the tap on, and water would come out. Sometimes the simplest, low-tech solution is the most reliable.

Illustration 5: A "first-flush system" between the gutter and your tank will help keep your water clean. Large debris is screened off the top and washed away. Small debris goes to the bottom and is separated from the rest of the water by a floating ball, allowing clean water to pass to the side and into the tank.

Let's start with the roof. To get an idea of how much roof space you will need, it is a simple volume formula (Depth of water times area of roof equals volume of water). Or you can simply calculate that 1000 square feet of roof space gives you 600 gallons for each inch of rain. Thirty inches of rainfall in a year on a 1000 sf roof will give you 18,000 gallons (600 times 30) of water per year, or about 50 gallons per day. Consider your water consumption needs as discussed above and you will find how much roof space that you need. If you are 5 people using 30 gallons per person per day, then you will need 3000 square feet to gather the 150 gallons per day that you require. If you also have two milk cows that drink 50 gallons total per day, then you will want 4000 square feet for all your water needs (4000 square feet at 50 gallons daily per 1000 square feet equals 200 gallons daily {with 30 inches annual rainfall}). Simple math, you get the picture!

Moving on, you will also need to consider the type of roof. Asphalt shingles are not ideal for this application because they will leach small amounts of hydrocarbons from the tar on the shingles which is hazardous to your health. Galvanized metal roofs may leach lead over time, so this is also not advised. You will, of course, meet people who tell you, "I have drunk plenty of hydrocarbons and lead in my life, and look at me, I is fine!" Just ignore the sasquatch look in their eyes and take my advice instead. A painted metal roof is the way to go; it is definitely the best option and should yield the cleanest water. Slate roofs would be even better, but the cost and architectural considerations make this an unlikely choice. Any type of gutter will work for rain catchment as long as you keep the leaves out as they can hang on to unsanitary debris, i.e. bird poop.

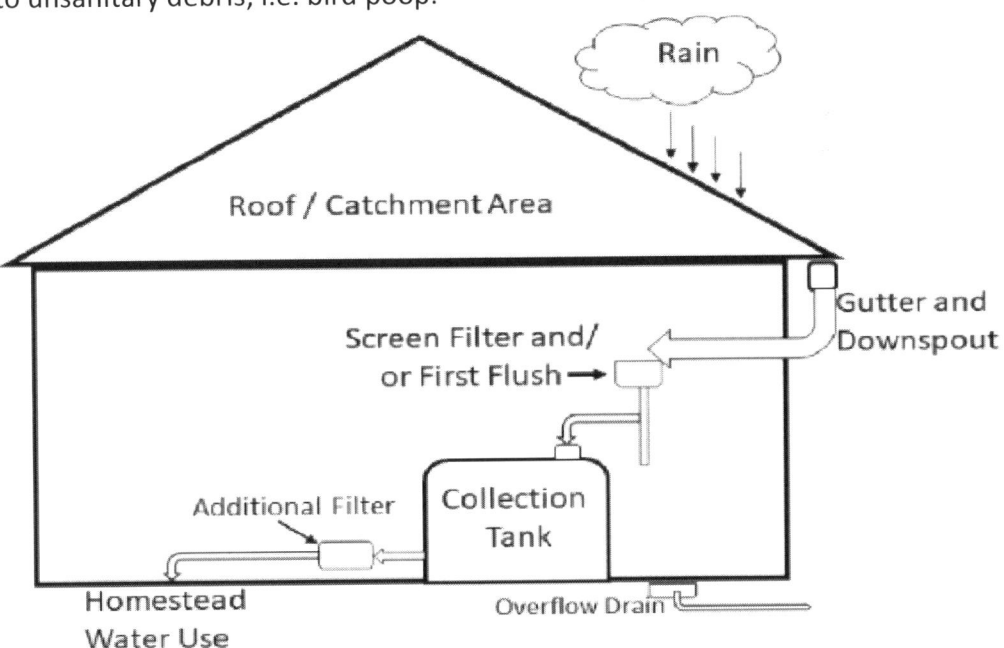

Figure 4: Basic Rainwater Catchment

Water storage is the next consideration. The amount of storage needed should be calculated by taking the daily usage of water in gallons times the maximum days of drought expected. My family uses about 100 gallons per day and in our area I would not expect a drought to last more than 4 months. So, I take 120 days times 100 gallons and thus I need 12000 gallons of water storage for a long drought. Keep in mind that this water storage should be in a tank that is safe for potable water. A friend of mine once proudly showed me his backup drinking water stored handily in an old 55-gallon industrial detergent container... But he got such a good deal on the detergent! DO NOT risk your family's health in this way. Make it potable. In the past, I would have recommended PVC pipes for your system, which is still fine, but PEX is a great easy-to-install replacement and will probably last longer without getting brittle. I have used black HDPE pipe for underground lines in the past, but I have had problems with couplings becoming leaky over time, so I now recommend at least 250 psi PEX with brass couplings underground. Drink bottled water or water from another safe source for the first week while you use any new pipes, in order to flush out any residues.

Gravity Flow

Finally, it is time to talk about gravity flow. Our family lived for years with a very meager 10 PSI water pressure in the house (PSI = pounds per square inch). This was fine for all practical purposes, but showers left something to be desired. Our visiting family chose to leave our house and stay in hotels after experiencing our water pressure. Nonetheless, we later raised our storage tank level and now have about 20 PSI, which is extremely satisfactory for showers, etc. To calculate how many pounds per square inch achieved by a gravity flow tank, you simply take the height or elevation in feet of the water level in the tank, minus the height or elevation of the faucet. Then, divide this number by 2.31 and you will get the pounds per square inch of pressure. The reason is that a 1-inch square water column that is 2.31 feet high, weighs one pound.

I absolutely love gravity flow tanks because they can eliminate extra pumps, wiring, and problems caused by broken pressure tanks. A pressure tank holds very little water by comparison and is guaranteed to have a limited lifespan. This all means that you are much more likely to experience a water outage when using a pressure tank than when using a simple gravity flow storage tank. You can use your imagination to find a way to get your water storage as high as possible above your faucets and achieve great pressure. Our family has been inspired by some homesteaders that had been living off-grid in our area since the early 1970's. They had a windmill built above a shower room that pumped water into a storage tank inside the roof. This allowed for gravity flow showers with minimal plumbing. Just using your imagination, you can think of how such a setup could incorporate a solar water heater or could be designed as part of the structure of a house. The sky is the limit when it comes to gravity flow.

Groundwater

While rainwater collection is very reliable and simple to install, groundwater is normally the cleanest and healthiest source of drinking water possible. This is because it is generally filtered, sometimes for years, through porous rock formations. Most rural Americans depend on ground water for their drinking water, but very few understand how it works. With a Masters in Geo-Engineering, I had a good idea of what to expect when the well-drillers came. The first company I talked to hemmed and hawed about the uncertainty of success as if we were just rolling the dice. This is not what you should settle for. In our area of the Ozarks, you can drill a well and hit water virtually anywhere, and depths can be easily predicted based on geological maps of your area. This is not true of all locations and is a good thing to research before moving to an area. The second company gave a bid based on aquifer depths that was within 5 feet of the actual. The owner of this company had 12 years of experience but most importantly, had enough courtesy and patience to explain every detail of the job, including how the drill rig works, to me the landowner. This is what you should expect from a drilling company as the cost can easily surpass $60 per foot.

First it is important to understand how aquifers work. Generally, an aquifer will be located in a permeable layer of rock which is porous enough to allow water to pass through, somewhat like a rigid sponge. These types of stones are known as bearing rock and typically include sandstone, limestone, and porous dolomite. This layer may be next to layers that are impermeable, that do not allow water to pass through. Impermeable layers are also called confining units and can keep water from sinking to further depths or even prevent it from rising back to the surface. They often include stone such as shale, granite, or dense dolomite. The water is not like an underground lake but instead occupies only a small portion of the porous rock, about 10% in my area. This means that out of 10 square feet of bearing rock (think sponge), 1 square foot will be water. It does travel, but often very slowly, often measured in just a few feet per year, going to lower elevations.

When drilling a well, well-drillers will talk of hitting "water rock." This means that they can actually see fragments of porous bearing coming up from the drill hole. The location of the level or depth of this aquifer stone can often be predicted by looking at well logs or data from your state's Department of Natural Resources. Otherwise, you can try to find out from your neighbors, if they remember. The DNR in many states posts this information on the internet so you can have a good idea of what to expect in your area. If a neighbor has a static water level (the surface of the well water) of 100 feet depth and is at 350 feet elevation above sea level, then the static water level is at 250 feet above sea level. Therefore, if you are very nearby, but at an elevation of 400 feet above sea level, then you could predict your static water level to be at 150 feet of depth, because you are 50 feet higher. This would just be an estimate as water levels rise and fall with the terrain, even in aquifers. In our area, the Ozarks aquifer tends to be lower near streams and higher along the ridge lines.

The static water level of your well is not necessarily the same as the level where you first hit water. The reason is that sometimes water sinks beneath impermeable rock layers or confining units. This water is under pressure because the water level of the aquifer is higher than the confining unit under which it is trapped. When you drill through the confining unit, the pressure pushes the water up through the hole to a level where it is no longer under pressure. On our homestead, we drilled a well and hit water at about 300 feet. It was flowing at only about 5 gallons per minute. We drilled another 55 feet to ensure a better flow rate (20 gpm), and then observed as the water rose to just 160 feet depth, 140 feet higher than the level we hit water at! This is known as the artesian effect and occasionally it will even push water above ground level.

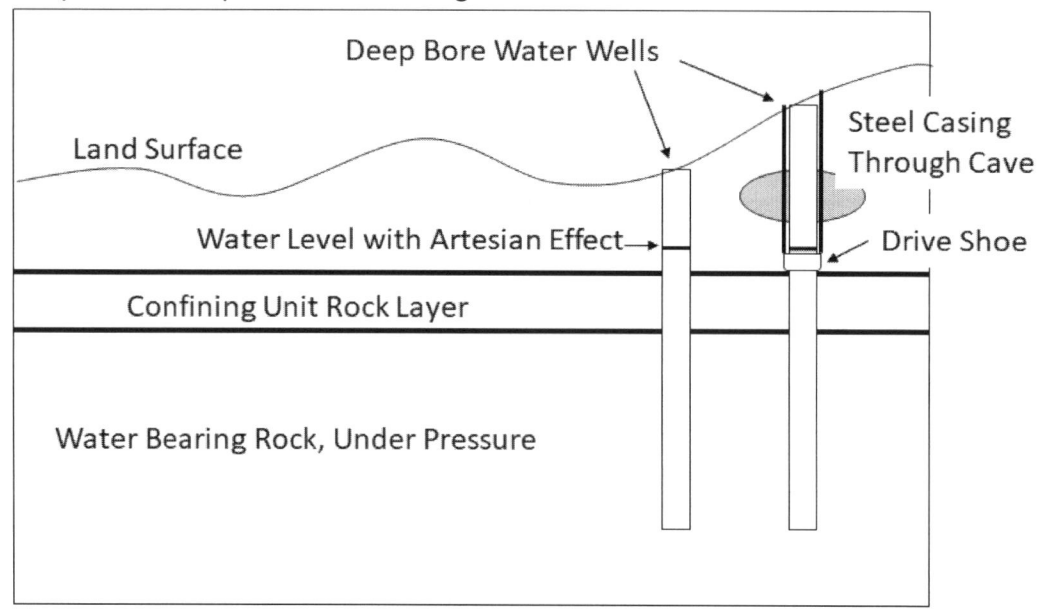

Figure 5: Water Well Basics

Notice that I said we drilled another 55 feet after we hit water. This has to do with flow rate. For most electric pumps, you want a flow rate of 10 gallons per minute or more, though some can pump slower. For a windmill or most solar pumps, 7-8 gallons per minute will suffice. In our aquifer, the flow rate was only 5-6 gallons when we first hit water. As we drilled deeper, the porosity in the rock over the larger surface area of the hole allowed us to get 20 gallons per minute by drilling just a little more.

You also need to know the depth of your well. This is easy to test as terminal velocity is about 40 ft/second. Simply drop a pebble down your well and time how long it takes to splash. Multiply the seconds by 40. If your stone is bouncing all over the place, try again. To avoid damage, don't do this after you have installed a pump.

The price of your well can really vary based on the nature of your subsurface geology. Steel casing must be put in down the hole if you hit a cave, a clay layer, or other loose or dirty material. It may sound special to hit a cave, but in areas with lots of limestone, you almost always hit a cave. Drillers may get away with only PVC casing in some areas, and often a combination of both steel and PVC are used. Using a combination typically means driving a larger 6-inch steel casing until significant resistance is met, or to the cleaner, cohesive rock layers. Then a 4-inch PVC casing can be put inside of that and can be driven down to the bottom of the well, ensuring that the walls stay clean and do not crumble all the way to the bottom. Drive shoes and other seals are used to keep shallow or murky waters from trickling down into the good water in the well. They add a little cost but are well worth it to keep your water clean. A drive shoe is typically used in conjunction with a grout that is like a cross between concrete and mud, and it is pumped down to seal between the bottom opening of your casing and the walls of the well to prevent debris from falling down the outside of the casing and getting in your water. Let your driller know that you really care about having a good seal and clean water in your well.

It is reasonable to ask a driller what they expect to use and then to explain the purpose of the liners that they choose. You can simply trust them, or you can also count the lengths as they are installed. Remember it is your well so you should know all of the details. You might feel like you are inconveniencing them, but you will have that well for decades and they are normally gone in a couple of days. Talk to your driller before you give them the job to make sure they are comfortable handling questions from customers.

Illustration 6: My Crazy Amish Friends installing a Windmill 60 feet in the Air with no Safety Ropes

Windmills and Hand-Pumps

Windmills and windmill pumps are not cheap, but they are a thing of beauty that run with a mechanical simplicity that is almost lost in modern times. If money is tight, research closely the costs of such a system and compare it with alternatives such as solar. The last thing you want to do is spend the money required to erect a windmill pump in a location where the wind speeds are too low. The limiting factors involved when choosing a windmill pump include the static water level of your ground water, the amount and quality of wind at your site, the amount of water you need, and the equipment you have chosen. The flow rate of water within your aquifer is usually not a big issue if you are anywhere close to 10 gallons per minute and often 6-8 gallons per minute will suffice. In this section, we will discuss both windmill pumps and hand pumps, because a windmill pump is normally just a hand pump with a windmill attached. When the wind doesn't blow, you just detach the windmill rod, and start pumping by hand.

Let's go over a few basics that you should understand. First, the static water level has nothing to do with the overall depth of your well. It is instead the level that the water rises to inside the well. You can put the pump deeper than this water level, but you still are only pumping against gravity after the water rises above the actual water level. Pumping water to the top of water requires almost zero force. Most windmill-capable pumps are able to pump from a water level no deeper than 200 feet below the pump. Even those that advertise deeper are not likely to be worth your effort, unless you are spending serious amounts of money on extremely heavy-duty custom equipment. For a deeper well it is much more economical to start thinking about electric or solar.

I have neighbors that went off grid back in the 1970's, when much of the renewable technology of today was not available or affordable. On a limited budget, they had a small windmill attached to a hand pump, but not more than 30 feet high, which doesn't get you far enough above the tree line or the terrain, unless you are on a tall hilltop. Even if trees are 200-300 feet away, they will cause massive turbulence and block the good steady flow that you require. My neighbors' windmill would whip around like a lightweight boxer in a heavy weight match, never able to face the wind and pump sufficient water. Good news, they have extremely strong arms to this day from all the pumping by hand.

Illustration 7: Hand-pumping water from a well more than 100 feet deep is hard work and it is nearly impossible if the water level is further down than 250 feet.

    The moral of the story is that unless you have no trees in sight and are at the top of a hill, go for the 60-foot tower and still cut the trees around it for 200 feet. If you like trees to surround your house like we do, then the windmill will need to be offset a little to a spot where you don't mind having a clear area.

    Did I mention that it is extremely helpful to put the windmill on the crest of a hill? It is very important to drill the well on top of the hill, even if there is only a remote chance that you will be erecting a windmill there. The Amish that I have often sought out for windmill advice have four farmhouses clustered around a valley, each house with its own windmill. When I visit, three of the four mills are often turning, but the one on the northwest side of the valley is just a bit lower and beside some trees. It almost never turns as far as I can tell. That sure makes for one expensive lawn ornament! The Amish seem to always insist that the mill be within 40 feet of the house. I understand that it is the lifeblood of the farm, and you want it accessible for maintenance, but it must pump water above all else, and so finding the right wind in the right location is critical!

    The first time I went to the Amish to research putting up our own mill, a huge water truck pulled up to deliver water to one of their barns. Many people might have turned around right then, convinced that it was a fool's errand. But then I found out that the barn contained 160 calves, drinking 2400 gallons per day! With an average of 5 hours of good wind per day, and a mill pumping at 5 gallons per minute, you still would only get about 1500 gallons per day. So, this farm would have needed two wells and two windmills. Make sure you do the math, especially if you own a bunch of thirsty cattle, who each drink between 15 and 30 gallons per day. For humans, the UN says that we need 35 gallons per day for each person for everything including hygiene. When my family and I first moved off-grid, we used closer to 15 gallons per day, but we used serious conservation measures. This was accomplished with a low-flow shower head, and by using grey water to flush the toilet and before we had to water gardens or trees.

When relying on a windmill, you should plan for at least a full week without wind. For a family of four, I would plan 4 times 35 gallons times 7 days which equals 980 gallons. So, round that up to a minimum of 1000 gallons of water storage to get you through a windless week, just for human consumption. Now, let's think about livestock. My Amish neighbor, in addition to his two wells, would need 17,800 gallons of storage to water his calves for one week, plus 2000 gallons for his family of 8. He needs a storage of 20,000 gallons! Keep in mind that he has scaled his operation to our modern economy, which is beyond what a survival scenario requires. In a survival scenario, you may have a milk cow that will drink up to 200 gallons per week or maybe a dairy goat that will drink no more than 10 gallons in a week. Doing the math, with a family of four, 2 cows, and 10 goats, you would need a water storage of 1500 gallons. If you have this storage and the wind is not blowing for more than a week, you are back to pumping by hand. You may also want to consider doubling this so that you have a buffer of two weeks for those sometimes-windless summer seasons.

As I may have mentioned a couple of times, your windmill could be placed at the top of a hill to gain some favorable wind. This also would allow you to place your storage tanks at the top of a hill to take advantage of gravity flow to your homestead. Don't forget that you need 2.31 feet of drop for every psi of pressure. In other words, 23.1 feet will give you 10 psi minus a small amount of friction. The friction is generally so small that at the homestead level you can leave it out.

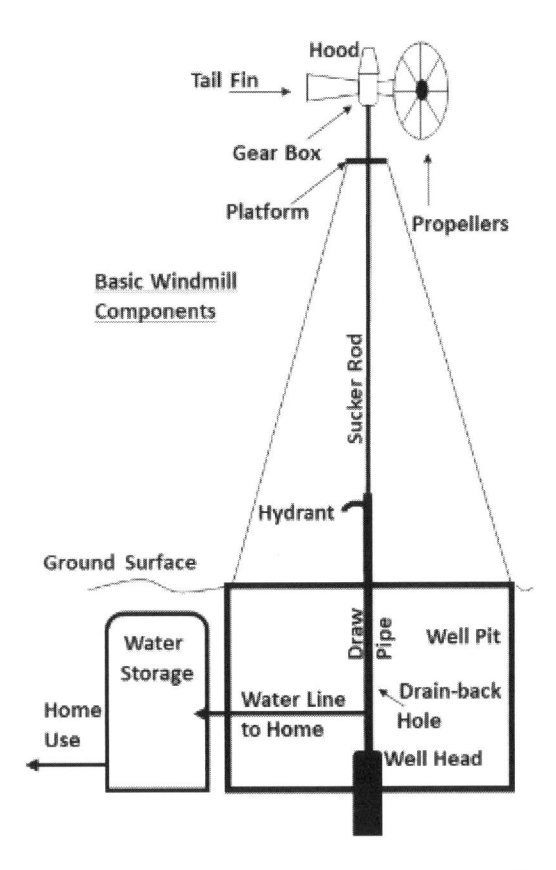

Figure 6: Components of a Water Pumping Windmill

Equipment and Erection

The steps of putting up your windmill pump include drilling the well, constructing your well pit or cellar, preparing footings and pipes, erecting the tower with windmill, installing your pump, and emplacing water storage.

Drilling the well is generally not a do-it-yourself task, so let's skip to construction of the well pit or cellar. A residential windmill pump is simply a hand pump that is attached to the drive piston of the windmill. Most of these hand pumps will pump water out of the spout, just like a garden faucet. These can be installed with a drain back valve so that you do not worry about the pump freezing, but you cannot leave a hose permanently attached or it will freeze. The drain back valve is often just a hole drilled in the pipe below the faucet which will leak a little, but can also get blocked by sand or dirt, leading to a frozen and ruined faucet. To solve this problem, we learned from the Amish to build a well pit below our windmill pump, which is a small underground room that houses the base of the pump and has pipes that pump water to underground storage tanks. This eliminates the freezing issue altogether. With the cool well casing and water pumping through the underground room, it can be used as a very effective root cellar.

The dimensions of the room are a minimum of 6x6 feet wide and 4 feet underground. It is strongly recommended to construct the pit or room before the tower is erected, so that you don't accidentally damage the tower with your digging equipment. It is constructed by pouring a 4-inch-thick concrete pad floor and then the walls can either be poured concrete or cinder block. The well casing is in the center of the room. Pipes will need to be placed at this point as close to ground level as possible with a pipe going to the storage tanks and a drainage pipe if necessary. How do you know if you need a drainage pipe? Unless you are in pure sand or gravel and well above the water table, then you need drainage. The well pit will not help you if it is underwater. If you are interested in using this as a root cellar, it may be a good idea to make it bigger than the minimum 6 feet by 6 feet and to insulate the concrete, especially towards the top of the walls. Blue board or other rigid insulation between the outside of the wall and the dirt works well. This insulation has a high enough compression strength to avoid being crushed by backfill. Backfill should be gravel or sand, allowing for good drainage of water. A drain tile or pipe around the base of the walls also will help increase drainage and reduce the weight of dirt and backfill around your pit after a rain.

Once you have built your pit, you are ready to dig footings for the anchors at the base of the tower. Many tower kits come with a four-foot leg that needs to be buried in the ground with the rest of the tower attached to this leg for stability. I also recommend putting concrete in the anchor hole to keep the tower from ever falling, although the Amish simply fill the hole with stones. In loose soil, rebar anchors should be driven deeply at an obtuse angle in addition to concrete backfill. An alternative method to using the legs is to bolt the base of the tower directly to a poured concrete wall of the well pit. In this case, you would need to be absolutely sure of the size of the tower before building the pit. This is a good time to make sure that all of your pipes going in and out of the pit are in place. A lid, preferably concrete will need to be poured at a later phase when everything else is complete.

After the footings, it is time to erect the tower. Many individuals will wish to simply put in the hand pump now and do a tower as funding allows. This works, but a drill rig or tripod with a block and tackle will need to be used to lower the rods into the well casing so leave room for this.

When you bury your anchor legs, it is very important that they be square, level, and at the same angle as the rest of the tower. To assist, a temporary square brace is assembled at ground level to hold them together at the right position while you fill in the anchor holes. If they are not perfectly level or square, then the tower will also not be level or will be impossible to anchor properly.

Next the entire tower is to be assembled on the ground. This simply entails putting all of the pieces together and tightening the nuts. Make sure everything is completely tight and use a thread-locking glue to keep it from coming apart. Otherwise, your whole tower may come crashing down. You may choose to put on the head of the wind turbine at this stage but if you are concerned about damaging it during the erection of the tower, you may also choose to put it on after tower erection. For the erection of the tower, it is recommended to get a crane that can pick the top of the tower straight up and hold it in place while it is bolted down. If you try to pull it up with a tractor, or with horses like the Amish, then there is more of a chance that it will buckle or fall and kill someone.

Illustration 8: Erecting a Windmill for our Homestead with the Help of a Crane

Once the tower is erected and bolted in place, then it is time to use the crane to raise the head of the windmill, if it was not erected with the tower. Two individuals will need to climb to the top of the platform to guide the head onto the spindle. They should be tied in with a safety harness. There is only one bolt to attach on the top of the spindle and then the gear box of the windmill must be filled with oil. To fill it with oil, all you must do is remove the hood on top and pour the oil in, filling until the gears are completely covered plus one inch. This oil should then be changed once every 6 months, with a 20 weight, zero detergent oil. The reason that there is no detergent is because detergent is generally for machines that have some kind of oil filter. When you change oil, there is a drain plug to make the job easy.

(Easy except for climbing a 60-foot ladder) Once the windmill is fully erected, installing the pump is next.

Hand Pump installation (attachable to windmill)

The pump I will discuss is the same type of simple pump that has been used for generations and is still used by the Amish and other off-gridders today. Installation starts with the piece that goes at the bottom of the well, and I will start there. The piece that goes in the bottom of the well is called the cylinder (see diagram). It is simply that, a brass cylinder that is hollow in the middle. On the bottom, there is a hole where the water enters when suction pulls the water up. When the suction is released, there is a brass weight that closes the hole to prevent water from escaping. The suction is applied by a piston in the brass cylinder that has actual leather providing the suction between the cylinder and the piston. These "leathers" are a replaceable $5 piece of leather that will wear out every 5-10 years, so have some extra on hand. This piston within the cylinder is pumped up and down by a stainless-steel sucker rod that is attached all the way to the pump and windmill at the top of the well. This sucker rod fits inside of a galvanized water pipe that carries the water as well as holding onto the cylinder. Both the sucker rod and water pipe generally come in 20-foot sections. It is really that simple; the pump handle or windmill moves the sucker rod up and down which pumps the cylinder, sending the water up the pipe.

When sizing your pipe and cylinder, keep in mind that the deeper the well, the harder it will be to pump. The reason is that the force required to lift your water is determined by mass times the acceleration. Acceleration is constant because it is determined by the stroke length of your pump, but the mass of the water becomes much greater if your water level is deeper. To decrease the mass, you simply use a smaller diameter water pipe, and smaller diameter cylinder. This means you have less water to lift with each stroke, making it easier on the pump. With most brands of pumps and cylinders, 200 feet is about the maximum pumping depth. Some manufacturers claim greater depths, but you start to run into the limits of physical possibility. The pumping depth is determined by the surface of the water, known as the static water level. The pump should be placed well below this level in the case that it drops in a severe drought. In our area, this means 20-30 feet below the water level. The depth of the pump cylinder below this static water level is of little consequence to the pumping effort because it requires almost no force to pump water through water in the well. The real force is needed when you pump water above the static water level. In most aquifers, the static water level will not change drastically under normal circumstances. In our area, levels may have dropped 5-10 feet in 20 years, due primarily to agricultural use. In desert areas where water is not recharged, levels may drop in response to industrial-scale pumping and industrial agriculture (one example is the Oglala aquifer)

In my experience, a 1.5-inch cylinder with a 1-inch lift pipe (water pipe), is the best fit for a 200 foot well. This is the smallest cylinder that is normally available, but still requires a great deal of force to pump by hand and if pumping with wind, it requires a large windmill with steady wind above 10mph. If you are lucky enough to have a shallow well, let's say 40 feet or less, you can go with a 2-inch pipe and a 2.5-inch cylinder. Increasing the diameters will increase the mass of water and the force required but it also means you will pump a very large volume with each stroke. A 2-inch lift pipe has a volume that is 4 times greater than a one-inch pipe, pumping 4 times as much water with each stroke.

Illustration 9: This 1.5 Inch Cylinder Pump is a very simple mechanism where the sucker rod (seen sticking out the top) pumps up and down to suck in water from the bottom. You can also see the 1 inch drop pipe that carries water but here is unscrewed and lying beside the cylinder.

Anyone can install a simple hand pump of the type that is attached to a windmill. As I mentioned, the lift pipe and sucker rods come in 20-foot sections. This means you will need an anchor point that is about 25 feet above your borehole (well). The anchor point must be strong enough to support the weight of your entire assembly of pipes. It must support them full of water if you need to pull it out to do repairs later. At the anchor point, you will attach a block and tackle, which will reduce the force required to lower or lift your assembled pipe. A threaded coupling that is the same size as your pipe with an attachment ring is attached to the block and tackle to lower the pipe sections. The first section to go is the bottom section. To prepare the bottom section, slide the first sucker rod into the pipe and screw it onto the sucker rod attachment on the pump cylinder. Then screw the lift pipe onto the cylinder itself. Usually, couplers are required at all attachments unless they are built in. Sealant paste should be used on the lift pipe threads and removable thread locker should be used on the sucker rod threads. The Amish screw a 10 feet black HDPE plastic "tail pipe" on the bottom of the cylinder. This is to keep water in the pump in the case that the water level drops in the well. All attachments should be secured snugly with pipe wrenches to prevent anything from falling into the borehole and being lost forever. Vice-grips are useful for tightening the sucker rod. Two people should do the tightening.

As this first section and subsequent sections are lowered into the hole, a brake-mechanism is used to prevent loss of the pipe. All pipe must be slid through the brake-mechanism and then down the well. One individual releases the brake as at least two individuals lower the pipe sections into the hole. After the first section is lowered, the brake is applied, the attachment ring is unscrewed, and the next section is lifted using the attachment ring and the block and tackle. It is a good idea to use vice-grips or a monkey wrench to secure the pipe that is sitting in the hole in the case that the brake mechanism fails. You do not want to lose your pipe in the borehole as it may even block the hole and render the well useless! After you achieve the desired depth with your pipe and sucker rod, you simply screw them on to the matching ends that come with your pump. There is a well cap that should come with the pump that has a gasket to seal the well with a hole in it to allow the pipe to pass through. It is also helpful to anchor the base of your hand pump to a small concrete pad around your well. The pump base should have bolt holes for this purpose. There you have it! If you ever need to fix the pump or replace the leathers, just pull it out in the reverse order that I have just described.

Solar Pumps

Solar pumps have become more affordable than windmills and are more versatile because good sun is easier to find than good wind. They are also quite easy to install because they do not require heavy, rigid pipe or sucker rods. I have installed solar pumps in various locations; in a shallow spring, an old-fashioned pit well, a cistern, and a deep borehole well. Solar pumps can be found that will pump water in excess of 200 feet, with price increasing along with depth capabilities. If the solar pump is installed first, a hand pump can also be installed in the same well, provided the diameter is large enough to accommodate both.

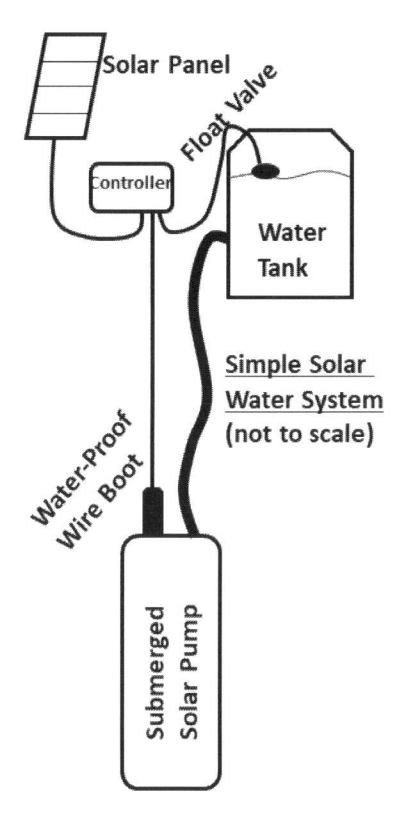

Figure 7: Diagram of a Solar Pump System

    The basic components of a solar pump include the pump itself, power cord, hose or pipe, solar panels, charge controller, and optional depth sensors. Pumps generally come with a screen filter, to protect the pump diaphragms from getting clogged with dirt. Nonetheless, you always want to ensure your pump will be sitting in clean water. I once installed a pump in a crystal-clear stream, only to have it clog up immediately during a rainstorm. They can be disassembled and cleaned, but this is a delicate, tedious process. Solar pumps should come with a waterproof rubber boot that protects the power cord where it plugs into the pump. Waterproof pump installers tape can be used to reinforce this. When selecting a solar pump, it is important to first know the height above water and the rate of flow at which you will be pumping. Pumps are rated to pump from a specific depth at a certain flow rate. Also, don't forget to include not only the depth of the well, but also the additional pumping height to storage tanks when calculating your total pumping height above water. After installing a sufficiently long wire, a flexible pipe is also hooked to the pump. Usually, ½ inch pipe is sufficient for deeper wells, with this small size meaning that less water weight has to be pumped all at once. With very shallow wells, you can attach larger pipes and attain a larger flow volume. It is acceptable to use black HDPE pipe, made for potable water applications, but black rubber ag hose is more flexible and doesn't pinch as easily.

Illustration 10: Solar Pump with three lines attached; water line, nylon lowering line, and electrical wire with waterproof tape.

With the pipe and electric wire hooked on, the pump should be lowered into the water using a long nylon twine, such as hay baling twine. It is bad practice to use the electrical wire or pipe to lower the pump as it may cause it to come loose. The pump should be lowered just a few feet lower than you ever expect the water level to be. The force required to pump the water to the surface is determined by the actual water level, and not the depth of the pump. Even so, the pump should not be placed lower than necessary because the voltage will be weakened by an excessively long power cord. This is especially true for low voltage DC pumps, even though higher voltage pumps may be less affected. The reason is that there is a voltage drop that occurs that is directly proportional to the length of the power cord. If the voltage starts at 12 volts, and drops to 10 volts, then that will affect the electric motor. For a 110-volt current to drop by the same amount to 108 volts, the effect will be negligible. A larger gauge wire compensates for the longer distance or greater depth of your well, but this can be pricey. A larger gauge wire is also dependent upon the amperage of your well pump. (See below chart for recommended wire size based on distance)

	WIRE SIZE / AWG (Max. Distance in Feet)									
AMPS	14	12	10	8	6	4	2	1/0	2/0	3/0
1	45	70	115	180	290	456	720			
2	22.5	35	57.5	90	145	228	360	580	720	1060
4	10	17.5	27.5	45	72.5	114	180	290	360	580
6	7.5	12	17.5	30	47.5	75	120	190	240	380
8	5.5	8.5	11.5	22.5	35.5	57	90	145	180	290
10	4.5	7	11.5	18	28.5	45.5	72.5	115	145	230
16	3	4.5	7	12	19	30	48	76.5	96	150
20	2	3.5	5.5	9	14.5	22.5	36	57.5	72.5	116
25	1.8	2.8	4.5	7	11.5	18	29	46	58	92
30	1.5	2.4	3.5	6	9.5	15	24	38.5	48.5	77
40			2.8	4.5	7	11.5	18	29	36	56
50			2.3	3.6	5.5	9	14.5	23	29	46
100					2.9	4.6	7.2	11.5	14.5	23
150							4.8	7.7	9.7	15
200							3.6	5.8	7.3	11

*Figure 8: Wire Sizing Chart for 12 Volt System: Shows Maximum One-Way Distance (**in Feet**) without Exceeding 2% Voltage Loss*

After the pump, it is time to install the solar panel and charge controller. Your solar panel should be facing due south if you are in the northern hemisphere, and the tilt should be about the same as the latitude of your location. If you are at 35 degrees of latitude, the average tilt should be 35 degrees measured from the ground surface. The size of your solar panel will be determined by the given specifications of your solar pump. In my experience, a 300-watt panel with the right pump can pump a 1/2-inch pipe of water to 200 feet of elevation at a slow rate of about 1 gallon per minute on average. This is enough to pump 400 gallons on a good, sunny day! This is approximately enough for two off-grid families of four or one family and a milk cow with a small garden.

All solar pumps need a charge controller in between the solar panel and the pump, to regulate the voltage to something that is acceptable to the solar pump. This will keep the pump from burning up from a voltage that is too high or too low. Charge controllers vary in size, but a good quality solar pump will come with a charge controller that is made specifically for the pump. It is just a small box with an inlet port for wires that come from the solar panel and an outlet port for wires going to the well pump. Installation of these charge controllers is very straight forward as long as you get the wires size right and keep it waterproof and safe from insects and rodents. It pays off to take a little extra time to caulk around wires and in ports or holes in your electrical boxes. If you don't you are almost guaranteed to be creating a home for insects to nest in, or worse, a rat nest!

There may also be a port for a float valve, automatic dry shut-off, and a manual on/off switch. A float valve for a solar pump is normally electric, not mechanical, and it is simply a rubber power cord with a floating chamber on the end that has a ball rattling around inside. You place the floating chamber on the surface of your water tank. When it is full, it will float and the ball will roll to the top end of the chamber, disconnecting the electric circuit, and shutting off your pump. When the tank is below the full level, the chamber will hang down freely, and the ball will roll to the end of the chamber, connecting your electric circuit and turning your pump back on. This will save a lot of wear and tear on your pump and keep you from overfilling your water tank.

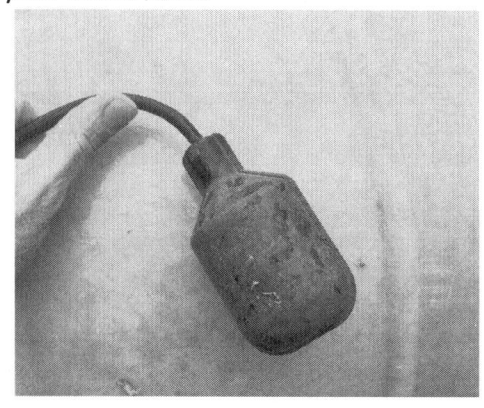

Illustration 11: A simple float valve will complete the circuit and turn on the pump when it is allowed to hang down because of low water. When the water fills it will float upright and turn off the pump.

An automatic dry shut-off on your pump will save your pump from burning up by not pumping when the well is dry. On most good aquifers, you shouldn't have to worry about this with the slow pumping rates of solar pumps. However, you may be in a location where you are dealing with a more variable aquifer or spring water, where the depth can fluctuate with the weather and seasons. For this scenario, some charge controllers will come with a wet/dry sensor, which will be attached with a wire all the way from a charge controller to the water level just above your pump. If that water level drops below the sensor, then the charge controller will shut off power to the pump, saving your pump. There may also be a second sensor, which will be placed a bit higher. This sensor will turn the pump back on when the water level gets to its higher level. The reason for the second sensor is so that the pump doesn't turn on prematurely.

When using a solar pump, you will obviously not be able to pump when the sun is not shining. Most conventional on-grid homes with wells will pump water into a pressure tank that holds less than 80 gallons. This will be insufficient for most off-grid needs. For this reason, you need to pump as much water into a holding tank as possible while the sun shines. The specifications for this holding tank are the same for the rainwater catchment and gravity flow scenarios that I outlined earlier in this chapter on water. Interestingly, you can have multiple types of pumps and water collection that can pump into the same holding tanks. For example, on my family's homestead, we have a solar pump, windmill, and rainwater collection that all use the same holding tanks. For even greater resiliency, I recommend using multiple, interconnected tanks instead of one big tank. Each tank should have its own shutoff valve so that you can disconnect it in case it develops a leak. Multiple water sources, multiple pumping devices, multiple storage tanks... This redundancy is how you create resiliency. In the military, the saying is, "two is one and one is none." This means that you must always have a backup because your primary is bound to fail sooner or later. If your solar pump fails, then you have rainwater collection and a windmill. If one tank gets a hole in it, then you have another, etc. Water is life; if you don't have water, then you don't have a homestead.

Ponds

Ponds are a great option for backup water. Pond water, when kept clean, is an excellent option for livestock and watering gardens, and can be filtered for drinking in a pinch. The key to a good pond is good site selection and a little know-how. The man that owned our property prior to us built two lovely and large dams, perfectly shaped, majestically tall, and embarrassingly empty of water. For this reason, this section focuses on how to successfully catch water with your dam, thereby avoiding the damn hard work for nothing and damn embarrassing dam. But first, let us briefly consider the use and purpose of a pond.

Pond water should be considered a last resort for human water consumption and can even be detrimental to the health of livestock. Our local agricultural extension agent highly discourages ponds, and instead encourages electrically pumped water. But, wait just a minute, what if electricity fails or the grid goes down?!? For this reason, in areas without year-round streams or springs, a pond can be the most reliable and fail-safe water source possible. On our farm we have water from the aquifer for our livestock, but we have also constructed ponds in case pumps fail, pipes break, or other mayhem occurs. For the health of the ponds and the animals, cows are fenced out unless there is such an emergency.

Now on to the important part. As a Geo-engineer who has built many dams in porous terrain, I can tell you that some sites are just not suitable and sometimes entire farms are not suitable for ponds. When looking for a good site, you need a large area with several feet of clay, and some year-round incoming water seepage or flow. Notice that I did not say you need to be in a valley, draw, or low ground. A rapid water flow is not necessary or even desirable; think slow and steady. Often water will follow the contours of the hills, not far beneath the surface. After rainfall occurs, it slowly seeps into the ground until it hits an impenetrable or impervious surface. This can be a clay lens or a dense rock layer such as shale. If this impervious surface is then exposed at the ground surface on the downhill side, the water will be seen leaking out. When you see this on top of a clay lens, then you are looking at a seep. If this carries water year-round and the clay is deep and wide, then you have a great spot for a pond. In some cases, the water is not seen leaking out, so you will need to dig a test hole to see if there is any flow. The best way to measure your flow is to get a gallon bucket and see how long it takes to fill it up. I would recommend at least one gallon per ten minutes for a small pond. This flow needs to take place even in dry, hot weather, so check it during a dry season.

What is a bad spot for a pond? Let's go back to the previous owner of my farm and his two dry pond dams. He put them both across deep, wide draws (small valleys between hills) that carried seasonal streams. The problem was that while there was water, there was no clay to build a dam or hold water. So, he built the dams out of rocky, sandy, loose loam soil. Try to make a bowl out of beach sand and put water in it. It disappears quickly. These dams made of rocky, sandy soil may hold water for a few days after a hard rain, but they are mainly useless. You should have at least 50% clay content.

Illustration 12: The Author building a pond dam at a site with excellent clay and abundant subsurface water.

Another problem that you need to avoid when choosing a spot for your pond is something called rock ledge. Often, even under a clay lens, you will dig and hit a ledge that may not be impervious to water. If this happens, the water can seep out the pores and cracks in the ledge and quickly drain your pond. You can tell when you are near a ledge because you will feel and hear your digging implements scraping across a big, solid piece of rock while you are digging. This can normally be detected while digging your test hole but could be found anywhere during excavation. Some rock ledges are very leaky or you may get lucky with rock that doesn't leak. To avoid problems, choose a site without a rock ledge or try not to dig all the way down to the ledge, keep it covered with clay, and hope for the best.

To avoid wasting your time on a high-risk dam site, it is best to dig several test holes.

to examine your soil horizons or soil layers. The best time to do all of this work is when the area is as dry as possible. That way you can avoid working in the mud and water. Simply dig a deep trench in different locations to make sure that you do have several feet of clay and do not have any rock ledge, or patches of sand and gravel or other porous material that will drain away your water. Pay closest attention to the test hole or holes near where your dam will be located, which is also the deepest area of your future pond.

Next, you will need to remove all vegetation, topsoil, and organic material from your pond area. Roots left in the ground can easily become a conduit for water exfiltration out of the pond. I have repaired ponds where individuals have let trees grow in the dams and they immediately begin springing leaks because of all the roots. You want to strip the area down to bare clay when building a pond if possible. At least the dam site needs to be stripped down to clay. You need to move all organic material, dark organic soil, and vegetation as all of these things cause leaks. Once you have done so, mark your dam site with some flags so that you know where you are working. If your pond is in a draw (miniature three-sided valley), then you can cut straight across the downhill side with your pond, from one side of the draw to the next. If it is fairly level ground, you will need to make a larger U-shaped dam, on the downhill side of course. If it is completely level, then your pond is simply a hole.

Before you build the dam up, you need to first excavate a key into the ground. A key is an excavation just below the dam, the same width that the dam will be. The depth of the key excavation should be at least 1 meter or three feet. This allows you to remove any traces of roots that remain and form a seal beneath the dam so that water cannot move between the dam and the ground beneath the dam. Once the key has been excavated, I like to sprinkle some bentonite into the key surface. This is an expansive clay that will act as a seal. Just a 1/8 inch layer of bentonite 3 feet wide will do the trick for most dams that also have enough clay content. Next, fill the key with good, clean clay, 6 inches at a time (6-inch lifts). After each 6-inch lift is added, it needs to be compacted. There are all kinds of professional compacting equipment, but for a farm pond, it will suffice to drive over each lift 2 to 3 times with a wheeled or tracked vehicle. Wheeled vehicles actually provide for greater compaction but sometimes you have to use a tracked vehicle to avoid getting stuck. Min-excavators and backhoes work great on small ponds, but large excavators and bulldozers are necessary for anything over ¼ acre.

Illustration 13: The Same Pond as Above; Ponds are a great source of backup drinking water, livestock water, and it is relatively easy to stock a healthy pond with high protein fish.

The layers of dirt that make up a dam, which are called lifts, must be patiently added and individually compacted until the dam reaches the height that is desired to achieve adequate pond depth. This depth depends on the terrain, your time, equipment, and the purpose of your pond. Ponds are often limited in depth by the presence of rock ledge or porous material beyond a certain depth under the soil. If you wish to keep fish in your pond, it is often necessary to achieve a depth of about 6 feet or greater in temperate climate areas.

After building your pond, you must think about how to avoid having the dam wash away by overflowing water. This is especially true when there is a heavy rainfall event. I recently built a pond on a large clay lens, away from all streams, where there was only a small seepage of water flowing. On the day I finished the pond, we experienced 3 days of rainfall, totaling about 8 inches. This is enough water to wash away a pond, in this case one which I had worked on for about two weeks straight! I had to quickly install a spillway, where the water can overflow the pond without eroding away the dam. A spillway can be a culvert, which goes through and over the top of the dam. It can also be a concrete path for the water to flow across, or sometimes a path made of thick-bedded gravel will suffice.

The important thing is that the spillway is big enough, and placed in the right spot, so that the water will not overflow or spill over your earthen dam in any other spot. This means that it must hold a sufficient volume to ensure that there is no overflow. It must also let water out lower than any other low spot on your dam. If you have another low spot on your earthen dam, then water will flow out there and wash away the dam. Heavy rainfall events can easily destroy a dam, especially if they are built in an intermittent or seasonal stream bed. This is why a sufficiently large spillway is crucial for the survival of your pond. And you want your pond to survive in perpetuity because it is one of the best options for long-term water redundancy and resilience on your farmstead.

Illustration 14: Castles were the only Safe Place in the Old Dark Ages, and we can learn from that example as we enter a New Dark Age

Chapter 6: Introducing the Homebunker: A Castle for the New Dark Age

My father-in-law was a builder in Europe for his entire life. He has given me loads of unsolicited advice, which usually began with a phrase that roughly translates as, "do you want to do this project with your ass..... OR WITH YOUR HEAD?!" This is a translation so I am not sure how it sounds in English but in Italian, it sounds hilarious, even though he is normally frowning at me when he says it. I have to keep from laughing and at the same time, I have to make him think I am taking him seriously, because construction really is a serious endeavor. In this section, I want to talk about how to plan building projects on your off-grid farmstead, using your head, and NOT YOUR ASS!

I have seen plenty of off-grid projects built with... let's just say built poorly; and the family that lives there continues to live with and suffer for the mistakes committed during the building process. Anyone that builds their own home will know its shortcomings better than anyone else, and there will always be shortcomings. I have seen homes situated poorly that collect too much heat in the summer, homes that are poorly insulated and have frozen pipes in the winter, and homes with poor drainage that flood when it rains. I know the mistakes that I have made and had to fix later, and I have talked with many other homesteaders about their building mistakes, even though it is not their favorite subject.

Now I want to share this information with you so that you can learn from the mistakes of others, and so that your family doesn't have to live with your building mistakes.

It is very common for individuals and I myself even used to have this fantasy of building a log cabin from my own trees somewhere on a lonely mountain retreat. After all, as Americans, this is what our forefathers did for centuries, carving out a living from the wilderness with their own two hands, living in a log cabin. But when it comes to survival, let us not appeal to tradition. Instead, let us use our heads and think hard about what will make it easier to survive as the world around us collapses. Survival requires not only skill and hard work, but you always must think hard, use your imagination, and ask yourself, "What is the worst that could happen?" In the military we had a saying, "If it can happen, then it will happen." This mantra is especially true when it comes to building your survival homestead. To survive the unexpected, you need to really consider building something more substantial than a traditional building.

There are a half dozen old chimneys within walking distance of my rural home. The homes have all burned, rotted, or otherwise fallen down within the 90 years or less since they were first built. There is even one story of a family across the creek just at the beginning of the 20th century. At this time most Americans still lived on small family farms, because big agriculture had not yet forced everyone off of these farms. This particular small farming family had a great setup; beautiful spring water, a bit of bottom land, rolling pasture, timber, good hunting, and a cozy log home heated by a wood cook stove. Unfortunately, their house burnt down a few years after construction and they ended up living in the root cellar for several years until they could afford to rebuild. It turned into a real nightmare. Conditions were unsanitary in the cellar, they had an infant child die of whooping cough, and finally the father died of pneumonia while trying to recover from a tree-felling accident. The family was ruined, and their misery echoed down through the generations! In those days, there was no home insurance, and neighbors did not always have the resources to help a family in need. Imagine the toil, trouble, and wasted resources that occurs generation after generation when building with materials that easily burn, rot, and blow away.

Contrast this with my wife's family in the foothills of the Alps, whose great-grandfather worked extra hard building stone walls 2 feet thick, anchored into the rocky mountain-side. It was also a great amount of toil and trouble. Still, he raised his family in it, and his son raised his family, and his son, and now two of the great, great grandsons are being raised in the same house, and no one has had to rebuild. I do think it is time for a new roof, as the spruce tree used as the original ridge pole is starting to sag; not bad for a century-old home. Now that hard times are again returning to Italy, building a home is one less thing that the family has to worry about. It is time we all start using our heads and thinking about thriving in the long term.

I know what you are thinking, "how can I afford to build a robust structure that will last 100 years or more?" But, let us consider the moral of the story the three little pigs. This is one of the favorite fairy tales told to children in the United States, yet we continue to build houses out if sticks, and not bricks! Even straw homes are gaining in popularity! Sustainable shelter goes hand-in-hand with survivable shelter. The reason is that a robust and efficient shelter not only keeps it inhabitants thriving in tough conditions, but it also lasts long enough for the return on labor and resource investment to pay off. For example, a well-insulated concrete-walled building will keep its inhabitants safe from fire, tornadoes, insects, and even gunfire. The same building, being made of concrete, will last for 50 generations. The building where my wife and I were married in Europe was an actual castle built in the 15th century, and it is continuously used up to the present day. If cost is a problem, then at least consider building a survival shelter or bunker on your survival homestead that will keep you safe in extreme circumstances. I have built many elaborate bunkers during and after my military career and in the following pages I can give you some basic guidelines to help you build this type of shelter and add to it the comforts of a civilian home. I like to call it the "homebunker."

The challenges of yesterday may pale in comparison to the challenges of tomorrow. While we don't have to defend our homes from slave-raiders (hopefully), the next century will likely see humans facing extreme weather, resource shortages, and social unrest. If this were not enough, consider nuclear proliferation. Ten countries are likely nuclear armed at the moment, and there are nearly 20,000 nuclear weapons on the planet. While we have all grown up with a nuclear-armed planet, many people seem to believe that these weapons will not be used again. But if you think about human history, when have we ever had the ability to destroy something and not actually done it? Nuclear weapons will be used again, and a high strength, reinforced concrete home can provide over 10 times the shear strength against horizontal force and nearly twice the compressive strength against vertical force as a stick frame home. It is the most durable, easily maintained material, which can be economically molded to any shape that you choose to design. Can you build a homebunker? You Can!

Worried about sustainability? While it is estimated that a stick-frame wood house uses 1/3 the energy and has 1/2 the carbon footprint as a concrete home, let us do the math. A stick frame home may last 50 years, on average. Concrete buildings can just as easily last 500 years, or even longer. My wife and I were married in a 500+ year-old building. So, if a modest stick frame building costs 50 thousand dollars, then, lasting 50 years, it comes to 1000 dollars per year. A concrete home of a similar size might cost 100,000 dollars, but lasting for 500 years, it comes to only 200 dollars per year. Plus, your great, great grandchildren will respect the hell out of you for building such an awesome house for them. This also makes it more ecologically sustainable to build one concrete home in 500 years than to build 10 stick frame homes in the same amount of time, because the fuel and resources required over the long term are much less. This is only one example of the advantages of a more robust home (homebunker), and a great reason why it is important to do the math.

Homes or bunker add-ons that I have built and wish to share with you, are based on the mass and durability of masonry construction and are designed around passive solar heating, use of thermal mass, and vertical air exchange. Such designs are not only robust and long-lasting, but they require very low energy to heat and cool and make life easier and more comfortable as well. The ancient Greeks used masonry and passive solar design which was considered an important sign of a civilized society. The skills required to build such a home or bunker are easily learned, and once you learn them, this type of construction becomes achievable and affordable.

The Basics of Masonry Construction

The advantages of masonry buildings become clear just by briefly examining the principles of passive heating, durability, and defense of the homestead. Still, many people find this type of construction to be intimidating and difficult to undertake. I still feel a little nervous when I hear a concrete truck pulling up the road to one of my off-grid project sites, but I have to remember that most of this is mental. As long as you give yourself the time to plan and prepare for a masonry build, then things can often go smoother than a stick frame build, except that you know you are building something that will last pretty much forever. For me, I draw inspiration from my travels in Europe, and seeing my father-in-law in Italy carry on a tradition that started there with the Etruscans. Moreover, seeing an 800-year-old building still in use is proof that masonry is the way to go when you want survivability.

Our goal when building such a home is not to create anything fancy or complex, because that can break in difficult times, when repair parts may not be available. Instead, I will focus here on the essential and simple elements of construction that will benefit the home's inhabitants for decades or centuries without maintenance. The following is basic advice that can be used to help plan the construction of a small bunker. It would have to be up-scaled significantly to build a bunker-home and remember any advice you read in a book does not take the place of a professional engineer that should be consulted for any construction project. Or you can just "ranger-up" and assume responsibility yourself!

Planning Considerations for building a Bunker

As a combat veteran in Infantry and Ranger units, I have built and used my fair share of bunkers. One of my favorite examples of a very expensive failure was a Cold War Era bunker at a decommissioned nuke site in Germany. I was attending a NATO reconnaissance school where we were expected to survey the site while remaining undetected by guards and dogs from the hosting German army. Fortunately for us, people and dogs alike are easily distracted, and we managed to slip inside the bunker to do our reconnaissance. It had many features that I liked, 2-foot-thick concrete ceiling, dry walls, and a long entrance with inner and outer doors. However, one major problem existed, 6 inches of water on the floor! Are you kidding me? This was a major nuclear site during the cold war, and while spending their millions, they overlooked drainage for the nuclear bunker! The problem was that instead of finding a way to allow gravity to take away the water, the site had relied on an electric sump pump. Now that it was decommissioned, there was no electricity to pump away the water. During any disaster that you may have to face, you may lose electricity, even with an off-grid backup. With this in mind, there are several important planning considerations that you need to think of ahead of time before building a homebunker.

1. Drainage: The most important detail of a bunker that needs early planning is ensuring that water will not fill up your bunker, meaning that you would have to spend the apocalypse in a deep, dark, underground swimming pool (Not Fun!). If you are building in a low-lying or flat, easily flooded area, consider changing your location. Floods are serious and common disasters that will ruin your hard work. Good drainage means that your building site needs to have at least a gentle slope. If you live in the mountains like me, drainage can be quite easy. A network of drainpipes covered in gravel can be placed so that they slope downhill, preventing any flooding of your construction. This will be discussed further in the foundation section, later in this chapter.

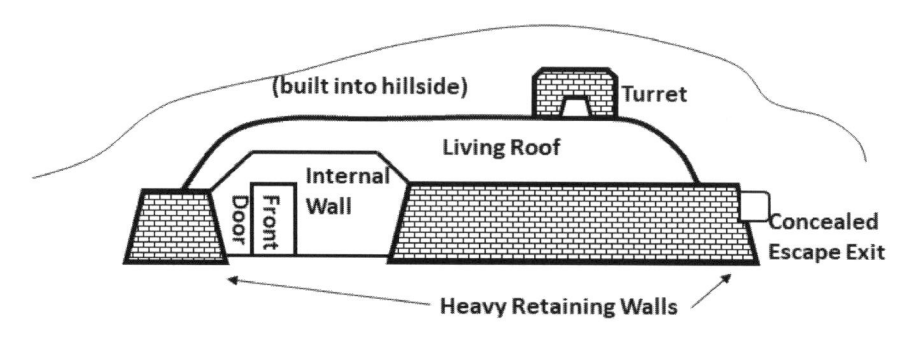

Figure 9: Sideview of Basic Bunker Shelter

2. Fields of Fire: "Fields of Fire" is a military term which means areas that you can see and effectively shoot at. Let me insert a quick disclaimer here; I am not advocating for rebellion, insurrection, etc. I am all for stability and peace, and I believe in the motto, "Leave to Caesar what is Caesar's." In good times, the power is all yours Brandon, but in case of unexpected disaster where the government has failed to keep us safe, then we all deserve to have a bunker. For certain types of natural disasters, this is unnecessary, but take a quick look at history or the news for that matter and see the savagery that people have committed against each other when the rule of law breaks down. You should be prepared to defend yourself and your loved ones. Many military bunkers, including the WWII German bunkers in Normandy, have a port for firing at invaders only in one direction. This is because

they worked together with other defenders in a large perimeter. As the Germans found out, you don't always know which side of the perimeter you will be attacked from (take it from a paratrooper). In fact, the Infantry battle drill for attacking a bunker is to fire into the port while someone else moves around to a flank that does not have a firing port. The moral of the story is that your bunker should have fields of fire on all sides, if possible, especially if it is a standalone bunker. This may mean installing a turret if you do not plan on having many defenders on your side to watch your back. If you do plan on having multiple defenders, then you can have multiple firing ports.

3. Escape Route: An escape route or tunnel is often overlooked when building a bunker, but it is not difficult to install with just a little prior planning. The easiest way to create an escape route from your bunker is to use a 2-foot diameter black plastic culvert. Excavation for your culvert is not hard, as long as you do it along with the initial excavation for the bunker site. Going back and installing it later is more expensive and tricky because you don't want to damage your existing construction. I recommend 4-inch perforated drainage pipe and gravel below your escape tunnel, just as I recommend in the section on foundations below. This will keep it from getting flooded, or worse, bringing water into the rest of your bunker. Obviously, your escape route will need to end somewhere that is slightly hidden, perhaps covered by vegetation or in a drainage ditch. The idea is that if you have holed up in your bunker and you are surrounded with seemingly no chance of escape, then a tunnel can give you the ability to escape. So, think ahead while planning and be creative when concealing the exit to your escape route.

4. Safe room Doors: There are a number of good options when it comes to entrances and exits for your bunker. The best, most cost-effective method is to build a multi-room bunker with one of the rooms being protected by a safe room door. This way, you can use your bunker without having to open a complicated lock every time you go in and out. This type of door has a built-in combination lock and cannot be breached without serious demolition tools. It needs to be anchored in concrete. The quality of your door depends on your budget and ranges from one thousand dollars to ten thousand dollars. The hinges are extremely important because they must be able to support such a heavy door. I have installed doors for customers with hinges that weigh 30 lbs. by themselves (just the hinges). Some safe room doors come as a 6-inch-thick steel form that is filled with concrete after it is hung. Yes, they are heavy! A great idea in a multi-room bunker is to have your safe room door in the room that contains your escape tunnel. This way, attackers will think you are locked inside, when you are really making your escape and are long gone.

Illustration 15: A Good Steel Safe Room Door has multiple bolts attached to a "boltwork" within the door and is firmly attached to a concrete doorway, then entering into the saferoom.

5. Radiation Air Filter: Your bunker should be designed to keep you safe in the event of any foreseeable event, including a nuclear catastrophe. A properly constructed underground bunker can protect you from a reasonable level of nuclear blast, but what about harmful radioactive dust particles? One thing that most people fail to realize is that most radiation fallout from nuclear weapons is simply carried in the dust. For this reason, a regular air filter will normally protect you from reaching dangerous levels of radiation inside your bunker. The key is to have an airtight seal on your bunker. This means that any firing ports or turrets need to have closeable, air-tight seals, as well as your doors. Once you have achieved his, you simply create a vent from the sealed space to the outdoors, or to an unsealed room. This vent is then hooked to a HEPA air filter, which will filter out radioactive and other types of dust, and then blow the clean air into your sealed bunker. Remember that in the event of a nuclear catastrophe, power will likely be out, so you need to have a long-lasting battery backup for your filter. Radioactive fallout is present at high levels for two weeks after a blast, so you need to be prepared to be holed up, with a way to power the filter, for at least two weeks. After that, you may still be wise to sleep and spend as much time in your bunker, with the filter functioning, but you can make brief forays outside when necessary. I would recommend direct 12-volt DC or other battery power to run your filter, so that you do not have to use an inverter, which could also break.

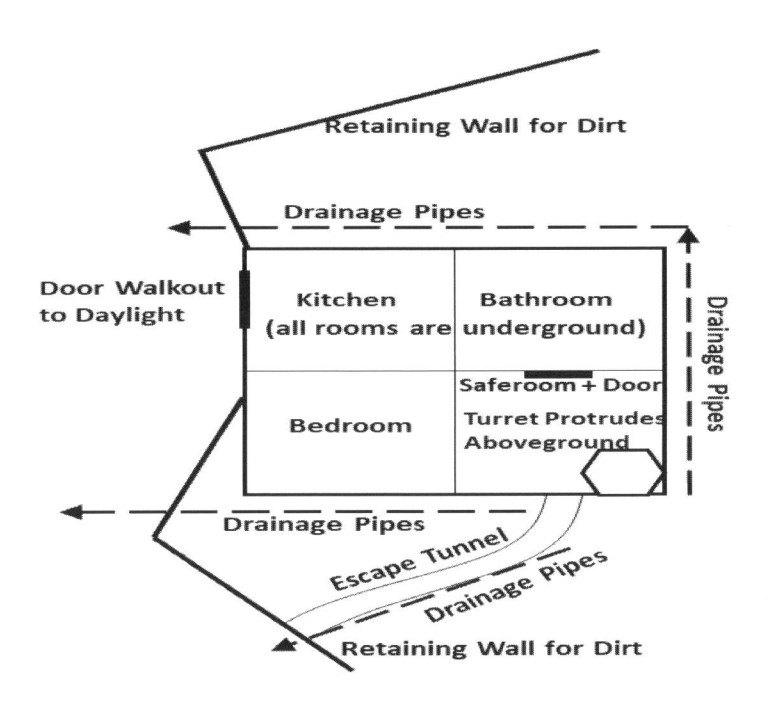

Figure 10: Floorplan of a Basic Homebunker

6. Water, Food, and Toilet: Do not forget that you will need access to your basic needs in your bunker. If you have water storage, such as rainwater storage tanks that are piped into your bunker, remember that they should be sealed off in the case of a nuclear event. Radiation in rainclouds is a serious hazard post nuclear war. One of the last things you do outside in the event of nuclear catastrophe is to cover and seal your rainwater or other water source that you will need in the future.
7. Where to put your bunker? Are you adding a bunker to an existing home? Is it a standalone, or are you building it along with a home as the basement in a new construction? None of these are the wrong technique, but some are easier than others. The most convenient and functional design is when a bunker is built as the basement of a home in a new construction. While many homes already have a basement, most of them do not have reinforced concrete basement ceilings and many other essential elements of a bunker. In addition, an existing home can get in the way of your fields of fire, meaning that you cannot easily see or shoot out of a basement bunker in all directions. One way to solve this is to create firing ports on all sides of the basement. If this is not possible, then using your ground floor as a defensive position might be necessary. This means that you want to be able to see in all directions from one floor in your bunker/home. In this case, if your ground floor becomes untenable, meaning that it becomes vulnerable or too dangerous, then you may be forced to retreat to your basement bunker, where you can "button up" and consider escaping through a tunnel.
8. Metal Door and Window Shutters: ¼ inch steel will stop some but not all light arms when fired straight into and at an angle it offers more protection.   More

importantly, these types of shutters, made of simple sheet metal, will stop or delay a typical criminal for at least 20 minutes, giving you time to escape or mount a counterattack. A ¼ inch steel door weighs around 210 lbs., meaning that it is easier to mount it with barn-door style rollers than it is to mount it on hinges. If you make your exterior window and door wall a cavity wall, meaning two walls with approximately 4 inches between them, then the sliding door and window shutters can slide between the walls when not in use. Interior barn-style dead bolts can be installed because this is a door designed to protect you while you are inside, so a key is not absolutely necessary.

Standalone bunkers make it quite easy to create good fields of fire for defense, and they allow for faster, easier construction than incorporating a bunker into a home, but they have to be located where you can get there easily in case of emergency, even in the middle of the night. By far the hardest option is adding a bunker to a pre-existing home. Professional help is strongly advised in these cases to avoid damaging the original home and especially the home's foundation and structural support. Are you ready to build your bunker? Let's begin!

Illustration 16: Footer and Rebar Applications Vary Based on Expected Loads, Existing Bedrock, and Subsoil

Foundations

A bunker or bunker home starts with the foundation, which can be the easiest part with proper planning, but it can be a disaster without proper planning. Foundation preparation or digging varies drastically based on your location, and with my background in Geo-Engineering, I have seen massive variation from one location to the next. First, and easiest: shallow bedrock. When dealing with shallow bedrock, you simply dig down to the solid, or fairly cohesive rock layer, and this is where you base your foundation. Unlike pier foundations or perimeter foundations, a masonry home's slab foundation height or elevation is often dictated by the underlying rock or soil. One option on raising this foundation height is to bring in rock and gravel. To raise the slab less than 6 inches, a one inch or greater size gravel will do the trick. The gravel will also provide great drainage under your slab. If you desire a height increase greater than 6 inches, then you will need to bring in 4 inch plus-sized gravel and rock, to avoid settling and movement under your slab. Every 6 inches of depth, you need to compact the gravel which is most easily done by driving over every square inch with a vehicle or equipment. I recommend an angular blasted rock such as limestone or granite for foundations. Rounded river gravel does not compact well and will typically continue to shift and settle.

If your bedrock is not accessible, then you need to dig down to cohesive soil, or hard-packed, undisturbed clay or hard loam. This undisturbed soil is known as hardpan. How can you tell if it is undisturbed? It needs to be difficult to dig through, and absolutely no organic material, roots, or soft dark soil should be under your foundation. Sand is also very ill-advised. You may encounter other types of soil which require engineering, such as placing geo-textiles or other reinforcing materials. In any case, with clay or other soil beneath your foundation, I always recommend first compaction, then putting down a geotextile, and then putting down 6 inches of 2 inch or greater diameter gravel for drainage. Compaction is critical for this type of subsoil. Many contractors will advise you to place plastic under your foundation, but this is normally not necessary or desirable. Plastic can hold water in as well as it keeps it out, and it doesn't provide an effective vapor barrier in most situations. The key is to use gravel and good drainage to allow moisture to drain away quickly. Now let's build your slab. You can do this!

Step by Step Foundation Slab Construction:
1. Around the perimeter of your pour, place perforated drainpipe, with the holes facing down, and draining out towards the downhill side of your property. That's right, I said holes facing down. It is not supposed to carry the water, it is just a place for the water to escape in the gravel. If you are building a huge bunker home, wider than 20 feet, place it every 16 feet (minimum), under your foundation. Not sure you need it? Do it anyway!
2. Cap the pipe ends with slotted caps and place landscaping fabric over the drainpipe to ensure that the pipes do not fill with gravel or concrete.
3. Next, place one-inch-thick rigid foam insulation on top of the gravel, across the entire foundation site, leaving a gap underneath where your walls will sit. "Blueboard" is an example of this type of insulation that will work; non-rigid styrofoam will not work because it will be crushed. It should be rated for at least 40psi.
4. Now place two rows of ½ inch rebar, on top of rebar cradles, under any wall locations. For larger walls, you will need larger rebar, and in case of larger buildings or in areas

where required by code, use an engineer. Wire mesh should be placed on top of cradles everywhere else. To avoid using wire mesh, you can use fiber-reinforced concrete, but this does not take the place of rebar under your walls. Rebar should also be placed under any location that is expected to have excessive weight such as a chimney, stove, water tank, or bathtub.

5. To start on concrete forms, place your corner stakes, using steel concrete pins that have holes in them that will hold your wood form boards. Once your corners are in and square, then run a masonry line string around the corners, and emplace additional stakes every 6 feet along the lines.

6. Now you get your elevation preferably by using a laser, and driving your stakes in to the laser height that marks the height of your desired foundation.

7. Place your form boards by screwing them to the inside of the stakes, flush with the top of the stakes, around the perimeter of your foundation. This is, of course, the step where you determine the depth of your concrete foundation. I recommend a minimum of 8 inches under your wall for a standard, one story cinder block wall, and more for anything heavier. Non-loadbearing concrete floors should be a minimum of 4 inches thick to prevent cracking. *(My own home has a foundation that is 20-24 inches of concrete all the way across, poured on bedrock, and it supports three floors, two of which are concrete and blocks, the third is wood –framed. There is also a partial living roof on one of the floors, very heavy! This thickness may seem like overkill, but it will hold anything that I wish to put on it, and it will never crack or move.)*

8. Next, add any desired plumbing, wiring, or ventilation into the correct location beneath the floor of your bunker home. Plumbing is normally all that is required, and you can often put wiring in the walls and ceiling. Most importantly, your toilet drain needs to be placed precisely, ensuring it is the right distance from the wall, and the right height above the foundation, keeping in mind any tile or flooring that you might emplace later. Other pipes need to be emplaced based on where you will want sinks and other fixtures.

9. It is a good idea to put extra floor drains in rooms that will not be near an exit in case of a flood or burst pipe, it can be very difficult to drain a bunker style home with no floor drain. These drains and pipe ends all need to be taped over prior to the pour to make sure that you don't get concrete in them.

10. Pour concrete. I will not waste time on the basics of leveling and smoothing concrete. If you have prepared properly as I mentioned above, and you have a little help, then the pour should go smoothly.

11. After the pour, before it dries, it is a good idea to place rebar, or threaded rod, sticking vertically out of your slab, in order to tie your slab to your walls. If using solid concrete walls, the placement of the rebar is fairly easy. If using cinder blocks, then

you will need to make sure that the rebar comes up inside the cores of the blocks. This completes your slab build. Now it is time to talk home/bunker walls.

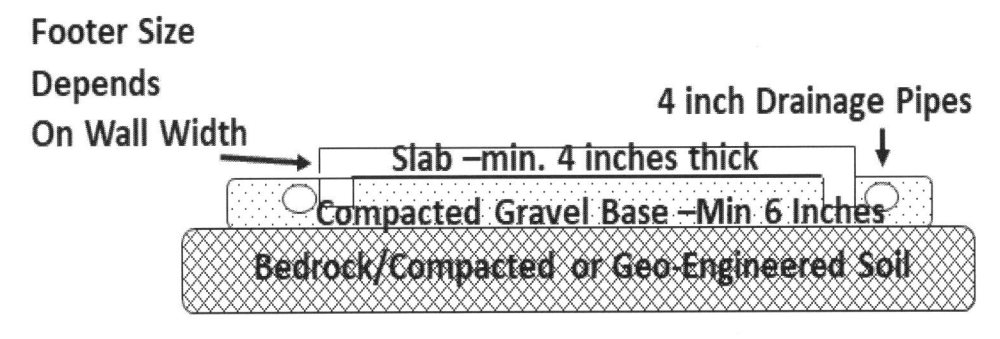

Figure 11: Foundation Side View

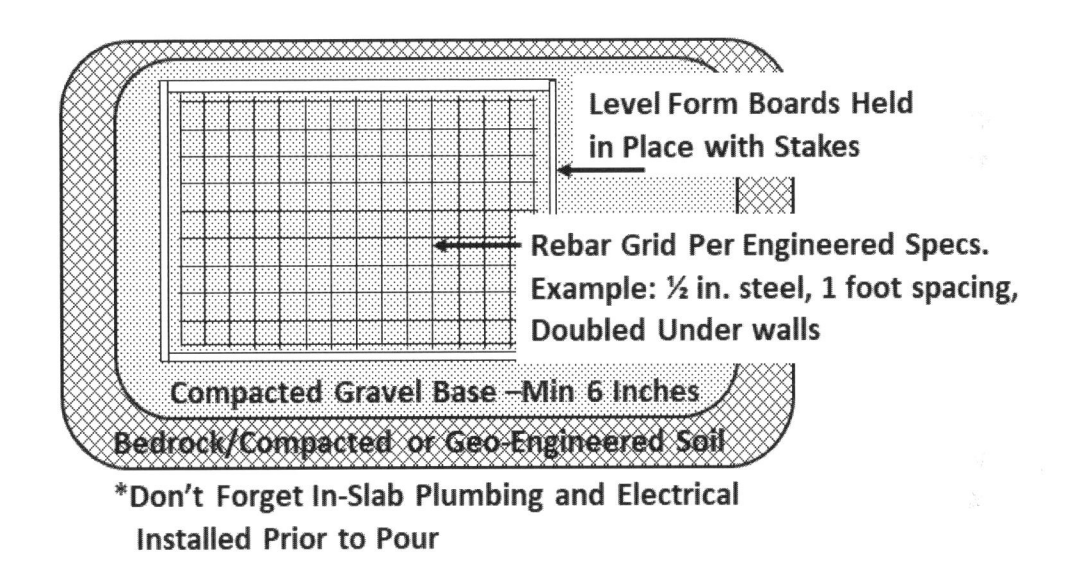

Figure 12: Foundation Overhead View

Bunker Walls

When choosing what type of walls you want to build, ask yourself these questions: Am I trying to be fast? Do I just want to save money, or is it more important to save labor? Do I want a beautiful bunker home, or do I only care about strength? For a fast and easy, but expensive build, consider ICF block, or "Insulated Concrete Forms." These are rigid foam blocks with plastic skeletons and 6 to 8 inches of space in the middle for concrete. The rigid foam means that insulation is excellent and effortless. They are extremely lightweight, and you put them together like Legos. Once this is done, you just add rebar and have a concrete pump truck come and fill them up. The drawback is that they are very expensive, about 20 to 25 dollars per square foot of wall for materials. I have built the walls of a small 700 square foot ICF bunker home in 3 days with two people using ICF and a good concrete pump truck.

Illustration 17: These ICF form walls are covered with Cement Board, Reinforced with Temporary Bracing, and Ready to Be Filled by a Concrete Pump Truck

Illustration 18: Whether your Walls are Poured Concrete or Block, you need to Install Adequate Rebar to Resist all Force placed on the Walls

For a build that is more labor intensive, but relatively cheap, consider cinder blocks. This can be built where pump trucks cannot go. They will cost you about 7 to 10 dollars per square foot of wall for materials, including a layer of rigid foam insulation. It can be labor intensive to place all of the mortar on the block joints. To save time, you can use surface bonding cement, which is a fiber-reinforced stucco that is applied to both sides of the block wall, after you dry stack the blocks. This means that you do not have to put mortar between the blocks as you would normally do, saving you loads of time. The horizontal shear strength of such a wall is actually greater than a traditional mortar block wall, meaning that it stands up better to underground applications. It will add approximately two dollars per square foot to your price, depending on how thick you put on the surface bond. Here is a quick step-by-step for building a block wall with surface bond:

1. Layout your first course of blocks, using the traditional method of mortaring all of the joints. This first row should be absolutely straight and level, so pull a straight masonry line from one end to the other, and use a bubble level on every block and, if possible, us a laser to check overall level.
2. If rebar were not placed in the concrete already, then holes need to be drilled in at this point and rebar placed with anchoring cement. I recommend placing ½ inch rebar at least every four feet.
3. After the first course of blocks has dried in place, stack the remaining courses, ensuring that you continue to check for level, plumb, and straightness. You may need to place small shims to keep everything level, because there is no mortar. Small pieces of sheet metal or roofing scraps make good shims, because they are the right thickness.
4. I recommend placing your surface bond cement after every 6 courses or every four vertical feet, to keep the wall from toppling over. For added strength, you can use a caulk gun to place polyurethane adhesive in between block layers. This will add about 75 cents per square foot to your wall building costs.
5. All cores of your blocks containing rebar must be filled with concrete to achieve the desired strength. You may also add a "bond block" course, every four feet, to increase strength for underground applications. This row of block looks like a regular cinder block course from the outside, but on the inside, the blocks are all left open on the sides, and they hold concrete that is poured inside just like water into a long trough. This, along with accompanying horizontal rebar, bonds the wall together horizontally.

Remember that your block wall still needs at least one layer of insulation. For underground applications, you can place a layer of rigid foam insulation, at least one inch thick, on the outside of the wall, prior to backfill. On underground applications you will also need waterproofing. The most reliable water-proofing method is to use a bituminous (petroleum-based) membrane. A common way to do this is by painting on the waterproof material, but I recommend the membranes that can be rolled on like a big strip of tape, over the entire wall. There are manufacturers that make 3-foot-wide rolls that can be put on directly to the rigid foam insulation, or can be put on block after a primer. The bottom of the roll will need to be covered with the paint-on bituminous material, just to seal the edge. After you place water-proofing, you should place a drain board or "dimple board" along the outside of your wall. This is just a 3- or 4-foot-wide roll of plastic with dimples that allow the water to pass or drain down the wall, instead of lingering on the surface.

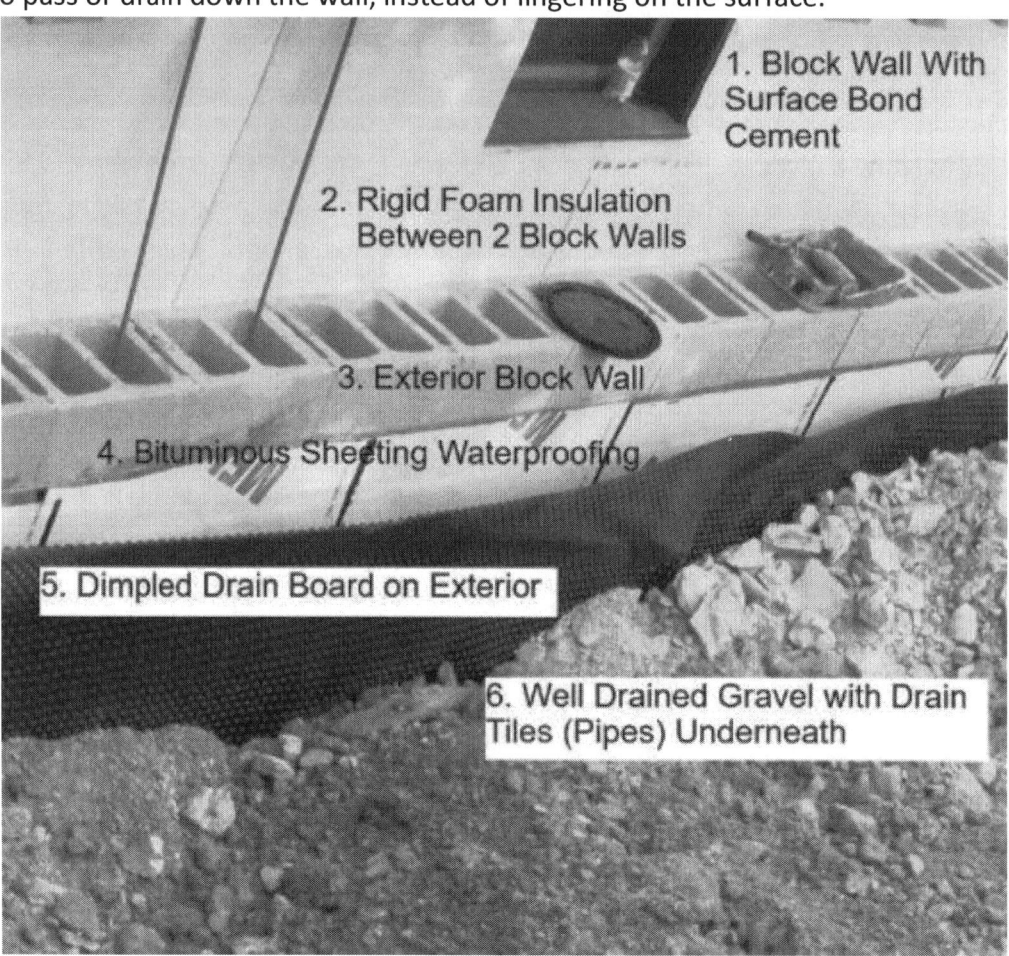

Illustration 19: Layers of a Good 2-foot-Thick Waterproof Underground Wall

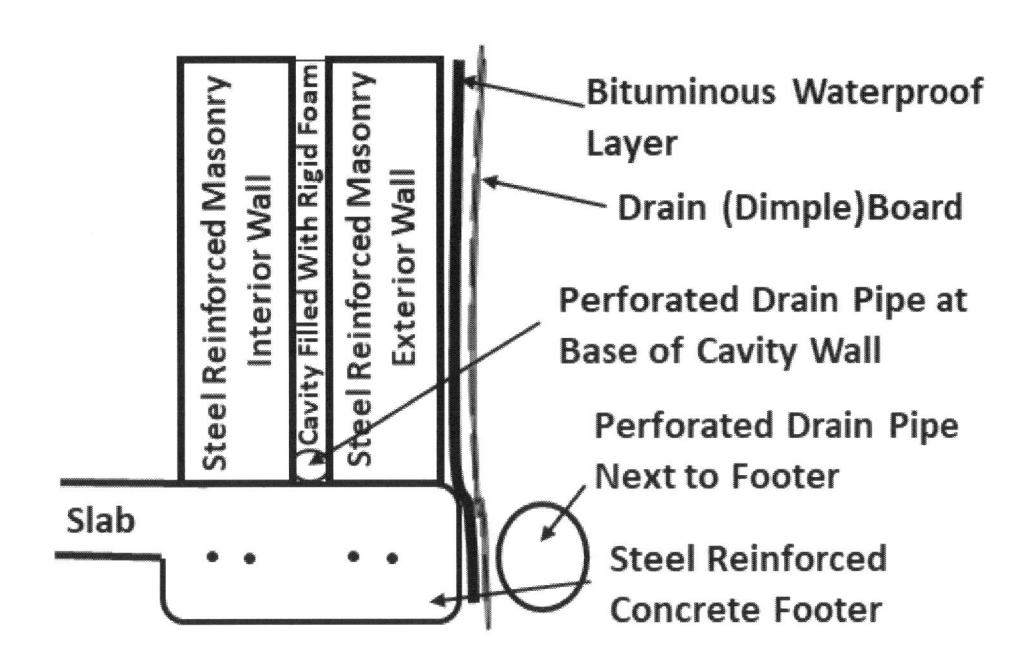

Figure 13: Cross-Section of Waterproof Underground Wall

When backfilling an underground wall, it is important to place a tile (perforated rigid pipe) along the bottom of the wall and draining out to an exit point downhill. You should place an additional drain tile every four feet of elevation that you backfill. All backfill should be clean gravel without too many fines, clays, or excess sand. This prevents any water from "water-logging" the backfill and making it heavy. Heavy, water-logged soil backfill will collapse your walls.

On above-ground walls, you will need to find a way to hold insulation in place. One option is to build a stick frame on the interior of your structure, instead of insulating the exterior. This stick frame can hold your insulation, pipes, and electric, and provides a surface to mount drywall as well. I do not recommend this for underground installations because condensation may occur, resulting in moldy drywall.

Another option for placing rigid insulation in your masonry wall is to build a cavity wall. In this instance, you simply build an inner wall and an outer wall, leaving a gap in the middle of 2 to 4 inches. This gap can hold your rigid foam insulation. It provides for not only better insulation but also more strength. You can also waterproof both walls. In the case that the outer wall is breached by water, then the inner wall will certainly keep you dry. A cavity wall is a great option for a robust structure, especially when building underground, but it will double your costs.

Bunker Roof

There are not many options for a bunker roof; you pretty much have to go with poured concrete, or else it is not a bunker. I visited Normandy to participate in the D-Day commemoration, where we jumped on to one of the old drop zones to honor the invasion that took place 60 years earlier. While there, we also visited some of the old German bunkers on Omaha beach that are still in working condition today. The roofs of these bunkers were fully 2 feet thick, reinforced concrete. With the exception of a full-on invasion force of 156,000 allied troops, this roof thickness will keep you safe in your bunker. Don't bother with anything thinner than 1 foot. Remember that because you cannot predict the future, this bunker needs to be able to keep you safe from anything.

Generally, you will have to build, rent, or buy forms for your bunker ceiling/roof. One shortcut that I have used is to build the forms out of heavy timbers and wooden decking that is sturdy enough to hold the weight of the concrete. These can then be left in place as an attractive ceiling for your bunker. The important thing is that you or your engineer check the rafter span tables for these timbers to ensure that they will hold the weight of the concrete while it is being poured. Then you need to make sure an engineer approves the strength of your concrete roof to ensure that it will hold whatever soil is to be added later.

Illustration 20: Properly Engineered Timbers Emplaced to Hold a Concrete/Living Roof

Illustration 21: An Alaskan Sawmill is a great way to Make Roof Timbers

The step by step of this technique is as follows:
1. Place your timbers across the top of the walls of your bunker, parallel to one another like joists, again checking the rafter span tables to ensure that they will hold. You need to leave a four-inch minimum gap between the end of the timbers and the outer edge of your bunker walls, to ensure that the roof concrete is tied into to the wall concrete, meaning that the concrete pours outside of the wood form and onto the top of the walls.
2. Rebar pins should come out of the bunker walls so that they will connect the concrete pour to the roof.
3. The roof does not need to be steep, but a flat roof invites leaks, so slope it at a minimum 1:12 pitch.
4. Next nail decking to the top of the timbers, which is now the base of the forms for the roof. I like to use one-inch-thick cedar or other rot-resistant wood for this purpose. I don't use treated wood because the chemical smell will not ever go away if you do. This should be covered with blue board or other rigid Styrofoam insulation to prevent unsanitary condensation on the ceiling of your bunker.
5. A bituminous water-proofing layer should then cover your rigid insulation, as an initial protection against water. Drip board or dimple board should be unrolled on top of this in case any water should need to escape to the edges. Remember 4-inches around the edges of the roof should be left open so that the concrete can tie into and make direct contact with the walls.

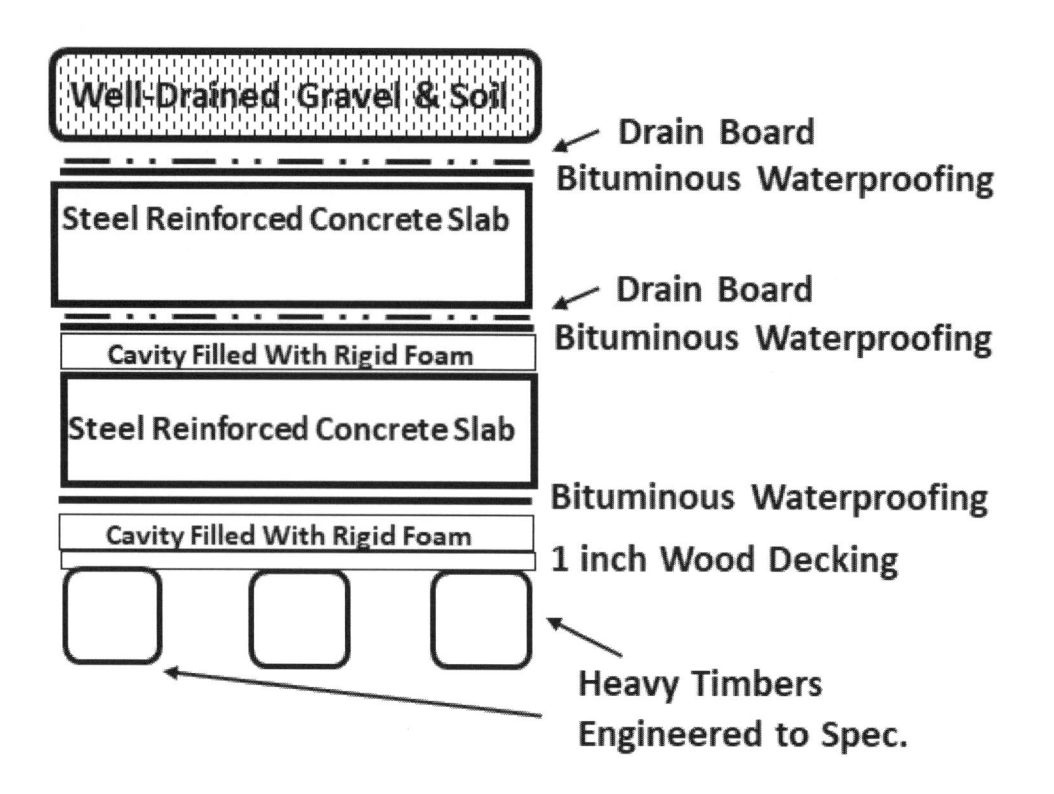

Figure 14: Cross-Section of Underground Bunker Roof, Can be Engineered for One Layer of Concrete but Two Layers Ensures Eternal Longevity and Virtually Guarantees No Leaks Ever

Illustration 22: First Layer of Insulation Installed Directly on Top of Wood Decking. This will be Covered By Bituminous Waterproof Sheeting and then a Layer of Rebar and Concrete

6. Next, place your forms around the edges of the pour, on the outside and above the walls. The form height of course determines the thickness of the roof. I recommend 2 feet to survive any scenario except for large caliber artillery or tandem-shaped warheads. The forms may need to be propped up and reinforced by metal stakes or 2" x 4"s on the edges of the walls. Remember that they will need to be able to resist the outward pressure of poured concrete.
7. Rebar is the next step and rebar size is again something which requires engineering calculation based on the size of the roof and the span between walls. Just remember that these calculations are based on minimum requirements under expected conditions. It is better to overbuild in order to be prepared for the unexpected. I have often used one inch rebar in sticks that run perpendicular to each other like a grid. One foot spacing of this rebar inside of a 2-foot-thick roof makes for a bomb-proof shelter.

Illustration 23: Ready for Top Slab Pour, with waterproofing, drain board, rigid insulation, and rebar. Note that insulation is not placed where it would block slab contact with supporting walls.

8. Concrete is then poured as in any other slab. Do not under any circumstances allow anyone to go into the rooms beneath the pour as they could be crushed and easily killed in the event of a collapse.
9. After the pour has cured, 3 to 7 days later, it is time to finish the outer layer of water proofing. Again, rolls of bituminous sheeting work great, or paint-on bituminous

material should also work. After this, another layer of dimpled drain-board should be added to ensure that water has an escape route. Remember that a 1:12 minimum pitch should be maintained on the top of the pour to allow for drainage.

Illustration 24: 2 foot thick Concrete Roof Slab, Bituminous Waterproof Sheets are tied in from the Roof to the Walls, and later Covered by Drain Board. Roller is for Primer that is applied before Bituminous Sheets

10. Finally, clean gravel, preferably rounded creek gravel should be added, at least 6 inches thick, to allow for drainage on your new bunker roof. Landscaping fabric on top of the gravel will keep the gravel clean and allow water to continue to drain quickly. Additional dirt or other materials may be added as your engineering calculations allow for. Soil types such as clay or silt are extremely heavy when water-logged so these should not be used so as not to add too much weight. Again, doing this without an engineer can be extremely dangerous or fatal. Even an engineer is advised to overbuild when constructing bunkers, so make it stronger than what you think you would ever need.

Illustration 25: Gravel for drainage on 1/2 of an Underground Roof

11. Once you are successful at completing your underground roof build, then you can add the final thin layer of topsoil on top of your gravel layer. Drought tolerant, sun-loving plants should be planted on the living roof because if constructed properly, it will drain quickly and not hold water. I recommend plants that are native to the drier niches of your region or biome. In the temperate U.S., nut sedges, little blue stem grass, rattlesnake master plants, and coneflowers work quite well.

Illustration 26: Living Roof planted on an Underground, Earth-Sheltered Home

Illustration 27: Underground, Earth-Sheltered Home

Concealment considerations

"Sun Tzu," the ancient Chinese text on the art of warfare, strongly encourages the reader to avoid conflict at nearly all costs, while preparing to annihilate the enemy should that fail. To avoid unnecessary conflict, and surprise attackers, it is essential to learn proper camouflage and concealment, without compromising your fields of fire and ability to defend yourself.

When I was training as an infantryman for the U.S. Army, a fellow soldier and I were tasked with building a machine gun pit or fighting position, by digging into the ground and reinforcing with sandbags, logs, and dirt. We worked hard all day, digging, sweating, and cursing. At dusk, we had finished with an 8-foot-long L-shaped pit, crowned with sandbags, a firing port, a shelf for the machine gun and tripod, entrance, and 18 inches of sandbags for overhead cover, supported by 8 inch diameter logs. We were so concerned with camouflage, cover, and concealment, that we dug the fields of fire down into the ground, so that the roof of the bunker, covered with leaves and sticks, looked like part of the ground everywhere else. We were nearly invisible! This was a live fire exercise, meaning that pop-up targets were already in place to our front. Prior to the live fire, we settled in to finish setting up our machine gun. Only then did we realize that the roof was too low for us to look over the sights of the weapon! It was far too late to raise the roof. The machine gun couldn't be lowered because it was already at ground level, and the live fire was about to begin, without our critical machine gun! Finally, we had to take off our helmets and crook our necks a bit, and we could make out targets well enough through the sights, without bumping our heads too much on the roof. We almost blew it, but we worked it out just in time to send 600 rounds of fury per minute down range! Luckily our platoon sergeant didn't come by to check if we were wearing our helmets!

The point is that while concepts like cover and concealment, and fields of fire seem elementary and easy to achieve, they actually require significant planning. While a field expedient bunker may be used for a week or less, your survival bunker could last for generations. It is worth your time to draw out defensive planning considerations like fields of fire on a piece of paper, and then get down on the ground to see if it all makes sense in person. This should be done in different weather and during different seasons if time permits, before you start pouring concrete and creating a permanent fixture. It will make the difference between a creation that will save your life and one that will just give you a false sense of security. Remember the 5 P's. Proper planning prevents piss-poor performance.

Passive Solar Heating and Cooling

While building a bunker is critical for short-term survival, long-term survival requires a home, which ideally is part of or attached to your bunker but can also be built separately. Because this home needs to be designed to function independently of the electrical grid, it is appropriate to start the discussion with passive solar heating and cooling. These two functions of a home are the most important basic necessities of any shelter, but they also are among the most misunderstood. Past human societies have proved that when necessary, you can live without lighting, refrigeration, and you can cook on an open fire. However, you cannot ensure survival without a shelter that keeps you and your family warm in the winter and reasonably cool in the summer. Doing this off-grid is not always easy, but with some basic knowledge and by learning from other off-gridders, it can be accomplished.

Always in search of more off-grid knowledge, I recently took my family to tour a newly built solar home constructed by our local university for a national competition of portable, renewable energy buildings. It was modern, spacious, open, and completely unsustainable, utterly dependent on backup power from the power grid. To prove the point, appetizers for visitors to eat were being cooked on hot plates that had to be powered by a grid-tied outlet. They had sacrificed the essential and the practical to create a superfluous, overly expensive, impractical design. After living off-grid in a climate with both hot and cold extremes since 2009 with my family, I can tell you that the number one energy challenge for a resilient and sustainable home is ease of heating and cooling. You could literally freeze to death or catch pneumonia in the winter, while suffering intolerable heat in the summer, if you do not carefully take advantage of passive heating and cooling considerations.

So, you can imagine my dismay when visiting the solar house created by the brilliant young minds at a nearby university, only to find that there were no realistic passive heating and cooling measures whatsoever. The home featured very few windows on the south side, meaning that the low winter sun would not shine in to passively heat the home. Instead, nearly half of the eastern and western walls were large glass panes! This means that the rising and setting summer sun would basically cook the occupants of the home, just like in a solar oven! The ceiling was open and reached high to about 12 feet, meaning that all the hot air in the winter would rise and not keep the living area warm.

In the display home, there were also windows at the peak of the "lean-to" roof, in the back of the house. These would open automatically to "let out hot air." This may work on cool nights, but during times when it is truly hot outside, you cannot simply "let out hot air." Where does cool air come from to replace it? At those hot times of the day, you need instead, to button up the home, ensure that you are not passively heating through windows, and rely on good insulation and, ideally, even thermal mass properties. Conversely, south facing windows and thermal mass take advantage of passive solar heat to stay warm in the winter. I would like to help other individuals, builders, and off-grid families like mine learn some of these concepts the easy way. So now, let us discuss some of the critical lessons that I have learned with my family through years of sobering experiences of off-grid living.

The first key to passive heating and cooling is home orientation, perhaps the most important planning factor in building your home or survival shelter. Passive solar heating allows for the capture of sunlight using properly positioned windows and eaves, and simple thermal collectors such as stone, concrete, or even water. It is important to orient the home with the long axis on an east-west plane, with large windows and the passive solar collectors facing the south. The reason for this is that in the winter, the path of the sun is lower and moves across the southern part of the sky. The farther north you are in the summer, the lower in the southern sky the sun will be, allowing it to shine further back in the room and heating more of the floor. I enjoy watching the winter sunlight creep further and further back into our home as the days grow shorter, bringing warmth and light, even as the days grow colder outside. When I see the sunlight hitting the back interior masonry wall of the house, I know we are receiving a huge benefit from passive solar heating. We are at a mid-latitude close to 35 degrees north and the sun will hit even reach and strike the back wall with all of its warmth, 16 feet from the windows in December and January. In the southern hemisphere, for our Australian, African, and Latin American cousins, the same concept is at play with compass directions and seasons being reversed.

    Modern windows have space between panes that often are filled with a gas such as Argon, which will help insulate the glass in your home. Low-E windows are a great idea that are highly misunderstood by passive solar heating advocates. Low-E windows have a special coating that allows them to block thermal wavelengths. These are heat wavelengths that do not come directly from the sun but come from objects that have been heated by the sun or other heat sources and even from warm air. Many people think that Low-E windows would block significant amounts of sunlight, reducing the passive heating effect, but this is not accurate. Direct sunlight will still shine in just as strongly with Low-E windows, allowing you to heat your home with the sun in winter. They will then trap the thermal heat in so that your house stays warmer in the winter. Low-E windows also help keep heat out in the summer and keep your home cooler inside.

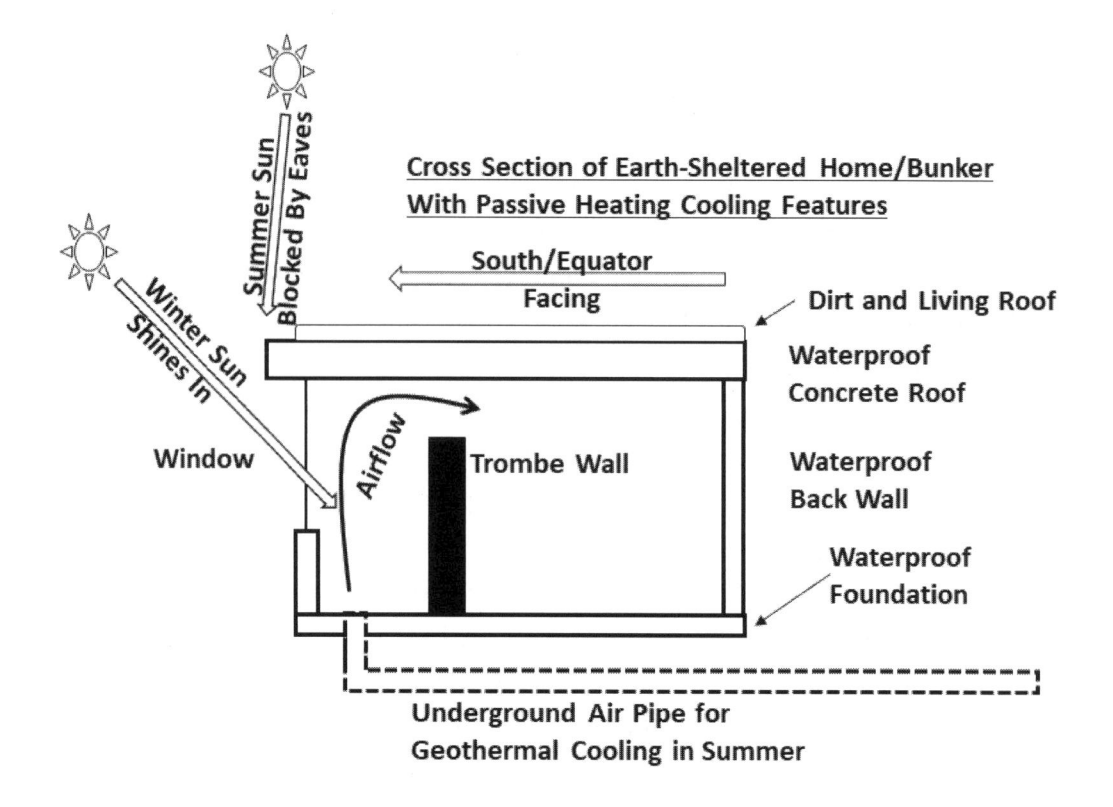

Figure 15: Side View of Passive Heating and Cooling of an Underground Home

Thermal collectors inside the house then absorb the sunlight and store it, releasing it over time as heat. Dark-colored thermal collectors such as a concrete floor with black tile make the process even more effective. Some off-grid home builders will install a *Trombe* wall that is placed just behind the south wall's windows. This is a name for any wall that provides thermal mass and is often dark-colored. It is designed to capture the sun's heat during the day, and slowly release heat throughout the night. Some builders will incorporate water containers as thermal mass into the *Trombe* wall. This is because water has a high thermal inertia and high amount of thermal mass, even higher than concrete, meaning that it will help to maintain a steady temperature. Other materials that have a high thermal mass include earth and stone. Materials such as metal, wood, vinyl, and fabrics tend to lose heat quickly, with no passive heating benefit. While the *Trombe* wall helps to heat the home, it can also block light, making the home a little darker in winter. For this reason, a well-insulated concrete floor, preferably with a dark, sun absorbing color, is also a very good and sometimes better option.

Living off-grid can be extremely challenging in the summer when oppressive heat is present. Humidity makes it even worse. Air conditioning is extremely taxing on an off-grid energy system and may cause it to overload and fail. Insulation is critically important, but this is standard for all homes. For off-grid homes, passive cooling is a unique way to keep your home cool without using great amounts of electricity. Passive cooling, while important, is more difficult to achieve than passive heating, and involves the use of shade, subsurface earth coolness, and ventilation.

In the summertime, the path of the sun is much higher in the sky and the eaves on the south side of the house are then necessary to create shade and block out the sun from entering your windows to create unwanted heat. For windows 3 feet above the floor, I recommend an eave length that is half the latitude of your home's location. If your home is at 36 degrees of latitude, then I recommend 18-inch eaves. If your windows are closer to the ground, the eaves need to be longer. For each inch closer to the ground than 3 feet, extend the eaves out one more inch. For each inch higher than 3 feet, shorten the eaves by an inch. Extremely high windows have low potential for solar gain. Using these concepts, you can create shade during the summer months to keep your home cool passively, while allowing in the heat-giving sun in the winter. Windows on the north, east, and west side of the house should be kept to a minimum to avoid heating the home in the summer with the rising or setting sun or cooling the house in the winter with drafty windows on the north side.

Another way to create shade for your home is to use the surrounding vegetation as shade. In a forest, the heat index can often be up to 15 degrees cooler in the shade than in an open area. At our house, we were in a rush to build a garage / toolshed as an afterthought to the home construction. We skimped on insulation for the roof, and it was extremely hot that first summer. As a solution, we planted grape vines and kiwis next to the north wall, and within a few years, had trained them to grow on trellises over the garage roof. It soon became the coolest space in the home, because of the shade that we had created over the roof!

There are simpler ways to use vegetation to cool your home. Deciduous trees on the east, west, and especially the north-east and north-west sides of the home are very helpful in the mid-latitudes of the northern hemisphere. I have seen doors and windows on the east or west side of a home that get absolutely cooked by the rising or setting sun in the summertime. Deciduous trees that provide full shade in the summer will keep these vulnerable sides of your home cool in the summer while letting the sunlight through in the winter.

It is a common misperception that trees planted on the south side of a home will help keep it cooler. In reality, in the northern hemisphere, blocking the sun on the south side only keeps a home cooler in winter, when the low southern trajectory of the winter sun should be heating your home. In the summer, the sun has a high trajectory, meaning that trees on the south side do not shade your home. Trees on the north side will provide some summer shade to your home at mid to lower latitudes, where the sun casts shade from north to south in midsummer. Trees on the north side of your home can be coniferous as well, meaning that they will retain their leaves in order to block cold northern winds in winter as well as the sun in the summer. While many of these seem to be insignificant details, they are worth your attention if you are planning to live off-grid or would like to be prepared to survive a grid-down situation.

Another property of physics that can keep you from overheating in the summer is the relatively constant temperature of the earth just a few feet below the surface. One of my hardest-working Amish neighbors that works construction once told me that when he gets home from a hard day, he likes to go down to his basement root cellar and lay on the cool concrete floor. The temperature of the earth at a typical basement level is about 55 degrees Fahrenheit, or 13 degrees Celsius. This is cooler than what most air conditioners will put out, and not difficult to utilize to cool your entire home with a little proper planning. When living off-grid, using an Air Conditioner can be an enormous load on your renewable energy system. This can require you to double or triple your electricity usage and possibly overload your more vulnerable renewable energy components such as the inverter.

Three ways to use this geothermal cooling include building an earth-sheltered home, ventilating from a basement to the rest of a home, or ventilating from an underground pipe. The first, building an underground home, is the simplest, but also the most expensive. In my time living in such a home, I can tell you that an underground home will not be as cool as the surrounding Earth because of air infiltration. However, it will be much cooler than a regular home because there is no heat coming in from the walls or roof if it is completely underground. Furthermore, if the soil on top of the roof is moist, the evaporation of water from that soil creates a natural cooling effect on the home, even if it is not incredibly deep. If an underground home is in an arid climate, not much else has to be done to cool the home. If it is in a humid climate, then condensation and mold on the inside of the home can be a problem. One way to help mitigate this is to keep the warm, humid outside air from entering the house by using an air-lock. This means that you have a foyer with an outside door and an inside door that you must pass through to enter into the house. It will decrease the air exchange and cut down on interior humidity. While this technique is useful, extremely humid climates make it impossible to keep out all humidity. In this case, a modest one room dehumidifier can be run from a renewable energy system, making a big difference in a small home.

Another way to keep a home cool without relying too heavily on electricity is to ventilate cool air from a basement, if you have one.   We have lived both in a totally Earth-Sheltered underground home, as well as one with an upstairs, so I will give you some tips for both with or without two levels. As I mentioned, the Earth's temperature just a few feet beneath the surface is around 55 degrees Fahrenheit. This means that your basement temperatures should be fairly cool. When building my home, we put multiple four-inch ventilation pipes running from the basement to upstairs. I recommend one pipe for every

400 square feet. We then installed simple 12-volt fans in the pipes to move cool air upstairs from the basement during summer months. 12-volt fans can also be installed with a voltage-reversing switch (3-way rocker) that changes the fan direction, allowing it to blow hot air downstairs in the winter. This is useful because hot air immediately rises to the top of your house in winter, leaving the lower levels cooler. When using the fans to bring cool air up in the summer, you need to be aware of humid conditions that might develop in your basement. It is important to keep the basement and the air free of mold or you can develop serious health conditions. Again, a dehumidifier will do a great job and use just a fraction of the energy required by an air conditioner.

The third way of keeping your home cool in the summer without an air conditioner is to use geothermal cooling by burying a 4-inch pipe underground. There are several pitfalls to avoid ensuring this works successfully. First, you do not want to undersize this system, or it will not be worth the effort. Ensure that your pipe is at least 4 feet underground to reach the true cool depth of the Earth. Your pipe should be 1 foot long for each square foot that needs to be cooled. It is best to have a closed loop where your intake air comes from your house and then the loop returns all the way back to your house. This will ensure that you do not have to pull in hot, damp air that is harder to cool.

The second pitfall is again, humidity. The far end of the loop that is farthest from your home needs to be the low point of the system, meaning that it is at the very bottom of a downward slope. It needs to have a small weep hole, about a quarter of an inch diameter, so that moisture and humidity can drain out. Without drainage, you can develop mold inside your pipe and contaminate the air in your home. Another pitfall related to moisture is the idea that some people get to use this pipe for a dual purpose drainage pipe. Don't do that! You don't want any moisture in the pipe because of mold concerns, so it needs to be separate from your drainage.

Finally, do not undersize the fan for this system. You need a reliable fan that will move the entire volume in cubic feet of your home about every hour. This means that if you have a 750 square foot home with 8 feet walls, then you have 6000 cubic feet to move per hour. Dividing this by 60 minutes, you know that you need a fan that is rated for 100 cubic feet per minute (CFM).

A last consideration for off-grid living is the use of windows for ventilation. Living off grid for so many years, my family has learned to watch the indoor/outdoor thermometers that we have placed throughout our home. We are always ready to open windows at night to let in the cool summer night breezes. In the morning, we never forget to close the windows, just before the exterior temperature rises above the interior temperature. Forgetting to do so just once will teach a new off-gridder an important lesson as they suffer in their hot humid home all day. It helps to have fans that you can place in the windows on cool summer nights to bring in the air and cool down the house. We place the upstairs fans to blow out the hottest air that has risen to the top floor. The fans downstairs are placed to suck cool air in. Even when we don't use the fans, the hot air convection currents cause the air to flow up the stairs so fast that it feels like a fan is on. An attic fan is also useful, and I even recommend having a remote thermometer in the attic so that you know what kind of heat you are dealing with there. Both the attic fan and the window fans need to be selected for maximum efficiency, and 12-volt fans are reliable even if your inverter breaks.

There are many ways to keep your off-grid home cool passively in the summer, even in humid climates. The trick is not to look at your home as an energy hog with a bottomless hunger for electricity. Instead, look at it as an old-fashioned sailing ship, that requires you to "batten down the hatches," opening and closing windows, turning on and off fans, and even using the occasional dehumidifier to keep your home afloat on those muggy, oppressively hot summer days. It may sound inconvenient in a world of automation, smart phones, and the easy button, but after years of this off-grid lifestyle, I will tell you that it becomes just part of your normal routine, and you will feel more in tune the weather and the world around you when you become an active participant.

Active Heating of your Home

From an early age, I remember riding in my dad's old pickup truck down to the log pile to cut firewood. In our drafty old farmhouse, we would burn 6 or 7 cords per year, more than twice what I burn in my current earth-sheltered home. Nonetheless, it was a growing and strengthening experience for me and my sisters. It taught us that cool, fall weather was for working, as we watched my father heft the axe and split wood for hours. Loading wood in the truck was fun as long as we didn't get carried away with a game of firewood dodgeball! But seriously, if you live in a forest, why would you pay the utility company to heat your home? In a world of growing scarcity, threats to the power grid, and weather catastrophes, wood heat is a great idea in any forested area.

When you live off-grid, it is important to remember that you cannot just cut down a tree one day, and then burn it in the stove the next. First of all, a green tree is very difficult to burn and second, it will cause dangerous flammable creosote to build up in your chimney and stove. Instead, I recommend cutting your firewood at least 6 months prior to burning it, to allow it to season. Hardwoods such as oak and hickory burn the hottest and cleanest. Locust can be cured quickly in a pinch, ready to burn after about a month of curing. A dead, standing tree can be cut in order to reduce cure time, but try to never try to burn wood that has started rotting. It produces very little heat. When curing your wood, I recommend keeping it in a dry place with a roof at least during the last month of curing, to ensure that it burns hot and clean.

In most climates where passive solar heating of a home requires supplementation, wood stoves are the method of choice for off-grid living. The advantage of a woodstove is that they can be used for multiple purposes to include stovetop cooking, oven cooking, hot water heating, and the enjoyment of watching a flickering flame through a glass firebox door. Among our Amish neighbors, their wood cookstove is one of their most prized possessions. They use it for all of the above purposes, except I have never seen a glass firebox door in any of their houses. Every time we invite one of them over to our place, they can't take their eyes off the flame in the glass door. It's like our little off-grid television. But no television for you if you're Amish, no, no, no.

When shopping for a woodstove, you may be shocked at the high cost of a stove that does all of the above tasks, but they are all critical to off-grid living, and well worth the cost. Obviously, it is important that the stove heat your home, but you also don't want a stove that puts out too much heat. When we installed a stove with a large oven and huge firebox in our 750 square foot underground home, we kept fires to a minimum to keep from overheating. Still, with the need to cook and heat water in the winter, we used the stove every day and on sunny days in January the house would hit 80 degrees and we would run around wearing shorts and Hawaiian shirts. We later doubled the size of the home and it was just right. Later, we learned that you can install a taller, "summer grate" in your stove, making a large stove put out less heat, while making your griddle hotter, thus downsizing the fire needed. A summer grate is just a metal grill with legs that holds the logs higher, reducing the size of the firebox. The Amish use these in warmer months so that they can cook on the stove top even while using a smaller fire.

Since it can be downsized, I recommend a stove with a large firebox for everyone. The wider the box, the longer the logs, and the taller the box, the more logs you can stack up. Shoot for a minimum of 20 inches wide but 24 is optimal. I would not recommend buying a stove without firebricks lining the box; all good stoves have them and they will hold the heat and keep your home toasty all night. Also, to keep a fire going all night without waking to add wood, it is critical that the stove be airtight when you shut the air intake vents. This allows for a slow burning fire overnight.

I would also mention that many old-time pioneer homes would have an outdoor kitchen, sometimes open-air, and always separate so as not to overheat the house in the summer. I have also seen old homestead chimneys that have a fireplace on both sides, one for indoor winter cooking and one for outdoor summer cooking. A wood cook stove is designed to circulate the smoke around the oven box before it goes out the flue. It should also have a door that is opened to allow the smoke to go directly to the flue without going around the oven so that you can add wood without getting smoke in the house. With all of this smoke circulating around the oven, it is important to have ports that can be opened to clean out the creosote that will build up like a black tar inside the stove. Clean this at least once per month when in use to prevent an oven box fire.

In addition, when keeping the circulation door closed for a period of time, you may cause gasification. This occurs when the thick smoke in the air becomes so dense that it will suddenly combust in the air. It looks like a fire breathing dragon has just blown flames into your stove, and the stove will puff out smoke and maybe a little ash. This will happen every couple of minutes until you open the flame circulation door. To prevent or stop the dragon, you have to increase airflow. Don't use the circulation door to damper down the flame too often and only use it sparingly when baking in the oven.

A cooktop or griddle can be made of stainless steel, which will really make your life easier for cleanup, and it means you can cook some food right on the stovetop without a pan, just like a griddle. There is nothing like pancakes straight from the wood stovetop. It is a weekend tradition to cook them at our house with our own blueberries and maple syrup. Some stovetops have removable eyes that can be taken out to put a pan directly over the fire. While this sounds like a good idea, the round piece of metal that covers the eye can often warp, and the seal often leaks, allowing smoke into the house. If the fire is not hot enough to use pans on the cooktop, you can use a grate inside the firebox to elevate the fire closer to the cooktop and create a hotter cooking surface. I would also recommend not having a water coil or water jacket above the fire in the firebox and below the cooktop, because this will absorb an amazing amount of heat and makes cooking on the cooktop much more difficult. Instead, the water coil or water jacket can be mounted on the side of the firebox, beside and not on top of the flame. This is something that we learned the hard way.

Illustration 28: This Wood Cookstove has a Firebox on the right, a Griddle on top, an Oven in front, and a Water Jacket inside.

A water coil or water jacket is a great way to heat the water for baths and showers in the winter. I can't imagine spending money on propane or electric water heaters in the winter when it is effortless and effective to heat the water with a woodstove. The process is really simple. The water coil is a coil of 1-inch stainless steel pipe with an inlet and an outlet with one or two turns in the middle. The water jacket is a 1-inch wide stainless steel box with a serpentine path for the water to pass from the inlet to the outlet. The inlets and outlets of either one must be threaded to allow for the connection of your water pipes.

This system can function without a pump if you use the thermosiphon principle. To do so, you simply place your water tank adjacent to and within 10 feet of your stove. The inlet pipe to your stove is connected to the bottom of the water tank and the outlet pipe is connected to the top of the water tank. The bottom or inlet pipe should descend down to the stove and be on the bottom. The top or outlet pipe should ascend up to the water tank. (see illustration 19) This creates a loop where the hot water is heated in the stove and then rises up the pipes to the top of the tank. The cold water in the tank sinks to the bottom and then down to the stove and is then heated, starting the cycle all over. The natural tendency of heat to rise and cold to fall means that this will all circulate without the use of a pump.

Illustration 29: A conventional propane water heater tank has ports in the top and the bottom that you can "T" off from to install a thermosiphon water heater to your stove and also for a solar water heater, meaning that one tank will hold water from three types of water sources. Do not completely remove your relief valve!

One of the greatest things about such a system is that it can be hooked into a regular old style propane water heater tank. This way if you have propane or gas available and don't want to use the stove to heat your water, then you just light your pilot. These tanks have an overpressure valve on the top that can be unscrewed so that you can thread in the top pipe. Just put in a "T" close to this part of the tank so that you can screw back in the overpressure valve. The water tank will also have a drain valve in the bottom that can be unscrewed in a similar fashion and replaced with the bottom cold water pipe. All of these fittings are normally compatible with one-inch stainless steel water pipes found at your local hardware store. In addition to the overpressure and the drain valves, it is a good idea to also have an occlusive air valve. This is simply another valve that can be installed via a "T" and it will allow air to escape if it is caught in the pipes. It should be placed on the high point in the loop and important so that trapped air doesn't block the circulation of your thermosiphon.

If you plumb your hot water pipes from your wood cookstove in this manner, then you should have dependable hot water for years and even decades. This system can also be adapted to accommodate a simple solar hot water heater which I will discuss in the chapter on home energy.

Vertical air exchange

Some of the best entertainment for a farming family with no television is to take the children to the livestock auction or sale barn. In the winter time, we would come in with heavy jackets, sit on the top of the bleachers, and then strip down to T-shirts because all of the hot air had risen to that top level. In the meantime, those at the bottom near the animal show ring were bundled up with mittens and scarves. It is quite amazing how hot air rises and cold air sinks. In a multi-story home, you can take advantage of this by controlling the air flow between floors, putting the warm or the cold air exactly where you want it.

Our home is small, but very tall, with three floors. We control the climate in the house with the use of small, solar-powered 12-volt fans. After we built the first floor, we moved right in and depended on a wood stove for heat. Heating this one floor was easy, but the air was dry and dusty. As we built up, we isolated each floor with doors between the stairwells. At the same time, we installed 4-inch pipes with 12-volt bi-directional fans between the floors. The first floor still provides the heat, but the closed doors between the floors allows heat to slowly rise and keeps the air in the upper floors clear of dust with a favorable amount of humidity. Occasionally the top floor becomes too hot, and the fans are used to push the hot air back to the bottom floor.

In the summertime, we use the same idea, but from the other end. A small, efficient solar powered air conditioner is located on the top or third story. The cool air will gradually work its way down through the entire structure. If we did not have closed doors between the floors, then the cold air would immediately sink to the 1st floor, or basement. In the summer, the basement often does retain all of the cool air. The fans are very handy when this happens, as the cool air can easily be brought up to the top floor of the house with very little electricity use, using only the 12-volt fans. This helps enormously as our off-grid lifestyle has very limited electricity for things like air conditioning.

Chapter 7: Agriculture and Sources of Protein

If you would like to be more self-sufficient, then I hope you enjoy agriculture, at least in one form or another. Personally, after spending a career in the U.S. Army Infantry and Special Operations, it has been extremely therapeutic to spend my second career learning to grow things and feed people, especially the people that I care about it. This chapter is not called farming, because surviving doesn't necessarily mean general farming. Instead, agriculture, particularly subsistence agriculture, is undoubtedly one of the most critical skills that you will need to learn. Many people, including myself, initially underestimate the skills and knowledge required to raise food in its many forms, from how much forage livestock need, to when is the best time to plant garden seeds, what diseases to watch out for, and how to keep it all from dying! There is so much to learn!

I remember when we got our first large livestock and we had picked a real dandy, the American Bison, also known as Buffalo!

My wife and I had meticulously constructed a 7-foot-high pen out of cattle panels to keep our first five calves in, while we finished fencing the larger pastures. We watched nervously as the calf seller backed up to our new gate with bison calves darting around inside the trailer. The first calf was released alone, and she commenced slamming her entire 500-pound body squarely into the weakest fence corner multiple times, popping every fastener and fence staple, and then bounding away to freedom in the Ozark hills! The seller looked at me, kind of embarrassed and said, "that was just the nervous one, I am sure the rest are fine." He continued, "Are all of your gates closed at the other end?" I looked at my wife, knowing that we had not even finished the fence. Then I coolly replied, "Of course, yep, I'm not that dumb, ha ha!" We quickly got the pen patched and reinforced, gave the man his money and quickly got rid of him so we could go chase down our first wild buffalo. The moral of the story is, do your research first, build your infrastructure next, and get your livestock after everything else is ready! (Horse first, then cart; but before the horse, build a fence and a barn.)

Now, here we are, many years later, we have attended the USDA grazing school, learned our lessons with bison, moved on to cattle and now we keep 30 brood mama cows that produce almost 30 calves every year, and about twice as many goats. We have come a long way, but it was a lot of knowledge learned the hard way, like quenching your thirst by drinking from a fire hydrant. With this in mind, save yourself a lot of trouble and consider the following sections on sources of protein and fat(livestock and hunting), sources of carbs (grains, nuts, and wild forage), and our favorite, the survival vegetable plot.

The ability to raise or hunt livestock for protein is critical in subsistence living. Many of us take this type of food source for granted, but it makes the difference between thriving and suffering. Many children in the developing world rely primarily on humanitarian rations for their diets. As a result, around 30% of children in these populations are visibly stunted due to malnutrition. Properly raised meat is a nutrient dense meal that is hard to mimic in a meat-free diet. Some survivalist-minded folks plan on hunting as their primary means of obtaining protein in difficult times. While some areas in the U.S. are indeed remote enough to do this, keep in mind that millions of others may be competing for the same wild game in hard times. During the Great Depression, it didn't take the hungry masses long to put white tail deer on the verge of extinction in many states. My great-grandfather was stopped by the local game warden in Southern Illinois for shooting a few squirrels out of season during the hardest years of the Great Depression. He told the game warden that he had 6 hungry children to feed back home and pointed out that he was then only man there carrying a rifle. Imagine everyone squabbling over a dwindling squirrel population post-collapse. Today, the world has many more mouths to feed than in 1930; and game wardens and other competitors are much better-armed. It is clearly important to know how to raise your own meat.

Livestock

Grazing Animals have long been a staple of human civilization both for meat and milk. These include animals such as alpine dairy goats from Switzerland, British meat cattle, the reindeer of Finnish Lapland, and the camels of the Arabian Desert. Where would we be without all of these critical animals? In a period of civil or economic decline, they become even more important, and becoming a grazier can be one of the most enjoyable parts of prepping. While there are millions of books on how to raise and care for livestock, this book contains a simple and relatively brief discussion on which ways the considerations for raising and the advantages or disadvantages of keeping various types of livestock during a subsistence or long emergency, grid down situation. It is based on my observations in Third World countries and my vast experience as an off grid homesteader.

Shortly after the cessation of hostilities in Kosovo, I found myself on a patrol in the dry shrubby hills of Kosovar backcountry, looking for weapons caches or any sign of continued violence. On such remote area patrols, it was not uncommon to come across a lone shepherd. They were often teenage boys with bare feet, a rope for a belt, and a critical food source on the hoof; sheep, goats, or cattle. A short time earlier, neighbors were gunning each other down as Apache Helicopters smashed Serbian tanks with their hellfire missiles. In the middle of all of this, shepherds still tended their flocks and herds and now they still stood happily, grinning ear-to-ear with a shepherd's staff and a belly full of goat's milk. We'd often come upon the lone farmstead at the end of a dirt trail where the shepherd's family could be found living a quietly happy life despite the turmoil just on the other side of the hill. Perhaps before the war, the shepherd's family members were seen as poor folk, even backwards and stupid. But during the war, they were well-fed and often safer in their remote hamlets. It makes you think about the real meaning of prosperity and wealth.

What do you wish for your family during hard times?

As turmoil bears down on this world of ours, you will also want to set your family up as well as a good shepherd knows how, and so we begin our discussion of grazers, browsers, and other useful livestock. Raising livestock is both a rewarding and challenging endeavor. The great advantage of raising livestock of all types is that they actually provide labor for you. They do this by mowing and fertilizing the pastures and even trimming back the brush if you know how to properly manage them. They can harvest food from land that otherwise would be too rocky or rugged to farm, and they can farm areas that otherwise would be labor or machinery-intensive when labor and machinery might be scarce. Rather than the current mindset of how to squeeze every ounce of productivity from the land, we need to examine how to keep your own land productive when the rest of the world has already been squeezed dry. While many conventional environmentalists believe that animals can ruin the land, I know from experience that they can also create fertility, abundance, and a livelihood for you and the generations that follow.

To harness the amazing potential of livestock, there are a number of fundamental questions that we must address. What type and how many animals should you keep? How do you keep enough animals for the spring surge of pasture growth but not too many for the bleak mid-winter? What is the carrying capacity of your land? How can you deal with disease and pests when veterinary and chemical options are not readily available? How can you afford the time investment with your livestock and how can you make them pay for their own upkeep? We will begin the discussion with types of animals.

Grazers

Let us not forget the importance of trusting and knowing where your food comes from. Milk from your best friend Molly the cow tastes infinitely better than any milk you could buy. Then you realize how much she eats! Our first livestock on our farm were bison. I remember hearing about how well they would forage and I would look at all of the oak leaves and broom sedge and think, "well look, there is plenty to eat in there, but why are they so skinny?" Then I finally went to the USDA grazing school and started to realize just how much land with quality grass is required to raise a large herd of cattle or other grazers for that matter. In areas with decent rainfall, around 30 inches or more annually, you can often stock 500 pounds of livestock per acre, but in arid regions with 15 inches of rainfall or less, the number drops to 10 pounds per acre or less.

At grazing school, I learned that grazers will consume between 2-3% of their body weight per day in grass and that they would lose weight and even starve on poor grass or other forage. I also learned that relying on feed can quickly bankrupt a beginning farmer. So, the key with raising livestock in a self-reliant manner is first choosing the right type and number of animals and then creating a healthy and well-managed pasture or semi-pasture.

It is easy to fall in love with the seclusion and beauty of forests but most of the real food production happens in the clearings, open areas, and pastures. Pastures are an asset that is worth demanding if you are looking to purchase property that will feed you and your family.

Illustration 30: One of our pastures with multiple types of legumes planted along with grasses as cattle forage.

Getting your Pastures and Paddocks Healthy

Grass types that you should encourage depend on your area but keep in mind that in order to keep demand for hay down, you will need your grass to last nearly year-round. In a temperate environment, this means both cool season and warm season grasses. For much of the country this includes grasses such as tall fescue, orchard grass, bromes, or perennial rye for cool season, and big bluestem, indian grass, eastern gama, blue grama, buffalo, or bermuda grass for warm season. Many pastures that have been abused by years of over-harvesting hay or over-grazing need to be brought back up to good condition as soon as possible as doing so in a grid down situation is difficult at best. Take a soil sample and find out from your local agricultural extension office what basic amendments are needed. A one-time fertilization or addition of key soil amendments should be enough to get your pastures back on track if you manage them carefully. Extremely poor soil may need amendments for a few years in a row. Your local agricultural extension office can help you find the specific soil amendments that are appropriate in your area. In ideal conditions, you would have the option of re-fertilizing every 3-5 years, but to prepare for difficult times, it is important to start with land that is topped-off with nutrients. This is an example of why preparation for hard times needs to be done sooner rather than later. Neglected farmland will not spring to life simply because you just realized that no one else is going to feed you and your loved ones anymore. It takes hard work and prior planning.

Once you have fertilized, doing so would be a waste if you did not also plant seed to get things going. Find out if any of the grasses mentioned above are already existent in your pasture and if so, encourage them to grow. Pasture mixes that are available at your local farm store often work well. For areas larger than 5 acres, it is very practical and advisable to rent a fertilizer buggy with your recommended fertilizer amounts together with seed pre-mixed to spread on your pastures. This should be done in the late winter to spring when the fields are fairly dry but you are expecting a good soaking rain, but not a gully-washer flood. It is good for some seeds such as clover to have a frost or two after you spread them. This timing allows for spring germination and prevents your fertilizer from dispersing and being wasted. Research the seeds that you think will do well in your area and plant them according to their specific criteria. Many native warm season grasses need to undergo scarification to break dormancy. Often this is best accomplished by planting in early to midwinter so that it can be exposed to several freeze thaw cycles. This is why it is important to research the best seeding techniques for all of your chosen pasture forages.

Illustration 31: Clover is easy to recognize but these are other legumes that can boost protein in your pastures.

It is very important to include legumes such as clovers or alfalfa in your pasture and get them established as soon as possible. These plants sequester nitrogen from the air and over a period of 2-3 years make it available to other plants in the soil as well. If you can get 30% of your pastures interspersed with legumes, you will never lack the most critical nutrient, which is nitrogen. This means that fertilization then becomes largely unnecessary. Legumes are also high in protein and a favorite of all types of livestock. Seeding is sometimes done after preparing the soil with a disc and some seeds can be planted with a grain drill.

Many farm supply stores or agricultural extension offices will rent these grain drills. Other techniques include broadcasting these seeds prior to an area being trampled by livestock or even prior to frost. Frost plants the seed into the ground because the expansion and contraction that occurs is able to work the seeds into cracks and crevices in the ground. A combination of discing, animal traffic, frost, fertilization, rainfall, and a sufficient rest period is a sure way to get any pasture to flourish. The beauty of growing perennial grasses as a crop is that once they are established, they can go without reseeding for a decade or more with properly managed grazing and light traffic.

Pasture Management and Fencing

Once you have revitalized your pastures you can then focus on your stocking and management of your grazers. This can be done even after the grid is down as it was done by our ancestors for centuries. My father-in-law growing up in post-WWII Italy spent much of his childhood managing grazers and herding them from one pasture area to the next. Such a system allows an area to be thoroughly grazed, mulched, and fertilized by manure, and then it gives maximum rest to plants before they are grazed again. In modern times, many ranchers just put livestock in large, fenced pastures, and let them graze at will. In this type of situation, the livestock tend to have a favorite spot where they graze the grass too short, kill it, and move to their next favorite spot, and so forth. The ancient practice of rotation by shepherds avoided this problem.

Today, with a small amount of help from technology, we can still herd our grazers from paddock to paddock by using electric fences, and solar electric chargers that are effective and easy to use.

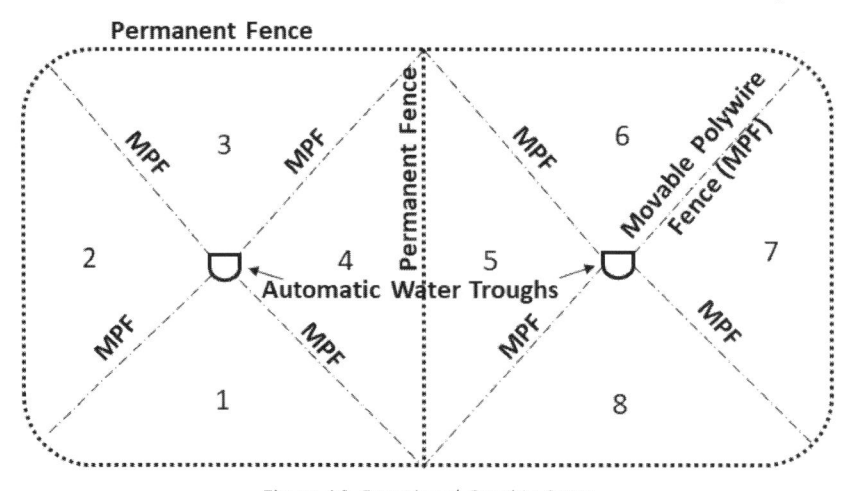

Figure 16: Rotational Grazing Setup

You may not have anyone available to serve as a shepherd for your livestock, but electric fences can do the trick. Many of you might be thinking that in a grid down scenario you won't have an electric fence available, but solar-powered fence chargers have gotten quite dependable and can persuade an animal to be good and do the right thing. Most cattle, once exposed to the shock of a single strand of polywire, will often not be tempted to challenge the fence again. In fact, a white string that is not electrified will keep trained cattle at bay for days, especially if they have plenty of forage and water. In a truly long-term emergency, even solar electric fences would begin to break down. But in this case, shepherds would probably not be so hard to find anymore.

Goats are also not so easily convinced by electric. Those with grid electricity can get a strong charger, with several strands of electric, which will hold trained goats. But, if just one part of the fence is grounded, the goats will quickly figure out that it is all just a ruse, and they will escape. For this reason, I recommend, for goats, woven wire that is 4 feet tall, with one stand of barbed wire on top, about two inches above the woven wire; at least for all of your perimeter fences. This may seem costly, but goats will save you from even more costly weed control and they will manicure your pasture better than a landscaping crew. Do not attempt to raise goats without a proper fence as they can be destructive and can destroy an orchard in minutes. Don't ask me how I know.

We have also kept Bison on our farmstead which was a learning experience, but also a real pain in the buttocks. I would lie awake at night wondering if they had found a way to escape; I could just picture $100,000 on the hoof rampaging through to the next county. Besides being difficult to keep in, bison are also nearly impossible to retrieve once they are free. We no longer have bison, but I often see news articles from across the country about various ranches that lose bison and are almost never able to retrieve them. They normally have to be shot. They are of course, big dangerous animals, but they are also as fast as a deer. Our bison fences were four feet of woven with two more strands of barbed wire and one electric strand on top, at least 6 feet tall in total. This was just barely enough to keep them in.

Illustration 32: Bison in the Snow on our Homestead, they Never need a Barn.

Once, we did have a bison heifer escape. She found a weak spot where a tree had fallen on the fence, and she went for it. She was gone for two months, and several of the neighbors saw her for miles around. She even tempted a few in their deer stands during hunting season. Finally, after several failed roundups and traps to corral her, we decided to hunt her down. After a good snowfall, I spotted her tracks and followed for about a mile before I found her grazing in a little meadow in the woods. She was in my freezer by sundown.

Cattle

Cattle are so much easier in many ways. A four-foot-high fence is sufficient for a happy cow and as I mentioned, one strand of electrified polywire facilitates the movement of a herd to graze your pasture evenly and thoroughly, not staying in one point for too long. Calves may not respect polywire fence, but you can't get too stressed about it. Let them be and they will not stray far from their mothers. If one of the mothers refuses to stay in the fence, then she belongs on your dinner table instead. Besides being docile, cattle are also relatively parasite resistant and can get by with less care than other classes of livestock. I keep my cattle without a barn and I have never had to help with calving. The reason that I am able to do this is that I do not breed cattle to calve in the winter and I don't look for a ridiculously large bull to breed my cows. These small considerations make keeping cattle much easier. As discussed below, the real challenge to running cattle is to keep such a large animal fed. In a grid-down, self-sustaining situation, this requires the right land, and some specific knowledge that I will focus on here.

Movement is the key to grazing cattle. Most cool season grasses should be grazed to no less than 3 inches while warm seasons should be grazed no shorter than 6 inches. We generally move our cattle every day or two in the summer, using a watering point as a hub for the rotation. Grazier's math can help you figure out how big of an area to allow for your cattle, based on how much grass volume they need to eat per day, compared to grass height multiplied by grass area.

Pasture Species	Stand Condition		
	Fair	Good	Excellent
	----- lbs/acre-inch -----		
Tall Fescue	250-350	350-450	450-550
Tall Fescue + Legumes	200-300	300-400	400-500
Smooth Bromegrass + Legumes	150-250	250-350	350-450
Orchardgrass + Legumes	100-200	200-300	300-400
Bluegrass + White Clover	150-250	300-400	450-550
Mixed Pasture	150-250	250-350	350-450

Table 1: You can estimate the amount of available forage in your pasture by roughly measuring the height of the grass and multiplying by the appropriate category listed here. (Tim Schnakenberg, Agronomy Specialist, University of Missouri, Stone County Extension Center)

Whole Season Grazing Efficiency	
Continuous	30%
4 Pasture	35%
8 Pasture	50%
12 Pasture	65%
24+ Pasture	75%

Table 2: This table shows why we rotate cattle daily. You can increase the grazing efficiency to at least 75% of available grass consumption. The number on the left means how many rotations per month. (Tim Schnakenberg, Agronomy Specialist, University of Missouri, Stone County Extension Center)

For example, I have a stand of fescue which produces about 400 lbs. of grass per inch of growth per acre. I don't want to graze it below 3 inches. If I turn the cattle in when the grass is 9 inches high, that gives me 6 inches to graze, or 2400 lbs. per acre. The cattle will waste about 25%, even when carefully managed, with a grazing efficiency of 75%. That means I can allow the cattle to graze only 1800 lbs. per acre, before they are moved. If I have 45 x 1000 lb. cows in the paddock, and they are eating 2% of their body weight per day, then they are going to need 1/2 acre (900 lbs.) per day. If the grass needs 30 days to recover and regrow, then I need to have 15 acres for my 45 cows, and they need to be moved to a new acre every day. In other words, they are grazing 1/2 acre per day and are on a 30-day rotation. In many areas, drought will double the time that it takes your grass to regrow, meaning that in the above case you would want 30 acres for 45 cows that are intensively managed. If you only rotate once per week, then the grazing efficiency is cut in half, so you will need twice as much grazing land. Again, you do not need a full fence for each paddock. Instead, you can maintain a good perimeter fence and then use moveable polywire fence between the smaller daily paddocks. While it may not be so easy to apply in real life, it is useful to understand the concepts in grazier's math, then you maintain flexibility and adapt it to the changing situation of your vegetation conditions and weather. Like many aspects of homesteading, it simply means that resources are limited, everything needs to be rationed, and you must plan for every mouth that must be fed.

To Review, this is the formula for managing your livestock and pasture using grazier's math:

To Determine the appropriate # of days a herd should spend on a pasture, divide the top line by the bottom:

$$\frac{\text{Total lbs. Forage per acre} \times \text{number of Acres} \times \text{Grazing Efficiency}}{\text{Daily Animal Forage Consumption in lbs.} \times \text{number of animals}} = \text{Days on Pasture}$$

Illustration 33: Thin and Portable Polywire Fences with Solar Chargers can help ration your Pastures, including during the early winter with stockpiled green forage such as Fescue and Orchard Grass

In wintertime, it is imperative to plan for stockpiled grasses, either in the pasture, or in the form of hay. Even many of our Amish neighbors pay for their hay to get baled because it is so labor intensive. But many of them still gather and keep loose hay in the barn loft as well. To do this without fossil fuel, you can use either a hand sickle or a horse drawn sickle mower. Then it can be hand raked, or raked by a horse drawn rake, and carried in a hay wagon to the barn. The key to baling good, high protein hay is to do it while it is dry, and to do it early in the season, before everything goes to seed, which is when it starts to lose protein. Only certain grasses can be left stockpiled in the pasture without any labor. Most noteworthy is tall fescue followed by orchard grass. In many mid-latitude temperate regions, these can be left untouched from August until February, and will be excellent winter stockpile in the field.

Taking the grazier's math and using the example of 45 cows above, let us say that we need 1/2 acre per day, because we have managed to stockpile about 9 inches of fescue. We might be able to graze our regular pasture until November 15, then we start into the stockpile from that time until January 15. This is about 60 days, which means we need 30 stockpiled acres to feed our 45 cows over the winter! With proper planning the previous summer, this same 30 acres can provide 60 additional days of winter hay from January 15 to March 15. Adding it all up, we see that off-grid homesteading requires more acreage than a conventional grain fed operation. In this case for our 45 cows, we need a minimum of 30 acres of good pasture for regular rotational grazing, and an additional 30 acres for hay and winter stockpiling. This gives a grand total of 60 acres for 45 cows or just under 1.5 acres of good pasture for each 1000 lb. cow. This is twice the stocking density for a farm with only once per week rotations, and it is calculated under ideal conditions. To give yourself some room for error, I typically recommend twice as much or 3 acres per cow, because a serious drought or hard winter will cut your grass supply in half.

There are other variables to consider, so this is a rough estimate and is designed for a mid-latitude temperate environment with at least 36 inches of rainfall per year. Keep in mind, this scenario is for a completely grass-fed, self-sufficient, long-term sustainable grazing plan with no external inputs. If the grid goes down, there is no feed store, there is no big tractor to bale hay, and there is no forgiveness or easy fix once you have exhausted your soil. For this reason, just like our ancestors once did, you must learn to ration, to plan for hard times, and to always keep something in reserve.

MINERAL

Speaking of keeping something in reserve, salt is a commodity that will be needed in large quantities in a long-term emergency. In the ancient world, it was a type of currency, in fact, the Latin word for salt was *sale,* which is the root for the word salary. It can be purchased relatively cheaply now, so it would be wise to stock up. While there are a multitude of human uses for salt, it is also critical for livestock. When livestock do not have the proper minerals, they do not efficiently metabolize their forage, meaning that they might eat a lot, but not gain weight.

Not only do animals require salt, but they also need other mineral supplementation to include phosphorus, magnesium, selenium, copper, cobalt, zinc, and more. These mineral requirements vary based on your location, your soil type, and they change based on the season. It is difficult to stock up on all of these minerals, but a two-fold strategy will get you by in an emergency. First, buy large amounts of all-natural raw, pink salt, such as Redmond brand. While not the perfect supplement, this type of salt contains many of the trace minerals mentioned above.

The second part of the strategy is to rapidly reduce your stock numbers in the case of a potential long emergency. Today's livestock manager is geared towards squeezing every penny out of their grazing acreage. This means that feed supplementation is often purchased in winter, in drought, or when livestock numbers surge. Historically, and in lean times, this type of supplementation is not available. Instead, you have to reduce your livestock numbers to what your land can support in adverse conditions. For example, if you would normally be comfortable with 3 acres per cow on your land, consider reducing your stocking rate to 10 acres per cow, and try to get by without feeding hay in the winter. This may cause an overgrowth of forage during certain times of the year. This can be solved by burning, which enriches your soil, and by grazing weed-loving stock, such as goats. Goats will be the next topic discussed.

Goats

For goat grazier math, figure 8 goats for 1 cow, meaning that it takes about eight goats to eat as much as a cow. There are several considerations for grazing goats that are helpful and good for your land. Goats will eat most forage types, including nuisances like ragweed, blackberry bushes, wild rose bushes, and sericea lespedeza. They can also thrive on mostly acorns in the fall if you have a lot of oak forest. Finally, they do not like to graze low on grass, and will graze more evenly than cows. This is good for your grass and allows it to retain more leaves and thus continue to send energy to stimulate root growth, but again, movement is the key. We generally keep the goats in one paddock for 5-10 days because they are not as likely to overgraze an area.

The wonderful thing about goats is that because of their eating habits and climbing abilities, they will do well on rugged land. If you notice in the security section of this book that rugged land is easier to defend and that steep land is cheap land, then goats logically seem like a good choice for many homesteaders in rugged locations. They can provide you with lean, healthy pink meat, and with milk that is nutritious, and easier on your digestive system than cow's milk.

Illustration 34: Goats eat these and most other invasive and noxious plants, turning them into meat and milk for you and your family.

Goats are not without their drawbacks. An Amish neighbor of mine once told me, "There are three things you need to know about goats; WORM, WORM, and WORM." He of course meant that goats are susceptible to all kinds of parasites and worms. In addition, being a prey animal, they tend to hide when they are not feeling well, so that predators don't pick them for their next meal. Unfortunately, this means that by the time you find out that there is something wrong with them, then they have likely hidden somewhere and dropped dead. To prevent this, I used to deworm goats once every three months. Finally, I found a good natural remedy that helped me cut this down to only once every 6 months. I started giving them loose goat mineral and diatomaceous earth at a rate of one cup of each substance per 10 goats every single day. The mineral strengthens their immune system, and the diatomaceous earth is sharp at a microscopic level and actually cuts and damages microorganisms such as worms.

I am also a big fan of vaccinations for all livestock and in the case of goats, the enterotoxaemia vaccine is very important. The best time to give goats their vaccines is once per year about three weeks after kidding. This allows you to vaccinate mamas and babies all at once without damaging any unborn kids. In a long emergency, vaccines will be unavailable, so your best bet in that case is to stock up on mineral. Selenium/salt blocks are inexpensive and becoming more widely available. High selenium in an animal's diet helps their immune system.

I find that it is advantageous to kid in late winter and early spring. You will need a good barn with dry hay and feed. A barn that is south facing and can catch the sun in winter is ideal. Kidding this early in the season allows the baby goats to be born without many of the warm weather parasites. In addition, the best forage in temperate climates is available from April to October, allowing the kids and nursing mothers to take advantage of the lush growth, growing fast and strong. This means that they will be big enough to deal with the cold when the next winter sets in. Meat goats are prime at 90 lbs. but can be eaten later if you like a stronger flavor. However, they should not have a terribly strong flavor if castrated. One technique to use when raising Dairy goats is to breed the dairy does with a meat buck in order to produce offspring that are good for use as meat, while the mothers are good for providing milk.

Illustration 35: Our Barn, A Good Barn is absolutely crucial to raising Goats in wet climates and is used for hay storage, milking, kidding, and as shelter during storms.

Rabbits

Rabbits have a reputation as a "prepper" food, but people often overlook their dietary needs. Because rabbits can breed and multiply rapidly, many in the prepper community have claimed that they are a wise choice as a food source. It is true that rabbits typically have up to 10 litters per year of 6-14 babies, but they have to be well cared for and well-fed. Many people who claim to be preppers often feed their rabbits nothing but store-bought pellets, meaning that they would be completely useless without our grid-dependent supply chain. It is hard work, but if you hope to raise rabbits during a grid down situation, they can survive on forage that you and provide yourself.

One of the first things that we noticed on our homestead when switching to wild forage for our rabbits was a huge improvement in our rabbits' health. They tend to have a lot of digestive issues, such as gut stasis and weaning enteritis when they eat nothing but pellets. Introducing them to wild vegetation almost completely eliminated these issues. The first consideration when switching to wild and domestic forage for your rabbits is that you should do so gradually. Don't feed 100% pellets and then the next day 100% wild forage. All animals, especially herbivores have microbes in their guts that allow them to digest the food which is normally in their diet. If you change this diet, the gut microbes (flora and fauna) can upset the pH and the general chemistry of the gut, causing the animal to get sick and die.

The second consideration when switching to this type of diet is that you really need to get smart on your weed identification and your knowledge of a rabbit's diet. It is always a good idea to provide simple grass hay to your rabbits, but they will also need some variety to meet their nutritional needs. In the spring, great rabbit foods include freshly sprouted grasses, dandelions (the whole plant), plantains, and tree branches with leaves. Favorite trees include elm, sassafras, and oak. Black cherry, white sumac, and certain others can be poisonous so get to know your trees! In the summer, you can add ragweed, clover, lespedeza, and domestics such as soybeans and garden vegetables. In the fall and winter, you can add honeysuckle, blackberry briars, multiflora rose, willow, poplar, and you will need to start relying more on hay, especially high protein hay with clovers, and preferably alfalfa. Chard and cabbage are also important fresh winter supplements, but you will need to rely on high quality, mold free hay during the colder months. This is by no means a complete list, but it is a good start. Don't feed iceberg lettuce, rhubarb, apple seeds, fruit pits, potatoes or corn as these items can kill a rabbit.

I find that it is useful not to put too much food in front of them; not more than they could normally be expected to eat in one day. One half day of food at a time works best. This is to avoid waste and trampling of the food. You also need to ensure that your rabbits get enough to eat. Again, put what you believe to be one half day of food in front of them and see if they run out too early, or if they waste and trample it. If they trample it then you are feeding them too much.

A final consideration when getting away from relying on store-bought pellets is that a diet of fresh and stored forage is not usually as dense in protein as a diet of pure pellets. With this in mind, they will grow a little slower and should be bred less frequently. I would recommend breeding no more than every 60 days. You will have to manage this because if you put the buck rabbit in early, he will often breed the doe just 30 days after she has her litter. The buck should of course only be kept with the doe during intentional breeding, but this gets into the details of rabbit husbandry, and we will focus only on grid-down survival considerations here. Rabbits are fast multipliers, but the best foragers are chickens, which will be the next topic of discussion.

Chickens

Utilizing Chickens in your grazing rotation can be beneficial, but it is difficult to keep them safe from predators. One of the main advantages of having chickens is that their manure is high in phosphorous, a key mineral fertilizer for all types of vegetation. When incorporated into your grazing rotation, chickens can really help to green up your pastures if they are rotated properly. They also have the added benefit of sanitizing your pastures by eating insect pests, and scratching through other manure which aids in the decomposition process. If a hen house is centrally located, chickens can be released in different paddocks on a rotational basis. Another technique is to use a mobile hen house, egg mobile, or chicken tractor.

Everyone loves to eat chicken; humans, coyotes, bobcats, vultures, even possums like to chow down on a drumstick. For this reason, predator deterrence is the key to raising chickens. I have designed and built numerous chicken houses. A stationary chicken house, located centrally between paddocks, should always have a concrete floor, or at least a concrete footer under the fence that surrounds it. Chicken lovers-like raccoons will dig under any fence that has no concrete underneath. A stationary hen house has the advantage of being easy to secure but it must be centrally located with access to multiple paddocks. Multiple paddocks are essential because chickens will scratch and dig around until all vegetation is stripped bare if they are not properly rotated.

The advantage of a mobile hen house is that it can be moved from paddock to paddock based on where it is needed to provide nutrients and sanitation. Mobile hen houses can be built in two main styles: the chicken tractor and the egg-mobile. Chicken tractors are most frequently used to raise meat chickens. A simple chicken tractor has four walls that are about 8 feet long and 2 feet high. The walls are covered with 1 inch mesh wire and the roof is normally metal. It is important that the structure is made from light weight material, so that it can be dragged like a shed on a daily or semi-daily basis.

Illustration 36: The Chicken Tractor, light enough to drag by hand, giving Chickens fresh forage and insects, and spreading their manure fertilizer in your fields

Illustration 37: Our Egg Mobile is big enough to need wheels and has place for chickens to roost, nesting boxes, and can be locked up securely at night

An egg mobile, which is most commonly used for egg layers, generally looks like a shed on wheels. The walls can be tall enough to accommodate a person to gather eggs and it can be as large as the vehicle pulling it can handle. I even had a 4x8 foot model with wheels that I could move by hand in the early days of our homestead. An egg mobile definitely needs nesting boxes, 1 for every two chickens, and enough roosting space where chickens can get up off of the ground to sleep. These hen houses are opened in the morning to allow the hens to forage and they are closed at night for safety. There are automatic doors available, complete with a timer and solar panel for the lazy homesteader, but you might just make it your routine to open them for feed time and close them when you gather eggs. Just don't ever, ever forget to close them, or some lucky predator will be a winner, winner, chicken dinner!

This movement of chicken houses allows you to spread the chicken manure throughout your paddock and gives the chickens access to the key vitamins and minerals in fresh greens as well as nutritious insects. You still need to keep their water full at all times and they will still need grain-based feed. Chickens with access to fresh pasture and insects will eat about 1/3 less feed than caged chickens during warm months. They will also be much healthier because of their rich diet and will almost certainly produce meat and eggs that is higher in vitamin D and Omega 3. One secret to keeping chickens without using bagged feed is to keep in mind that they are omnivores, and they can eat scraps, and also meat. Old timers have told me that in the winter, they would sometimes kill squirrels, possums, or even fish that they would throw to the chickens so that they could have extra protein. Animal carcasses with maggots and bugs on them are also good for chickens as the chickens love to eat insects.

As mentioned, it is very difficult to keep chickens safe, and I always recommend keeping them close to the house. Even with a concrete floor and cinder block walls, we have awoken to squawking chickens that had been invaded by the local possum or raccoon. Once a raccoon dangled from the eaves of the chicken house with one hand long enough to rip open the screened, ventilated window at the top of the house with the other. When I caught him stealing eggs, he dangled himself upside down inside the cinder block wall, holding himself up with one foot. I figured he would be stuck and just left him to die, but he hoisted himself out of the hole by his toes and jumped back out the window as soon as I turned my back. Double 007 raccoon!

Our predator problem was so bad that instead of closing the door on the hen house, we started placing a live trap on the inside of the entrance. We even caught two possums at once that way. They probably were just high-fiving and congratulating each other for having made it into the front door, when the trap door slammed shut and closed them in. The next morning, the possums would of course play dead, even spitting up and vomiting on themselves and each other to convince me that they were just carcasses. Disgusting! Raccoons, on the other hand, will always give you this innocent big-eyed look like they are so sorry and will promise not to do it again. Then if you come close to them, they will hiss and growl like a murderous demon. I don't like the idea of executing captives so I would always take them and release them far from our farmstead. Out here in the country, city folks often come and drop off their unwanted dogs along our road. To repay the favor, I go to the city to drop off our unwanted raccoons and possums. (Just kidding all of you animal control officers, settle down!)

Livestock Guardian Dogs

Eventually, I wised up to the fact that possums and raccoons are in endless supply in our neighborhood and so I figured out how to use livestock guardian dogs to protect chickens. LGD's can be imprinted on chickens just like goats or sheep, when the dogs are just puppies. Our favorite bitch was born right next to the chickens and has been around them her whole life. She has a particular hatred for birds of prey, especially vultures, and she always lets them know to stay away from her territory with her loud and ferocious bark. You do have to keep an eye on the LGD's when they are puppies to make sure that they don't make a game of chasing the chickens. Puppies are very playful but a very quick reprimand or especially a shock collar will break the habit quickly. People think shock collars are cruel but in reality, you only have to use the shock 2 or 3 times, then the bell on the collar is a sufficient reminder. The people that say the shock collar is cruel are the same ones whose dogs have chicken feathers hanging out of their mouths when you visit. Then they dump the dog off in the country so they can go on vacation to Cancun, after they have totally ruined the dog through lack of discipline. If you are using a mobile chicken house, then the dogs can simply patrol outside of the chicken area, which is a great deterrent for predators.

Illustration 38: A Trained Livestock Guardian Dog Behaves just like the other Members of his Herd

At our stationary hen house, we sometimes let a dog roam unfenced areas, to keep the predators back. The only problem here is that sometimes LGD's like to roam too far and even run off. To fix this, we always keep a pair of dogs. We normally keep the bitch in a very sturdy pen with a large yard by the chickens. She raises her puppies there and also provides near security for the chickens. Her partner, the male, is for security and can be placed with goats or sheep, or can be released in the unfenced areas as needed. As long as the bitch is in the pen, the male will never roam too far or run off. The female can also provide a litter of 8-10 pups per year, adding to your farm's production.

Hunting for Protein

How and what you hunt will of course depend largely on where you live and the game that is available in your area. I will focus on whitetail deer first and get into smaller game later. Whitetail deer can be some of the most unpredictable and challenging prey for a hunter and can be a source of lifelong enjoyment as well as a great source of healthy lean meat for those who are up to the task. As you build your hunting skills, you will find that they can readily be taken with a bow as long as your hunting knowledge is adequate. In many poverty-stricken areas, such big game have become scarce, and so you should also have skills for hunting small game, birds, and even rodents. In hard times, desperation will drive many people to hunt wild game, and this food source could disappear, so have a contingency plan. When my grandmother was a child, the Great Depression created this type of desperate scenario in Southern Illinois. Her father Frank, my Great Grandfather was hunting squirrels on his own land out of season in order to feed his 9 children during the depression, when a game warden caught him in the act. My Great Grandfather, a World War I veteran, lowered his shotgun and told the warden, I've got children to feed and I am not afraid to use this gun so you'd better turn and walk away. Great Grandpa got his way. This will quickly get you killed by the game warden today, but the point is that a man will kill the last squirrel on the planet to feed his children, so treasure and guard your wild game as you would your livestock. Keep in mind that current laws and wildlife code should always be obeyed. You do not want to experience the coming Dark Age from a jail cell. Many of the techniques discussed in this section are for survival situations only, and do not take into consideration current wildlife regulations that you should always obey.

I should first mention how a good hunter cares for game animals by managing them properly. Just as humans need natural resources and should not exceed their carrying capacity on the planet, so too should deer be managed to stay below their carrying capacity. This means that it is wise to cull and hunt deer so that the size of their population does not require more food than what their habitat can produce. A hunter should spend enough time in the wild to be familiar with the number of animals in a given area as well as their general appearance and health. A great hunter will not always be after the trophy buck. Many of the deer that I have hunted were culls; a buck with a deformed antler, a doe with an injured hoof, or members of a herd that is obviously too large for the amount of forage available in the area. I like to thin a herd like you prune a fruit tree. After the weak and crowded branches are thinned, you remove the leader, and then leave the healthy upcoming branches to become the leaders next year.

Apart from aiding in natural selection, humans are often inclined to encourage nature, even going above carrying capacity when possible. During a hard winter, I too am guilty of this. I take seriously that God gave dominion over animals to humans, to care for and utilize. Even if you are non-religious, you have to take into account our powers of reasoning and our ability to do long range planning unlike any other species on the planet. With this in mind, I have fed wild animals, grains and mineral supplements, keeping them from suffering and starving during hard times. I notice right away when the acorn crop in our area has failed, and I begin to stock up on corn for the deer, turkeys, and woodland mammals. Nonetheless, keep in mind that God also has not hesitated to "put the smack down" on mankind when we stretch ourselves to thin, lose humility, and generally misbehave. In other words, use moderation and judgement, feeding wildlife only in times where their food becomes scarce and feed them at a sustainable level. The minute that it becomes unsustainable, you need to cull and thin the herd to keep them from overgrazing and destroying their own environment. Used in this way, hunting is a form of good stewardship, and can be enjoyed for generations to come.

Illustration 39:On A Homestead, everyone can Help Put Food on the Table

Hunting Big Game, post-collapse considerations

In an area with abundant game and few people, you may find that you do not need to raise livestock at all, but keep in mind that everyone else will be looking for food in the event of an economic or social collapse. In terms of whitetail deer, we try to take one average 120 lb. animal for each member of our family every winter. We use every scrap of meat, and it provides over half of all meat that our family eats. (Livestock provides the rest) And remember, waste not, want not.

There are volumes upon volumes of books about hunting big game, so I will not hit all of the details here, but I will hit upon those morsels of information that are unique to long term emergency survival. First and foremost, one needs to realize that you cannot be a non-hunting vegan one day, and then switch to being a deadly big game predator right after your food supply chain fails. I once overheard a dear non-hunting friend of ours say that deer season was like "shooting fish in a barrel." Nothing could be further from the truth. Hunting requires skill and patience beyond measure, and it takes years to become a good hunter. Furthermore, as soon as the game understand that they are being hunted, the difficulty of the hunt increases ten-fold. The bottom line is that you must start developing your hunting skills now, before a crisis hits, in order to provide long term food security for you and your loved ones during a long emergency.

When preparing for a long emergency, you must think first and foremost about the durability and sustainability of your hunting gear. You will not be able to run to Walmart and buy a new scope or more ammunition. Scopes that require batteries are totally unsustainable, but instead, opt for iron sights or at least a simple fixed magnification scope. Also, think about stocking up on ammunition and using bows or crossbows that you can make new arrow for in a pinch. When storing ammunition, never buy a large quantity of ammo and then leave it in an unsealed container. Make sure your ammo box or bucket has a rubber seal and then throw a couple desiccant packets in there to suck up the humidity. Small boxes are good because you will not want to open more ammo than you can expend in a short amount of time during a survival situation. Reloading ammo is a great skill, but I consider it more of a money-saving craft than a survival aid. This is because it is just as easy to stock up on ammo as it is to stock up on reloading supplies.

Use of bows and crossbows requires a whole new level of skill than hunting with a rifle. This is because you must be much closer to your target to achieve a kill shot. Nonetheless, it is a huge advantage to be able to make your own ammunition in the form of arrows (bow) and bolts (crossbow). I recommend buying a modern compound bow or crossbow because they are so much more effective than the old-style wooden versions. They will also last for decades if not abused.

Making arrows for these composite bows is a little different than for their wooden counterparts. A composite bow shoots much harder, so you must choose a wood for your arrow that is very hard. Splitting a straight-grained wood such as Osage orange, walnut, or a very straight hickory is a good place to start. These split, dry, shafts then must be whittled down, rounded, and well-sanded. A knobby shaft such as a cane pole shaft will not function smoothly with a compound bow. To ensure the arrows are straight, bend out all the curves over an open fire, without burning the shaft. Once straight and smooth, you are ready to fletch and mount your arrow tips.

I find feather fletching and stone arrow points to be beautiful but also somewhat impractical and time-consuming. From a practical standpoint, in today's world, there will never be a shortage of plastic for fletching or metal for points. Survival means using these available, abundant materials. The flat sides of plastic milk jugs or other flat bottle sides make perfect fletching. Simply cut the plastic to the proper shape, super glue, and then reinforce the top and bottom of the fletching with fine wire or string. For arrow points, simply cut a triangle from any type of sheet metal, notch the arrow, and use resin, superglue, or epoxy (best option) to mount the point. This is not artsy or crafty, but these arrows will certainly work as suitable replacements when disaster prevents you from purchasing arrows. Since the materials are widely available, bow and arrow technology will be critical for any future scenario where ammunition for firearms becomes scarce.

Whitetail deer are one of the most reclusive and unpredictable large game animals in North America. You might see dozens of them along the roadways, but they are not ignorant animals. When you start hunting, they will melt away into the forests and hollows like ghosts. I once took my young daughters out for their first hunting season. To make things a little easier, I set them up in an abandoned old shed, on the edge of a field that we never hunt, where female deer congregate carelessly year-round. The old shed worked perfectly to hide the sounds and smells of two fidgety girls and their stinky father. When the does made their daily appearance, my oldest daughter easily made her first kill with a rifle at 115 yards. There was no containing the excitement and joy at her first kill, but to the deer, it was a lesson they wouldn't forget. For the next three months, through our bow season, not one doe stepped out into that field, even though it was the greenest, most delicious feeding spot in all the valley. The moral of the story is that white tail deer are intelligent prey animals, and you must always be on your toes to bring home the venison.

These and other deer species are also very prolific and widespread, making them the perfect game animal to hone your skills and keep your family fed. While this is not a book about hunting techniques, there are a few considerations that must be taken into account when hunting deer in a "post-collapse" world. Today it is common practice to hunt the deer "rut" or mating season using scents, calls, plastic decoys, and lures. It is also common (where legal) to use bait such as corn or mineral licks, or to plant a food plot where deer will gather. In a post-collapse world, there will be no store-bought scents available, calls will eventually break, plastic decoys will not always be available, and grain will be saved for your own family, instead of feeding it to the deer. Fortunately, there are excellent and viable alternatives to all these techniques, some of which were used for centuries before the modern era.

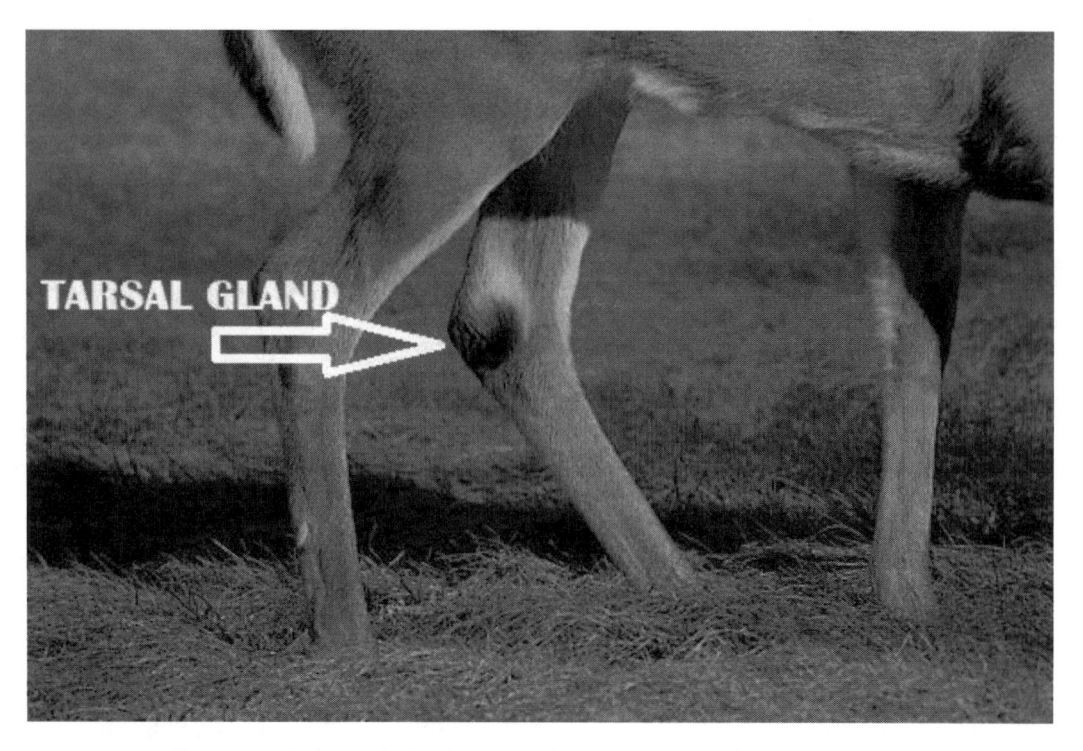

Illustration 40: A Tarsal Gland on a deer has a strong scent that will encourage other bucks to come and fight.

    First, during the fall rut or mating season, there is no scent or lure that can match the real thing. Hunting where a group of female deer is present is almost a sure way to kill a buck. And killing a buck does little to reduce deer numbers when you are looking to maintain a large herd. Once you kill a buck it is useful to cut off the tarsal gland, which is on the "heel" of the deer, about 16 inches from the hoof, on the back of the leg. It is just a dark oily patch of fur where the buck will excrete a scent to attract does. It has a strong nutty smell almost like a putrid walnut. I like to tie these on a string and carry it with me. Dragging it along the ground while approaching a hunting location lets other bucks know that a competitor is present and gets them to act aggressive and careless. When butchering you can also preserve the bladder and urine of females as well as bucks. This can also be put on the ground or hung in a tree near your hunting area. Getting the deer "in the mood" makes them easier to fool. These simple solutions were commonplace and known to be highly effective before modern scents came along.

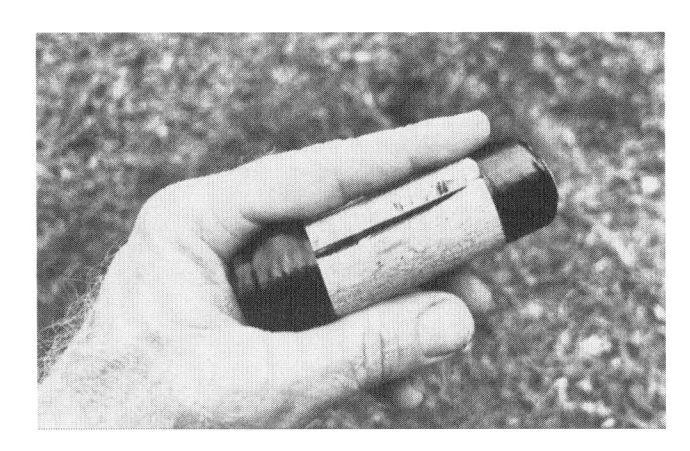

Illustration 41: Easy to make doe call from a split piece of wood with a gap and piece of elastic in between.

Another way to get a deer "in the mood" is through the use of deer calls. A few years ago, I was hunting in a quiet valley where there was a smallish 8 pointer that I had seen earlier and planned to let grow for the next season. He was so turned-on by the deer call that I was using that he was ready to fight, and he crashed through the brush, out into the open, and charged across the dry creek bed right toward my location. I was so startled myself that I leveled my rifle and fired reflexively, as in self-defense. He dropped and skidded toward me in the gravel about 8 feet from where I sat. I was sold on the idea of white tail deer language, and noises.

Illustration 42: I called in this Ozark Whitetail with a homemade buck grunt call

Modern deer calls are highly effective, and they may last a long time in a post collapse situation, but it is not as difficult to make a homemade deer call as one might imagine. Doe bleats and buck grunts are usually only effective around the fall rut season. To make a doe bleat call, you need a small stick, 1 inch in diameter by 4 inches long, a rubber band, and some duct tape. Split the stick in half, and carve a 1/8 to ¼ inch size gap, two inches long, in the middle of the split sticks. Put one rubber band around one of the halves and put the two sticks together so that they have an elastic in the middle. Then take the duct tape and wrap it around to keep the two halves together. This elastic "sandwich" will make a very feminine doe bleat almost like the sound of a loud woman's sigh when you blow on the gap between the two halves of the call.

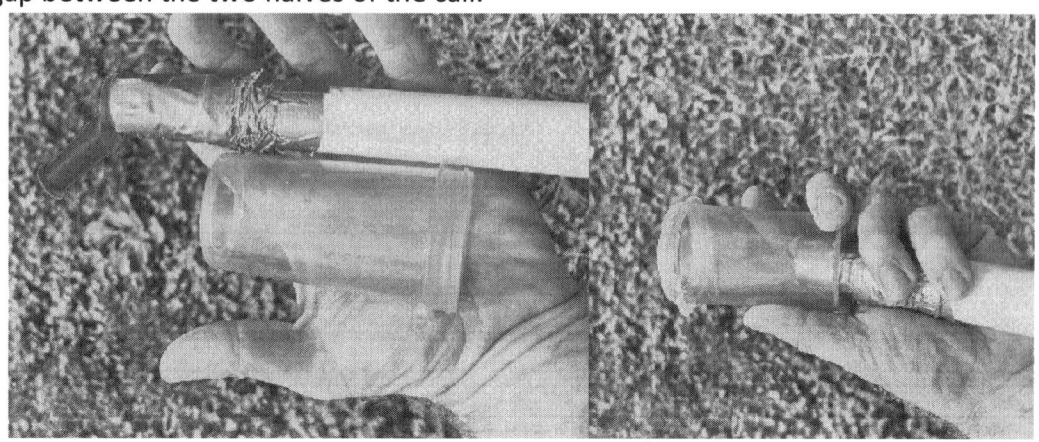

Illustration 43: You can make a simple homemade buck call out of a pill bottle, PVC pipe, a balloon, and duct tape. I personally think this works better than one from the store.

To make a more masculine, buck grunt call, you will need a foot long hollow ¾ inch pipe, a balloon, duct tape, and a container the size of a large pill bottle. Simply cut the round end off the balloon and shove the pipe in that end. Tape it so that the mouthpiece of the balloon is centered on the edge of the pipe and hangs off about 1.5 inches. When you blow on the other end, the balloon should block the airflow enough to sound like a whoopee cushion. After it makes a good, deep gurgling grunt sound, you can then put the balloon end of the call inside of the large pill bottle, with the taped in facing the open end of the bottle. This means you drill a hole the same size as the pipe in the closed end of the bottle, and just thread it through. The taped end will be inside the bottle, so when you blow, it will sound deeper and echo, just like it is coming from the throat of a white tail buck. Put the pipe in at an angle so that the side of the bottle doesn't interfere with the balloon flapping. Cupping your hand over the end can add deeper, more realistic effects to the buck grunt.

"Rattling antlers" are another tool that works to draw in bucks before, during, and after the rut. I prefer to use real antlers, but dry, hard, de-barked sticks that are the same size as antlers can be used in a pinch. Oak, hickory, or best-of-all, ironwood can be used. Simply place several 6 inch long, 1-to-2-inch diameter sections in a cloth bag. Rattle the sticks together in the bag to make it sound like two bucks are sparring. If you have a set of smallish, real antlers, they can be left whole and rattled together for a nice, realistic sound as well.

You also rub them against a tree, which gives a nice sound effect just like when a buck in rut is excited and starts rubbing the bark off of trees.

While mating calls, grunts, and rattling work during the fall mating season, it can be a little trickier to attract deer during the rest of the year. If they are not finding a mate, deer are mainly interested in food sources and water. This sounds simple, but the huge variety of food that deer consume can make the perfect spot a bit hard to nail down. One way to simplify things is to create a deer feeding area, or food plot. Besides a food source, a good food plot has fresh water nearby, a place to hide, and is isolated from human traffic and other predators such as dogs.

In modern times, many deer lovers just go to Walmart or a feed store and pick up a bunch of deer corn to create an instant food plot. In a post collapse scenario, things will not be quite so easy. Our world grain supply is entirely dependent on mechanization, cheap fuel, expensive chemical fertilizers, and particularly, non-renewable phosphorus. Someday, you will not be able to go pick up a bag of cheap corn for the deer. Instead, you must grow the food plot yourself. The easiest way to do this is to use an existing meadow that has the water and the isolation that deer need. Unfortunately, many hunting retreat spots that are affordable, are also heavily forested and may have no existing meadows. In this case, you will need to remove the existing forest canopy, to allow for the sunlight needed to grow forage. Leaving mature oak trees will help keep acorns on the ground but most other trees are of limited food value to deer. It is a good idea to also leave some thick vegetation such as mountain laurel or cedar trees near the food plot, if possible. Deer are more comfortable in an area if they have some place to bed down and hide.

Currently, many deer hunters plant a lot of grains such as oats and wheat, as well as brassicas such as turnips. These are all annuals, which have to be planted year after year. In order to plan for potential scarcity, and make your life easier, it is not a bad idea to plant perennials, which will come up year after year. All types of clovers are great perennials that attract deer, and a number of wildflowers make great forage as well. These include chicory, yarrow, butterfly plant, snakeroot, purple coneflower, and more. Orchard grass is an excellent addition to this mix, as it will stay green and hold protein well into the winter. For some tall sheltering grass and summer forage, eastern gama grass and big bluestem are great additions. Buckbrush is often seen as an invasive plant, but I have often split open a deer's gut in the winter to find it full of these berries. Blackberries are often a bramble that is avoided, but deer eat the leaves just as well as the berries. If you can plant at least a half-acre of these deer forage species, you will have to hunt deer just to keep them from taking over! In fact, such food plots sometimes get grazed too heavily, and you will see clover nibbled right down to the ground. To avoid this, get out there and hunt!

There are many other skills required of a big game hunter. You need to know how to set up a blind, how to build a tree stand, how to stalk a deer. You need to know about using the wind to your advantage, camouflage, and noise discipline. These are all elements of common hunting knowledge that are not unique to post-collapse hunting and survival. The best way to learn all of these tricks of the trade is to get out their and hunt now. Hone your skills, take only what you need, and be a good steward of the land!

Small Game and Trapping

Hunting for small game for recreation is one thing, but for survival, it is completely different. In the event that you are faced with the necessity of becoming self-sufficient in your lifetime, every minute of every hour in your day becomes precious. You will no longer be killing time, sending text messages, while you wait for your tall vanilla latte. Instead, a wasted moment will feel like you may have just cheated yourself and your loved ones out of the opportunity to survive another day. In terms of hunting, this means that big game is well worth the effort, but small game becomes a time management issue. This is because big game provides dozens of meals per kill, whereas a squirrel is maybe one meal, *maybe*.

For this reason, and to use time efficiently, I highly recommend learning to trap to catch small game. While I won't pretend that animals do not suffer in a trap, I am willing to put an animal through suffering for the sake of providing for my loved ones. Doing so for pure profit or pleasure doesn't really turn me on. And, if you get overly aggressive and trap all of the furbearers off your property before the shit hits the fan, then you are just up shit creek without a paddle (a dumb shit).

There are three basic subsistence traps that I would recommend learning, the snare, the leg-hold, and the conibear.

There are various types of snares, but the wire noose snare is the most basic. The ideal wire to use for this is a three- or four-foot piece of thin but stiff, strong wire such as picture frame hanging wire. You simply make a small end-of-the line bowline knot with loop on one end of the wire, and then slip the other end through the loop. This creates a free-sliding slip knot, or noose. The other end must be securely tied or anchored to a tree or other immovable object. Then you simply set your noose a couple of inches larger than your intended prey's neck, and you set it on the animal's burrow or along a favorite trail or food source. Remember that if you disturb the area or leave your scent, then you may make the animal suspicious, and they will avoid the trap.

You can increase the effectiveness of your noose snare by adding an "engine" and a trigger. The engine is normally a flexible sapling that is tied to the end of the snare and set with tension so that it pulls the animal up into the air after the trigger is tripped. By far the easiest trigger to set is the hook trigger. Simply carve an equal size notch in two sticks so that their ends overlap and fit inside of each other. When you put them together and try to pull them straight apart, they hold together. One of these is then anchored in the ground, and the other has the engine tied down to it to provide tension. Put the two together with upward tension, and the trap is ready to spring. You then put the noose tight next to the trigger. If you leave a small branch on the trigger stick, you can add bait to it, which will make it easier to trip. This kind of trap should be checked often so as to avoid unnecessary suffering of your prey.

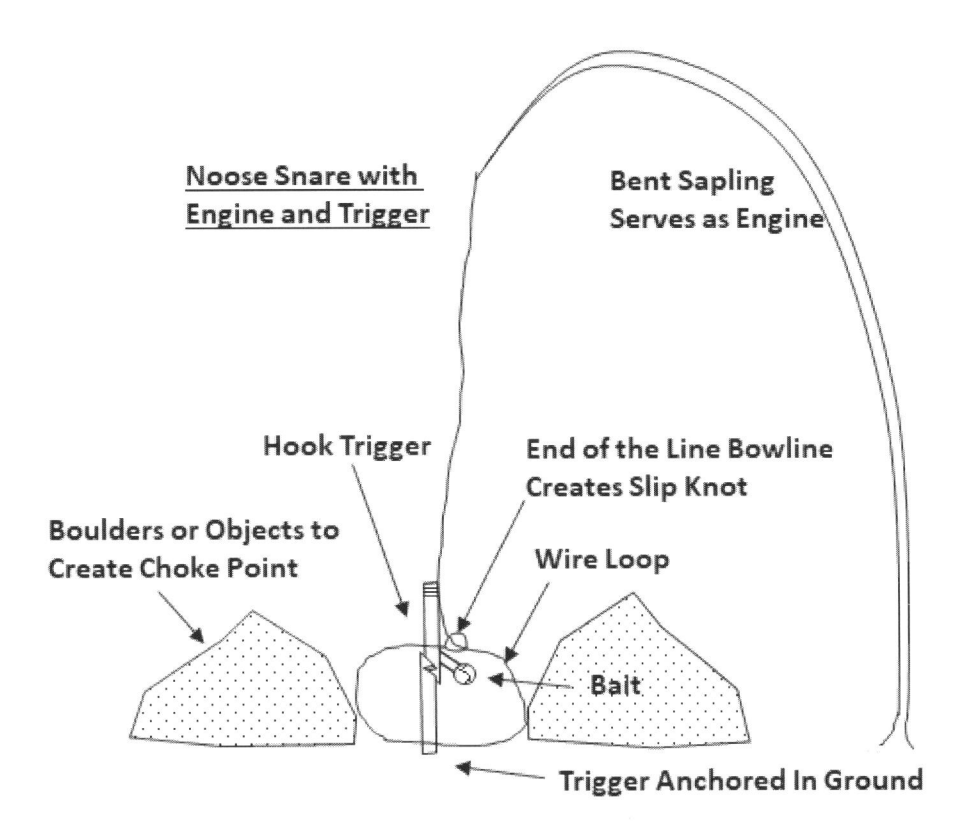

Figure 17: Example Noose Snare

    The next two traps have to be purchased so this is a survival item that needs to be planned for now, before any long emergency. The first is the leg-hold trap. This works similarly to the snare trap, except it is designed to always lay flat on the ground and it only requires the weight of the animal to be triggered. I only recommend small leg-hold traps for small game because it is not worth risking the chance of catching a person or especially a child in a larger version of this trap. Leg hold traps are very easily set; just separate the jaws and set the trigger catch. The most important factor is choosing a known trail, preferably on the trail of a tasty critter. If you don't master this last part, you may be stuck eating possum when the grid goes down. Camouflaging the scent is very important with this type of trap. This can be done by first storing the traps outdoors, dry and protected, but away from man-made odors. Secondly, you can use various types of animal urine around the trap to draw interest. A good trapper learns where the scent glands are on each animal, and also saves the contents of the bladder, to use as a lure.

    Conibear traps are a third type of trap that is somewhat difficult to set, but it is effective and often lethal to the prey, reducing the chance of animal suffering. A conibear is simply two large springs attached to metal jaws that are placed under tension by the trapper and held apart by a trigger. When the prey hits the trigger and releases the spring, the jaws snap down and crush the animal. Conibear traps are the preferred method for water animals such as beaver and muskrat because they can be used under water in streams and ponds. To set the conibear, just compress the two springs and set the trigger. It is easiest to do with two people. If you accidentally get both your hands caught in the jaws, then you will definitely need someone to help you as it will be like painful handcuffs until you get loose. The two springs have loops on the ends which can be placed over stakes that are driven in the ground to hold the trap suspended in the air or water at a height that the animal will walk or swim through. The trigger can be baited to give the prey more encouragement. There is also a chain on the conibear that should be attached to an anchor so that a large animal doesn't walk off with your trap.

    Game cameras are useful in trapping for locating animal trails and alerting you when your trap has an animal in it. They are now often equipped with rechargeable batteries and solar panels, meaning that they can last for years in a grid-down situation. I use a model of game camera that sends the pictures to my home over radio waves. This does not require cellular service and is totally free of the grid. With these cameras, I do not need to check traps until the camera sends me a picture of the trapped prey. These cameras are also discussed in the chapter on security.

Chapter 8: Sources of Carbohydrates

While your body craves protein during times of food scarcity, carbohydrates are the fuel that you need to survive and to keep you moving in hard times, and especially to keep you warm in cold times. In today's modern world of massive grain yields, subsidized corn products, and overabundance of sugars, we barely think about how to obtain carbs, in fact, the overabundance of carbs in our diets has caused an obesity epidemic. This will change drastically as hard times bring our standard of living to a much lower level.

This impending crisis is really a self-inflicted wound. For years, the U.S. taxpayer has been forking over about $7 billion dollars annually to subsidize grain and animal feed production. In addition, the mandatory addition of corn ethanol into gasoline has meant that farmers have been encouraged to plow up highly erodible land that was once set aside as protected, fallow land. In addition, other farmland has been squeezed for every available nutrient in order to make a lucrative profit for farm corporations and other large farm owners. As a result, non-renewable nutrients such as phosphorous have been applied in greater and greater quantities to keep up with the enhanced demand. By 2040, most experts agree that phosphorous mining and production will no longer be able to keep up with demand, and by 2060, it will be mined out completely and exhausted. Without phosphorous, say goodbye to modern agriculture, grain surplus, and all of those lovely carbs that we have been beasting on.

In the future, fertilizer shortages, fuel shortages, soil depletion, and deterioration of social values and farming knowledge in general will mean that American farmers will no longer have the means nor the incentive to bring their grains to market and feed the nation and the world. I have laid out in the previous chapter how to obtain protein for you and your loved ones, but hunting and raising livestock is simple compared to the planning, labor, and skill required to provide the energy-laden carbs that you will need to survive the coming struggles. Next, I will provide a list of viable sources of carbohydrates in the order of easiest to produce to most labor intensive.

Illustration 44: Chestnuts from our Homestead; these were a European Staple During the Ancient Dark Ages

Nut Trees as Carbohydrates

Oddly, I first learned the value of nut trees during my first solo date with my girlfriend who is now my wife. I was living in her home country in Northern Italy, and it was her birthday weekend, so I wanted to take her somewhere fancy to eat. So far, we had been only on group dates with friends, which was a social norm in Italy in those times. The first solo date was a big deal, so I called ahead to a place known as "Romeo and Juliet's Castles," a refurbished pair of medieval hilltop fortresses in a place called Montecchio. My Italian was coming along but I soon became frustrated with the receptionist as she tried to explain that the dinner was some kind of special medieval dining experience. I was like, "Va bene, va bene, that's fine just book me a table for me and my girlfriend, you all can do whatever you want. When we arrived and were seated, I realized that just for that night, all the tables were placed in a circle together, and everyone else was dressed in medieval costumes except for us. So much for a romantic first date! Luckily my girlfriend, now my wife, is a patient person, and she helped translate as they brought out course after course of medieval dishes explaining the significance of each one. As it turns out, most of them were based on chestnuts, and chestnut flours, not on grains. It was delicious, but I had to embarrass myself again, by asking why chestnuts were so popular during the dark ages. The master of ceremonies explained to me that while grain fields and flat croplands were often burnt by Moorish raiders and plundered by rogue armies, the forests were full of chestnuts that were less-easily burned and more difficult to reach. In short, chestnuts are a great staple in turbulent times! What is not so clear is how on earth my wife did not break up with me after taking her on a first dinner date where everyone was dressed in medieval leotards!

What I came to realize that day is that in dire circumstances, the easiest to produce source of carbs for producing breads, cereals, and high energy snacks is no grain at all, but instead a nut. Nuts require no tilling and only one-time planting, and some nuts are quite easy to process as well. With the proper foresight and a little investment, you can plant nut trees that can produce a crop year after year. The concept of food forests that require no tilling and annual planting is known as permaculture, and this is not some kind of impractical environmentalist scheme. Instead, it is a way to make your life easier, and richer, without relying heavily on modern luxuries such as cheap labor and expensive, high-maintenance equipment.

The way it works is that you must dedicate an area of land that is productive to your food forest, and a significant portion of this should be in nut trees for carbohydrates. Many people mistakenly choose land that is unsuited for annual crops, relegating it to the orchard. Instead, set aside your best land for the orchard, and your deepest, richest soil for your nut crops. This will pay off with a huge bounty of life-sustaining carbohydrates. For example, a single chestnut tree that is 10-15 years old, when properly cared for, can produce a 1/2 bushel of chestnuts, which will yield 25 lb. of flour, or about 25,000 calories! A healthy survival diet for one person could draw 50% of needed calories from nut flour, which is about 25,000 calories per month. This means that one chestnut tree per person per month can replace grains and provide the necessary carbohydrates for an individual year after year. In other words, about 50 trees can produce enough flour and carbohydrates to feed a family of four for an entire year. With 400 sf of spacing per tree, this amounts to about 2 acres. Intensively farmed grain can produce more calories per acre, but in hard times, grain is a less obvious target for pilfering. Grain fields are also a huge temptation for wildlife and livestock whereas chestnuts are generally left alone. We have kept chestnut trees for many years on our homestead. They are not within eyesight of the house and not even the squirrels have robbed the nuts. In fact, we often find the nuts a couple of days after some of them have fallen to the ground and they are still perfectly fine. The reason that they are not an obvious choice for squirrels is that the chestnut husk has very sharp spines that are painful to handle without gloves. When you do the math, it quickly becomes evident that woodland permaculture is a promising strategy for survival.

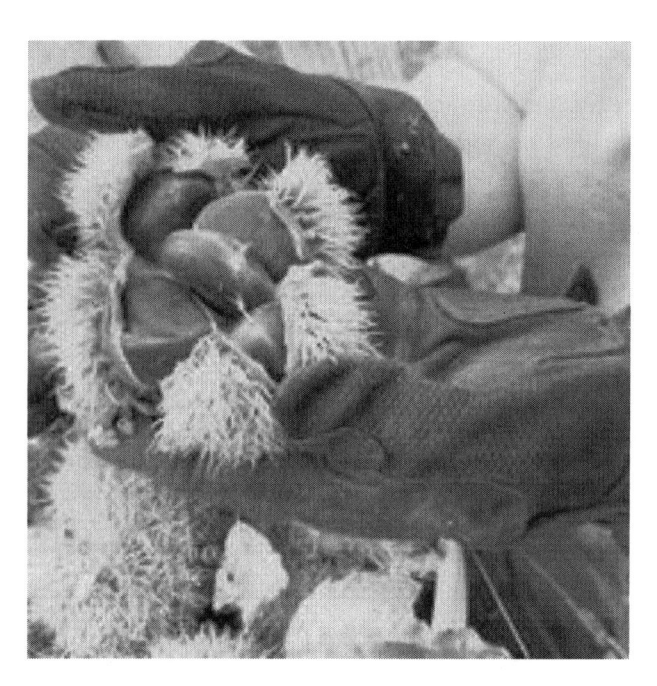

Illustration 45: Chestnuts Have Sharp Spines on their Husks that help Protect them from Squirrels.

Chestnuts are an excellent first choice as a source of carbohydrates, as long as you have the space, the planning, and decent soil to plant them in. As our global civilization moves into the next Dark Age, we need to remember the lessons of medieval Europe, when chestnut flour became a more important food source than wheat or other grains. Chestnuts can be more easily grown in the rocky soil near fortified hilltop retreats than grains. In the Old Dark Ages, slave raiders scoured Europe, burning, raping, and pillaging. It became too risky to tend annual grain crops, and people turned to the forests to provide. One of the reasons that chestnuts are preferred over other nuts is their ease of shelling. When properly ripe, the hull can be pulled right off with gloved hands, and it is fairly large, maybe twice the size of an acorn. Chestnuts are also very high in vitamin C and monounsaturated fats, as well as a number of phytonutrients. They are starchy and are nutritionally closer to potatoes than to other nuts.

The main considerations when planting chestnuts include moderately moist soil conditions and protection from pests. They will grow a little slower if they are not planted in dark, loamy, well-drained soil, but I have had some success in rocky areas, but only after they are established and make it through the first two years. Like many other trees, Chestnuts attract critters that like to chew on their bark in the winter time. Excellent fencing is required, even fencing that keeps out rabbits. Guard dogs can also be kept in your orchard area. Our orchards are fenced with 6-foot-high woven wire deer fences and 2 strands of barbed wire at the top to keep out deer. This is quite effective. We also keep one of our livestock guardian dogs in this paddock to discourage smaller pests from chewing on the bark of these trees. While they are a huge temptation when small, once the tree matures to about 5 years, it is not usually as appetizing for bark-eaters.

Hazelnuts or filberts are another shrub-like tree that can replace chestnuts, and they will tolerate slightly rockier soils with heavier amounts of sand. They are slightly harder to shell. Because hazelnuts are shorter in stature, they make an excellent fill-in for the gaps between chestnut or other taller trees. Walnuts or hickory nuts are much harder to shell, but they can often be gathered in the wild. Like everything else, proper planning can make life much, much easier, and less labor intensive.

If you have failed to plant a nut orchard, you are not alone. Fortunately for you, there are acorns which are not only edible, but are considered by some to be a superfood! For every 28 gram serving of acorns, there is a whopping 12 grams of carbohydrates, and a high amount of vitamin B-6. Acorns can also be found in the wild, and are not so difficult to shell. The Acorns from all varieties of white oaks are less bitter than those from red oaks, and chinquapin oaks provide acorns that can be eaten raw. White oaks have rounded fingers on the leaves, while red oaks have pointed fingers. Chinquapin oaks have an oval shaped leaf with undulating ridges all around. Most acorns are very bitter due to the high tannin content and usually need to be boiled through 3-6 changes of water before they will be ready to consume. Boil the acorns until the water is no longer brown and it becomes clear, then they will be ready to eat. As a teenager on a wilderness trip without other food available, I gorged on several cups of uncooked acorns. They will fill you up, but you will have to fight not to vomit, even if you are starving. While choking them down is possible, I definitely recommend cooking as it is well worth the effort.

Making Flour from Nuts

Ancient humans ate many of these nuts for centuries. Besides eating the nuts raw, you can also dry chestnuts or acorns and make flour out of them. They can be used to make flat bread or polenta, or even pancakes. Grinding stones are commonly found at prehistoric sites, but a great item for your off-grid bugout kit is a hand-driven grain mill. The first thing you will need to do with chestnuts or acorns is to roast them in an oven or, better yet, a Dutch oven for about 25 minutes until hard but not burnt. They will need to be rotated or shaken so that they don't burn on one side. You want them golden to light brown but not dark brown. You will need to crush the nuts to the size of corn, as most grain mills will accept only this size at most. If making polenta, crush or grind the flour until it is coarse, about the size of cornmeal, but go superfine for other recipes. Insert this flour into any recipe that does not require the use of yeast.

Cattails as a Major Food Source

Did you know that an acre of cattails can produce 6500 pounds of food per acre annually? This equals about 6.5 million calories per acre of cattails. Corn produces around 15 million calories per acre, so cattails aren't too bad considering that they basically cultivate themselves. In a world of 8, going on 10 billion hungry human mouths, it doesn't hurt to live near a cattail pond. Immature cattail shoots can be boiled and taste a bit like cucumbers.

They were a favorite of the native tribes of the U.S. Northern Great Plains. Cattail pollen can also be harvested and substituted for flour. Cattail roots are the kings of starch production, though you will have to work a bit to harvest them. Cattail roots will have to first be dug out of the water. Next, they need to be peeled, while they are still wet, don't let them dry or this will be impossible. They then need to be pounded, adding water to keep them wet and mushy. There will be a resulting mush and fibers will emerge which need to be removed. The remaining mush can be dried and used as a starchy flour in any recipe. In a more desperate hunger scenario, you can boil the root and chew it, spitting out the fibers. This will hopefully give you the energy to go get something a little tastier!

Illustration 46: Cattails just pulled out of the pond bank, make sure and peel the roots immediately before they dry.

Planting Grain Without Machinery

Our modern palate is certainly more used to grains such as corn (maize), wheat, and rice. Of these, corn is the easiest to produce and consume, and it produces 15 million calories per acre. This means that if a person obtains half of their calories from corn, then 50 people can be fed from 1 acre of corn for a whole year. Or if you are feeding just one person, it will take about 900 square feet, or a 30 x 30-foot plot.

The trouble with corn in a post-collapse scenario is that it is generally planted by plowing or tilling the earth. While this can be done by hand, this is labor intensive and time-consuming. One option is to use livestock to plant your corn. Pigs are by far the best at tilling land without machinery. One option is to keep two enclosed grain plots, or some might choose a greenhouse. Pigs can be kept in one plot, tilling the ground until it is suitable enough to plant corn. The pigs can then be rotated to the next plot. When the corn is tall enough for its own protection, chickens can be introduced to keep down weeds and pests. After the harvest pigs are rotated in and the plots switch places again, one being planted and the other being plowed. Keep in mind that pigs will consume an average of 6 to 8 pounds per day, so you will need this much surplus slop to feed them. The good news is that they will eat anything that humans eat, plus raw acorns, clover rich hay, and even roots. A pig snout is a plow just waiting to be used.

Most corn does very well only when heavily fertilized. Like other crops, it will not grow without the proper amounts of nitrogen, phosphorus, and potassium. In a post-collapse scenario, chemical fertilizer is difficult to come by. This means that you will need to use old-fashioned methods of soil fertility and maintenance. Corn grows best in dark, rich soil, often found in the valleys and draws that are alongside rivers and streams. If you are lucky enough to own this type of soil, plant your corn there. If not, you will have to work hard to enrich your soil with manure compost and organic litter. The best manure compost comes out of barns and is mixed with sawdust, straw, or even leaf litter. Sawdust works very well and can be obtained by a sawmill. We have a small sawmill on our homestead that provides a constant supply of sawdust for the barn. Spreading the sawdust in the animal pens, we are able to absorb the excess manure and urine, creating a nutrient rich fertilizer for gardening. This type of mixture is perfect for growing corn. It can be applied directly to cornfields, even after the corn is growing. The only exception is chicken manure compost. It is so "hot" that it should be allowed to cure for about a month and mixed with sawdust, straw, or leaf litter in order to preserve the nitrogen properly and avoid burning the plants.

In small corn plots, it is highly useful to plant the three sisters, as was done for millennia by Native Americans. Corn is the primary sister, and the other two are climbing pole beans and ground squash. The corn needs to have a head start of about two weeks to get established, then the beans and squash can be planted. The climbing beans will grow up the cornstalks and therefore do not need a pole or other structure to grow. They are also legumes and so their roots add nitrogen to the soil that other plants like corn desperately need. You can use any type of bean with a vine that climbs. The squash will spread out as ground cover and help keep the weeds down. If you keep the weeds down by hand for the first month, then the squash should totally drown out all the remaining weeds. You can use any type of squash with a ground vine. In this scenario, maintain adequate spacing with the corn 18 inches apart, one bean on every other corn plant, and the squash three feet apart.

Survival Vegetable Plot

In WWII, many of America's farmers were on the battle lines, and those still at home had to depend on themselves for many food staples in order to survive the war. The concept of victory gardens emerged, whereby Americans were encouraged to till up their yards, break out the garden tools, and get back to their agricultural roots. Urban gardens became commonplace, kids got their hands in the dirt, and gardening became the pass time of everyone in the neighborhood.

Years later, backyard gardening is often seen as tedious, a waste of time, even something banned by certain neighborhood homeowner associations. As a result, we have centralized fruit and vegetable production and have become alarmingly dependent on the state of California to supply the nation's produce needs. In fact, California produces over 90% of many fruits, nuts, and vegetables such as broccoli, walnuts, plums, celery, cauliflower, garlic, artichokes, kiwis, and more. California alone also produces over 50 percent of most other produce such as spinach, carrots, and melons. California is heavily populated and is going to be a major hotspot for any future pandemic that strikes our nation. It also relies heavily on migrant labor, which will be cut off in the case of pandemic or other disruptions. In addition, California is more and more often seen in the headlines as the scene of wildfires, drought, and even economic and civil unrest. What would happen if just one of these disasters or even a disruption of transportation was to cut off the supply of crops in this vital region? Prices would soar and most of these crops would simply not be available. While this may be hard to imagine in our well-fed nation, all nations in history have been subject to famines at some point, although no one historically has centralized food production to the same extent as the United States or other similar modern countries. This potential famine is something to prepare for now, use it as motivation to plant your garden every year.

The good news is that most of these crops can be grown in our own backyards. The time to reintroduce victory gardens is now, before we are faced with further crises and while we still have the resources to build and install the infrastructure to support backyard gardens. There are volumes and volumes of writings about how to be a good gardener, but this book will simply touch on a few aspects of gardening considerations when preparing for a long-term disaster and shortages. They include primarily setting up fail-safe gardening infrastructure, how to garden without chemical inputs, how to maintain a garden that is secure from pests and pilferers, and how to extend your growing season to increase and maximize your harvest.

As we all know, the best time to prepare is before a disaster hits, because after it hits, resources and labor can be difficult to obtain. First, let's examine gardening infrastructure that can be prepared now, before the next disaster strikes, that will make your life easier in hard times. Many people take for granted that they will be able to find adequate water, soil, sunlight, and nutrients. Unfortunately, these four simple elements are not readily available near everyone's home.

Illustration 47: Raised Bed Gardens are Among the Easiest Gardens to Maintain

Good soil can be the most difficult necessity for gardening to come by in some places. When I was still in the military and moving a lot, my wife and I purchased a home in a new subdivision where we lived for a couple of years. It was so new that the grass had not even been planted. The developers had simply scraped the topsoil off, exposing red Georgia clay that became our yard. You could not grow grass, let alone vegetables, or fruit trees. We came upon a great solution for our backyard by immediately building a retaining wall and hauling in good soil to fill it in. This type of uncompacted, rich soil grew the best tomatoes that I have ever seen! This solution works because while it can take decades or longer to improve existing soil, a terrace or raise bed can place good soil on top of anything.

Years later, while building our own homestead, my wife and I built raised beds to achieve the same effect. Raised beds are just four little walls placed on top of the ground. These are typically at least 12 inches high, and normally narrow enough that you can reach from one side to the other to cultivate and pull weeds. You can make the walls of your raised bed out of wood or masonry, or even spare tires if you are not worried about contaminants from the rubber. In our case we used cedar log sides, that were left over from milling cedar trees for our home. Cedar is rot resistant and non-toxic. The cedar log sides are fastened to fence posts that are driven into the ground for extra support. We made our walls 3 feet high so that we would not have to bend over to plant, pull weeds, or harvest. Our raised beds are each 4 feet by 8 feet in width and length. We lined the inside of our walls with black plastic, to help protect the wood from moisture, but not the bottom. The bottom must allow water to drain. With a taller raised bed such as ours, it is necessary to fill the bottom 18 inches with gravel, so that it will not retain too much water. Only the top 6-12 inches must necessarily be rich soil to raise good produce.

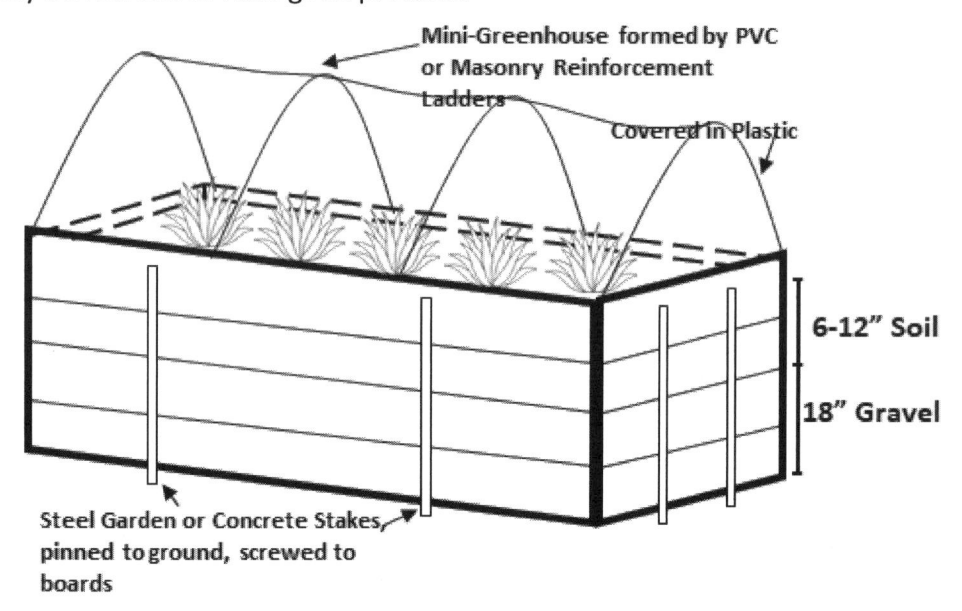

Figure 18: Raised Bed Garden

Illustration 48: Raised Beds can be covered with Clear Plastic During Cool Seasons to Extend Your Growing Season

In situations where you do not have the time or resources to build larger raised beds, you can simply fell trees to create a four-sided raised bed or one-sided miniature terrace that will hold soil and keep it from washing away and down a slope. Our oldest raised bed is made from raw cedar trunks and it has lasted for 12 years. We have raised a ton of strawberries there, and it is now home to blueberry bushes.

The second piece of infrastructure needed to raise produce during a long disaster is a source of nutrients or fertilizer that is not purchased at the store, but instead is produced at the homestead. When I used to sell at the farmers market, customers would sometimes ask if I had any free animal manure that they could come get. I would usually answer with a long, awkward laugh as they walked away nervously, "hahahahaaa…ha." This is because I know true value "the other black gold," the key ingredient to fertilizer, also known as manure! You create rich soil by combining organic material, such as mulch or compost, with animal manure and urine. Blood and bones from slaughtering animals is also quite beneficial, but harder to come by in quantity. The necessary organic material component is plant-based and is made of carbon-based material such as woodchips, peat moss, and straw. If added by itself, straw, wood chips, or other similar mulches will kill your garden. This is because the carbon in those substances draws the nutrients out of the soil and holds onto it. For this reason, you need to combine the carbon-rich wood or straw with manures and urine, which contain nitrogen, phosphorous, and potassium. On our farm, we have two main sources of this mulch fertilizer combo. The first is leftover straw covered and mixed with goat or cattle manure. This is found in abundance after we feed hay to our livestock in the winter. Ideally, this mixture will be shoveled into a pile which is kept moist to encourage limited decomposition. You have to be careful not to expose it to a drenching rain, because this will wash away the nutrients, so just keep it damp. Also, do not keep this close to anything flammable as the heat from a decomposing manure pile can catch fire. See the below chart for amounts of nutrients in different types of fertilizer.

Table 1. Typical nutrient content, moisture content, and weight of manure.

Type of Animal Manure	N	P[2]	K	Moisture, percent	Weight, lb/cu yard
	lb per ton as is[1,2]				
Chicken with litter	73	28	55	30	900
Laying hen	37	25	39	60	1,400
Sheep	18	4.0	29	72	1,400
Rabbit	15	4.2	12	75	1,400
Beef	12	2.6	14	77	1,400
Dry stack dairy	9	1.8	16	65	1,400
Separated dairy solids[3]	5	0.9	2.4	81	1,100
Horse	9	2.6	13	63	1,400

[1] Manure analyses are usually reported in terms of P and K, while fertilizer labels use phosphate (P$_2$O$_5$) and potash (K$_2$O). To convert from P to P$_2$O$_5$, multiply P by 2.3. To convert from K to K$_2$O, multiply K by 1.2.
[2] These values assume that manure has been protected from rain.
[3] Separated dairy solids are produced when dairy manure is pumped over a screen, separating the solids from the rest of the manure.

Figure 19: From Washington State University Ag Extension (https://extension.wsu.edu/animalag/content/manure-on-your-farm-asset-or-liability/)

Another source of organic mulch-fertilizer that we use on the farm is poultry litter combined with sawdust. Sawdust from woodcutting on our farm makes the perfect bedding for poultry. When it has been soiled, it is then shoveled out and kept moist, just like the manure and straw. I like to add blood from any animals that we butcher for extra nitrogen, and bones add extra phosphorous. You can also add charcoal, but don't add ashes, because ashes will cause the compost to become caustic. We keep these compost piles moist in a pile for at least two months before shoveling them onto usable garden areas to ensure that any pathogens from the livestock die, and to ensure that the manure is not so rich that it burns the plants. It is also good to mix the compost every week or so. Some people have special tumblers to do this, but our piles are too large, so we just make sure that the chickens have some access to the pile so that they can scratch through and mix it. They will scratch around and mix it thoroughly and then all you have to do is keep it piled up. Moving it around with a shovel or a tractor when available also helps speed up the decomposition process but is not completely necessary. Adding this type of compost before each planting will totally ensure that your garden remains fertile year after year.

Keeping your garden safe from pests and pilferers should also be a top priority. We once had a USDA agent come to help assess the agricultural value of our land. She suggested a garden site down in the fertile bottomland, in our richest soil, but out of view of the house. Being quite inexperienced, we tried it for a year. I built a monumental deer fence, 8 feet high with offset electric around the bottom. Months later, after a hard season of tilling, planting, and cultivating, we were amazed at how our produce would disappear right before we could pick it. We caught a couple of moles, rabbits, and even a racoon pilfering, finding a way to steal a free dinner. Then one day, we even found an empty soda bottle. We never did catch the two-legged thief, but our lesson was learned; you can't protect what you can't see. Your garden needs to be close, and if you can live right in the middle of your own little garden of Eden, that's perfect!

Many of us have had the privilege of growing up where law and order was deterrent enough for anyone thinking of pilfering gardens or crops. But as anyone who has visited other, less fortunate parts of the globe can tell you, food sources are the first to be pilfered when times are difficult, and families are going hungry. We all want to help a neighbor in need, but private property is key to ensuring good stewardship, and so your survival garden should be the most well-defended part of your homestead. It should be right next to your house. Your home has the most surveillance, and hopefully will have a guard dog and maybe a perimeter fence. That survival garden belongs inside the fence. When you think of fences, think about keeping out two-legged pests, but also consider something as small as a squirrel. Fences with 2x2 inch or smaller openings are ideal, but chain link is not bad at all. Standard woven wire works as well but should be used in conjunction with a dog that will chase away squirrels and rabbits that will fit through woven wire. One option that we use on our farm is to take a rigid cattle or hog panel, and cut off the top strip of wire. This leaves a row of spikes on the top that will deter anyone or anything from trying to hop over your fence. We put this on the gates or any other area that is normally easy to climb over. This can be a real liability issue so if someone climbs over it and gets impaled, then you will have to deal with it, so don't blame it on me.

Other pests that are difficult to deal with are of course insects. Remember that we want to prepare even for serious hard times when you won't be able to just run to the store and get pesticides. You could stockpile pesticides but keeping a bunch of poison on your homestead is just a bad idea, and dangerous for everyone. Once again, in dealing with insects, it is critical to have the garden near the house, so you can act quickly when something like squash bugs, tomato worms, or Japanese beetles appear. Having your raised beds at a comfortable elevated height is very helpful when dealing with these pests. This way they are closer to eye level, and you can simply smash them. Don't be squeamish about doing so, bug guts are easy to wash off of your hands. You need to check for harmful insect pests every day during the growing season because some, like potato bugs, will ravish your plants within 24 hours. In modern industrial agriculture, it is not as profitable to rely on manual labor to kill insect pests, but this is the most tried and true method historically and in hard times.

Another helpful preventative technique is to take common house soap and mix it with water until you see a few soap bubbles. Then put this mixture on your plants to deter insects from feasting on your hard work. Planting marigolds around your vegetable plot will also help deter harmful insects. Insects simply do not like the natural oils of the marigold. Oregano works in a similar way. This will not prevent all of these pests, but it could very well prevent a full-scale plague of locusts from destroying your garden. Finally remember to plant more than you need because will be some plants that don't make it.

Part of the trick here is to learn which pests afflict your particular region. Where we live, in the Ozarks, we have had problems primarily with Tomato worms, potato bugs, Japanese beetles, corn earworms, bag worms, and squash bugs. By identifying these insects and learning when they start to be a problem, you can keep an eye out for them at the right time of year. Potato bugs generally hit when the potato plants are fully grown, and you will notice yellow and brown patches first. Squash bugs will generally come out along with the first squash flowers and you will notice several tick-size gray bugs all on one spot. They will spread out if you don't kill them early so it is best to check early and squish the squash bugs immediately. Japanese beetles normally show up in July and need to be treated, killed, or baited and trapped every day for about a month. They will affect grapes, fruit trees, and berry bushes more than anything. Corn worms will be in your corn often just after the tassel comes out if you don't treat early. For us, there is normally a different crop that has difficulty each year. One year, the potato bugs will ravish the potato plants, the next year it may be squash bugs. Plant about 25% more than what you need and plant a variety so that you will compensate for losses.

Sunlight is not only necessary for the survival of your garden, but also can be used to extend your growing season. Green houses, high tunnels, low tunnels, and cold frames are indispensable as you move into higher latitudes and where the growing seasons are short. Getting an early start on your growing season not only gives your crops plenty of time to grow, but it also gives them a head start so that they can grow tall and strong and begin producing before the majority of insects come out in midsummer. We have had epic struggles against potato bugs here and the best way that we have found to prevent them is to plant our potatoes early, in late February and early March, with the help of cold frames. By the time the potato bugs get really rampant, the potatoes have already matured.

There are books upon books of cold weather growing techniques. I will just share one with you that has been the most useful for us. Once again, the small, raised bed garden is the key to an easy solution. To turn your raised bed garden into a cold frame, construct it in such a way that the rim, the top board of the retaining wall for your raised garden, is actually 12 inches above the inside soil. In this way, you can place a lid on this rim, keeping your seed bed warm in the early spring when frost threatens to kill everything. A way to raise soil temperatures early in the season is to use a clear plastic lid on your raised bed. You can use rigid plastic, or you can staple on plastic sheeting. This allows the sunlight to enter and warm the soil, and the plastic will prevent the heat from escaping. On particularly cold nights, a piece of rigid foam insulation, such as blue board can be placed on top to really keep the heat in. If you make the size of all of your raised beds 4 by 8 feet, minus one inch all around, then a standard piece of blue-board or other insulating material can be placed on top as a perfect fitting lid.

To determine when to plant your crops, you must consider your location. My homestead is in the Midwest, in the USDA plant hardiness zone 6. This means that my family generally plants our raised bed cold frames no earlier than February 15, but later if the forecast is poor. This means that by February 15, we are paying very close attention to the two-week forecast. Crops that can germinate this early include lettuces, spinach, kale, peas, carrots, and potatoes. We usually wait at least another month for Tomatoes, Zucchini, Squash, Corn, and Melons. Again, this is the earliest date possible and with a cold weather forecast, we push it back by another 2-3 weeks. Don't forget to protect your plants once they sprout. This can be done by turning your cold frame raised bed into a hoop house raised bed. Do this by inserting flexible sticks or thin metal rods from side to side on your raised bed, creating a hoop to protect crops and hang the plastic on top of that. By using a raised bed and a little plastic, we have found that you can really increase your yields and even make the difference between a failed crop and a successful one.

You will find volumes upon volumes that have been written on how to grow different types of vegetable crops using many techniques. My advice in growing your survival garden is to keep it simple, and to start growing before there is a food shortage so that you can have some time to learn. My family's experience was that the first year was a bust, the second year was mediocre, and after three years of gardening, we were growing nearly all of the vegetables that we needed for the year. We found that, most importantly, for efficient, survival-ready crops, raised beds with good soil and water were the essential components. Secondly, these easy access raised beds, planting a surplus, vigilant supervision, and a few non-toxic pest control methods helped preserve the harvest. Finally, our harvests were extended and enriched by using a little plastic and also foam board insulation on top of the raised beds. Apart from reading volumes upon volumes of gardening books, this brief advice on using raised beds, along with a couple of years of experience, is all that you will need to create a long-term, sustainable survival garden plot.

Chapter 9: The Homestead Dairy

When we first moved to our homestead after my military service, our first lessons were shaped by our new Amish neighbors. I remember visiting them one of the first times and stopping in front of their amazing Amish barn to talk to a couple of teenage boys that were hitching horses up to a couple of buggies. They were dressed modestly and looked humble, but they were clearly showing off as they spun their shiny black buggies around while pulling sharply on the reins of sleek black Arabian geldings. When they were done, I asked them about the milk that they had for sale on a plain black and white painted sign at the driveway. They were selling "fresh daily" raw milk from their small herd of tall, boney, black and white Holstein cows. I told them that I had never drank raw milk; they totally laughed at me. I'm not sure if they laughed because they were incredulous or if they laughed because to them it was like seeing a 40-year-old virgin. Whatever the reason, I demanded to buy some raw milk right then and there. I handed them a $20 bill for a $5 gallon of milk; "keep the change," I said. "Not even old enough to grow more than 5 whiskers on their chins, and laughing at me… 18 years old and don't own a smart phone, ha ha!," I thought to myself as I unscrewed the lid on the milk jar. But after I gulped down that raw milk for the first time, I realized that I really had been missing out! It was the best milk that I had ever tasted, milk the way that God intended for us to drink it. I had a little chuckle myself, laughing at the 40-year-old raw milk virgin that I used to be. I laughed all the way home as I drove off with a thick milk mustache still on my face and dripping down my chin.

That day sealed the deal for me. One day, our homestead would produce our own raw milk. The benefits are obvious. Raw milk provides valuable nutrition and antibodies. It is a way that livestock can harvest the richness of the land for you, and transform it into highly nutritious sustaining liquid, coming directly from a rich farm environment that you have a hand in creating and nurturing. It is a way to harvest a food source that you can trust because you know exactly where it comes from. Raw milk can also be converted into homemade cheese, butter, yogurt, and more. This is a way of harvesting, extending the harvest, and incorporating it into a rich diet.

Illustration 49: Dairy Animals will produce a massive amount of nutrition daily and harvest wild forages and grasses for you, but they require excellent care.

Despite my initial enthusiasm, it would be a few years before we were able to put all of the pieces in place and start milking a herd of our own. There were many lessons to be learned first. Above all, remember that milking animals is usually a twice-per-day task, and you should not even try it if you don't have time. For many homesteaders, this means that you should finish building your homestead and learn some important lessons about animal husbandry before committing to such a huge time investment. Raising dairy animals requires a higher level of proficiency in livestock care than keeping other types of domestic animals. It will certainly test your homesteading skills. They need to have a rock solid, dependable shelter; a crooked shed made from old pallets and recycled scrap metal will not suffice. Their feed needs to be of excellent quality. They will be providing high quality nutrition for your family everyday, so you need to do the same for them! Can you produce or obtain high quality hay or fodder? Can you produce and properly store nutritious grains or other protein sources for your stock? Finally, keeping one or more dairy animals requires a high level of animal husbandry skills. Do you have some experience with this and have you kept livestock before? A dairy animal needs to be tamer than other livestock, which means you must learn to read the emotions of the animal and understand when it is safe to approach, when it is feeling unwell, or even when it is thinking about kicking you in the face! For all of these reasons, I recommend keeping livestock, usually meat varieties, for a few years before you decide to commit to dairy animals. Keeping beef cattle such as Angus and meat goats, such as Boers, is a great way to work up to the task of keeping a milk cow, such as a Jersey or Holstein, or a dairy goat such as a Nubian or La Mancha.

Concerning the different breeds, I have now owned many types of these Dairy animals. I can tell you that Holstein cows produce a lot of milk, often 9 gallons per day, but they are big and temperamental, and a Holstein bull is the most likely farm animal to kill you. If you don't need as much milk, consider buying a Jersey cow, which still produces around 6 gallons per day. They have a better temperament, can even be sweet, they eat less, and they have better parasite resistance. As far as dairy goats, Nubians will produce up to one gallon of milk per day, and they can be extremely docile and sweet. They can start to act like you are their own kid when you are milking them. Nubians can be extremely vulnerable to parasites such as tape worm and barber pole worms, so you have to have a good worming routine, especially in warm humid climates. La Mancha goats produce about the same amount of milk as a Nubian, but with less milk fat. They are not as docile and require more coaxing to get on to the milking stand. La Mancha can also be very resistant to parasites, which makes them a better choice for a dairy breed that doesn't need as many external inputs, dewormers, or medicine. Nigerian dwarf goats are small and easy to manage, but they produce much less milk, only about two quarts daily at best. Their milk has 10% more fat than other breeds, and 10% more protein, so it is very rich. It is very important to keep Nigerian bucks far away from your milking animals, because they are very stinky and they will cause your milk to smell and taste like buck pee. I recommend consuming all unpasteurized goat milk within 24 hours of milking otherwise it will start to taste "goaty."

  Of course, there are numerous generic "how-to" books describing what you need to do to produce milk and dairy products at home. This book focuses on the important subjects that are typically ignored, such as how to raise dairy during a long emergency, when supply chains are disrupted, and it is totally up to you to live off of the land. I have seen great instructional videos on how to make butter and cheese, where the instructor pours the milk or cream out of a store-bought carton. Thanks, but any chump can do that! How do you produce your own cheese with nothing but what you have on your homestead? Now that is a true skill! How do you do it when there is a supply disruption and you cannot simply run to the feed store for grain, medications, fancy teat wipes to clean udders, etc.? Welcome to the world of high-skill-level, self-sufficient homesteading!

  To keep your dairy herd healthy and the milk flowing during the Neo-Dark Age, when supply chains fail, you will need to focus on self-sufficient feeding of your dairy animals, homeopathic medications, and de-wormers, and building and maintaining shelters and fencing. After I describe these requirements, I will tell you how to reap the rewards by harvesting, processing, and preserving dairy products.

  Imagine yourself as a newly minted home dairy producer. You are milking a couple of goats or a cow, you have learned how to make delicious butter and cheese, and you make a trip to the feed store every week to stock up on feed and other necessities. Wait, stop right there! As we all know, in a long emergency, supply chains are disrupted and in an emergency such as an extreme global pandemic, it might not be safe for you to go to the feed store. You need to become self-sufficient!!

Nutrition for Dairy Animals

First, you need to learn how to feed your herd from what you have on your own land. Feeding a lactating dairy animal requires higher levels of protein than any other class of livestock. Most dairy rations contain between 14% and 19% protein, which is difficult to achieve from wild forage. This is why it is important to consider what kind of forage your land can produce. If you have mostly pastures, then you need to focus on high quality legumes, such as Alfalfa. Alfalfa can contain between 18 to 26 % protein as long as it is harvested while vegetative, meaning that it has not fully bloomed and matured. Clovers and Korean Lespedeza are also sufficiently high in protein, between 16 and 22% protein before being fully vegetative. These types of legumes drop to 12-16% when they are allowed to fully bloom and are harvested after the vegetative stage. As a comparison, grasses such as Orchard grass can be as high as 16 to 18% protein while vegetative but drop down to 8-10% after fully maturing. When you are trying to achieve an average of 14-19% protein for good milk production, it is important to incorporate plenty of legumes into your pastures. While pure stands of legumes can occasionally cause an animal to bloat when they are grazed too early, legumes that are allowed to bloom and harvested along with grasses can provide the perfect balance of nutrition for your dairy animals. All of these forages will lose 1-2 percentage points of protein during the process of being harvested and stored as dried hay.

Type of Forage	% Protein	Value for Dairy Livestock
Vegetative Alfalfa before Maturity	18-26%	Bloat Risk
Vegetative Red or White Clover	16-22%	Excellent
Mature, Fully Bloomed Alfalfa or Clover	12-16%	Good
Vegetative Orchard Grass	16-18%	Good
Fully Mature Orchard Grass Gone to Seed	8-10%	Very Poor
Vegetative 50/50 Grass Alfalfa Mix	14-18%	Good
Mature 50/50 Grass Alfalfa Mix	14-16%	Good
Vegetative 50/50 Grass Clover Mix	12-16%	Good
Mature 50/50 Grass Clover Mix	10-14%	Somewhat Poor

Table 3: Legume and Grass Protein Content

In the normal, pre-disaster economy, my primary crop in the summer is grass and legume hay that I sell to picky horse people customers. I take pride in my ability to properly cultivate, harvest, cure, and store good hay. While I normally harvest conventionally with tractors and all the modern equipment, I have worked with my Amish neighbors, and I have learned how to bring in hay without technology. It is backbreaking work, and even using horses, it takes them at least two months to bring in hay just for a couple of horses and the home dairy cow. The most common method that I have seen the Amish use is to first cut the hay with a horse-mounted sickle mower. This can also be done with a hand sickle if you're strong and about 18 years young! I have been in a field when 4 Amish horse teams are mowing, perfectly on-line with each other. Instead of the deafening sounds of a tractor engine, you just hear the sounds of the horses breathing and trotting, and also what sounds like 4,000 pairs of scissors snipping along as they glide over the field in unison. It sort of sounds like what I imagine a chariot of the Roman god Helios might sound like gliding through the sky; just magical.

After the hay is mowed, it needs to be cured, which can take 1 to 3 days depending on the conditions. If it is 90 degrees with low humidity, one day will suffice. If it is 80 degrees and humid, three days are needed. If it rains or is too humid, you should use a tedder or find some other way to flip the hay over and fluff it up. This too can be done by horsepower or by hand with a pitchfork. Properly cured hay will begin to rattle just slightly when you pick it up in your hands. It smells sweet and should look dry, especially when you bend the grass blades. Preferably it will still retain its green color, even when dry. Once the hay is properly cured then, it needs to be raked and stored. Obviously, this can be done with tractor power, but if gas supplies are interrupted, then the easiest thing to do is to load the loose hay in a cart, and to store it in the barn loft.

Illustration 50: Amish Hay Forks, about 3.5 feet tall. They are attached to a rope and pulley and when pulled up, it automatically grabs hay so you can hoist it into the barn loft.

A dry barn loft is something that you see in a lot of Amish barns, but not in many modern barns. This is why the old beautiful hay barns had high roofs, like the stereotypical old red barn with a 30-foot-high gambrel roof. This wasn't for decoration, but instead was for hay storage, often just loose hay. I have watched the Amish use a pulley system with a large set of hay forks, that look like tongs, that can be guided to grab the loose hay out of a cart and lift it into the loft, using only pulleys, horsepower, and the 6-foot-tall metal tongs on a rope. It makes it easier to feed livestock when you just have to throw the hay down from the hay loft. If you don't have a hay loft, then you can improvise and achieve some proper airflow by using pallets that will at least get it off the ground and allow the air to circulate beneath the hay.

Illustration 51: Putting good hay up in your barn every summer is critical if you want your animals to survive through the winter.

How much do you need? One Dairy cow will eat about 1000 lbs. of hay in a month. Average to poor hay land can produce 2000-3000 lbs. of hay per cutting. If you are lucky enough to produce 2 cuttings per acre, then you might plan on getting 5000 lbs. per acre in a good year. In poor conditions, cut this amount in half. On the other hand, if you really take care of your field with fertilizers, etc. then you can double this amount. Taking our average yield, then just one acre of average, properly seeded pasture, with around 30-40 inches of annual rainfall, decent soil, and no drought, should be able to produce enough hay to feed one cow from November 1 to April 1. If you produce two cuttings of hay, then don't plan on grazing that acre for the year, unless you have some exceptional fertility. To be conservative, you should have at least two additional acres for one cow in order to be able to graze for the rest of the year without running into a shortage. So, plan on 3 acres per dairy cow in a temperate climate with average soil and 30+ inches of rain annually. For planning purposes, you can easily raise 6 large goats or 10 dwarf goats on the same amount of pasture.

Many new homesteaders will be priced out of good farmland and will instead have to purchase something of poor to marginal quality. Raising a dairy animal on this type of land is challenging, but not impossible. Our homestead had been abandoned for forty years when we bought it. It was rocky with steep terrain, and covered in small juniper trees, brush, and brambles. This type of land is worthless to most classes of livestock, except for goats. Goats, including dairy goats, thrive on this type of land!

There are several types of invasive plants that only goats will consume, and many of these serve as high sources of protein and nutrients. These include but are not limited to kudzu, sericea lespedeza, multiflora rose, autumn olive, ragweed, and many more. Among these, kudzu contains up to 18% protein, on par with many traditional legumes such as clover. This level of protein is perfect for milk production in goats. Anyone who has visited the southeastern United States has undoubtedly witnessed this invasive plant, taking over acres and acres of land. But with goats, you can turn an invasive plant into highly nutritious milk, cheese, and butter.

Sericea lespedeza dominates many mid-latitude and northern pastures, but it is also particularly beneficial to dairy goats, as it is a legume and contains up to 16% protein, right on par with other legumes. While this plant is a foreign, invasive, and noxious weed to most ranchers, many raisers of goats are starting to plant it because of its nutritional value. It is also known as a natural de-wormer and will keep your goats healthy without chemicals.

For those who live in the forest or prefer silviculture goat-rearing, I'd like to introduce you to the honey locust tree. This tree is often seen as a menace to farmers, as it grows readily in open areas, and it has thorns long enough to poke a hole in a tractor tire! If you have seen this tree's thorns, you probably know what I'm talking about. These thorns are a genetic remnant of the Pleistocene epoch and the end of the last ice age. During this time, mastodons and wooly mammoths would down trees with their powerful tusks, consuming their leaves and branches. The honey locust is a particularly nutritious tree, so to protect itself, it evolved black thorns up to 14 inches long, covering the trunk and branches. Today, the leaves and especially the seedpods can be harvested from the branches of these trees and fed to livestock, especially goats. If the thorns bother you, you can also find a large percentage of wild honey locust trees that no longer have thorns. Gather and plant the seed pods from these and you can create your own forest of thorn-less honey locust trees. While the protein content of the leaves and seed pods is relatively low, right at around 5%. The sugar content, on the other hand, is very high, around 30%. This makes it a great high energy supplement. You can also harvest the branches of these trees, removing up to 50% of the small branches each year without harming the tree. A relatively young ten-year-old tree will yield about 50 lbs. of animal fodder for goats each year. It should be harvested in late summer, usually towards the end of August. At this time of year, the seed pods will be large, but will still be firmly attached, green, and nutritious. You can store bundles of the small, leafy branches in the barn, just like hay. While other trees can be harvested and stored in this same way, honey locusts are among the best. The benefits of these trees don't stop here! They fix nitrogen in the soil, just like clover or other legumes, and their canopy is relatively thin, letting in a great deal of sunlight to the ground below. This means that pasture can be grown beneath trees that are properly spaced, and that the grass will actually benefit from the nitrogen fixation. While this tree may be a menace to tractor tires, honey locusts can be a real blessing as an excellent forage for all types of goats, especially those producing milk!

Caring for the health of your dairy animals

The care of your dairy animals is similar whether they are cattle or goats, but dairy goats require more care. If you can keep a dairy goat alive, then you can also care for a milk cow. While I have sung the praises of dairy goats, their weakness is definitely parasites. I give them high ratings for their wide-ranging diet, the quality of their milk, and their potential for great demeanor, but they have to be cared for more than cattle to keep them healthy. There is a saying about goat health; "they are either healthy or they are dead." This means they can be perfectly healthy one day, but as soon as a health issue arises, they can die very quickly with very little warning. With that being said, I will tell you that after you keep goats for a few years, you can spot and treat warning signs that something is wrong with one of your goats before it becomes a bad issue. I will often notice a goat that is slower than the others in coming to feed or won't feed at all. If they have scours and a wet tail from diarrhea, then that is something that you need to notice immediately within hours of the onset of the problem, and not let it become more serious. If a goat gets scours and you are in a grid-down collapse situation, you need to feed the animal blackberry or raspberry leaves, and the bark from the blackberry roots. These can be from wild plants that they forage on their own or you can harvest these and store them in a dry barn. If they are limping from overgrown hoofs or hoof rot, it needs to be taken care of and trimmed without procrastination. When you make the leap and decide to start keeping dairy animals, then you need to check on the herd twice a day. On most days these visits will take 10 minutes, but sometimes they will take an hour, and to keep a healthy herd, this is necessary 365 days a year.

Imagine yourself off-grid without the ability to access a veterinarian or feed store. You rely on goat milk for one of your main food sources, and your goat shows signs of worms. She is getting skinny; her eyelids and mouth are pale instead of bright pink. She may even have scours. What do you do? First, remember that an ounce of prevention is worth a pound of cure. The number one thing to avoid parasites is to rotate your livestock frequently. Most parasites will die off in a sunny pasture after one month. This means that however many paddocks you have, then they need to not be revisited for at least one month after the animals have grazed there. If you have two paddocks, then they need to be grazed for one month straight. If you have five, then they need to be grazed for one week each, etc. The more paddocks, the better.

The second thing that you can do for parasites is to provide your livestock with natural dewormers. While cattle are able to handle low amounts of tree foliage in their diets, goats need to have a great deal. Ideally, they should always have access to oak tree leaves and cedar or other evergreen needles. The natural tannins in these forages can save you a lot of trouble by keeping your herd parasite-free. The livestock must still have enough grass or hay, especially cattle. They need to have constant access to grass and/or hay. Underfed animals will succumb quickly to parasites so keep them well-fed. As part of their grass and hay diet, sericea lespedeza is not only nutritious but it is also a natural dewormer. Cattle will graze this only when it is under 6 inches tall, and goats will eat it at almost any stage of maturity. Both cattle and goats will also benefit highly from this plant if it is in their hay. Finally, a great natural dewormer for cattle and goats is vinegar. Add vinegar at the rate of 1 cup for 10 gallons of water. They will not like it at first so limit them to this water source so that they will get used to it. Cattle will never have a problem with this water but there is a risk to goats that it can acidify their rumens and cause them to get sick. To avoid this, add 1 tablespoon of baking soda to each gallon of goat feed daily. If you are not able to obtain baking soda, then providing them with one cup of plain cultured yogurt per animal in their feed on one day per week will also work. This is good for goats all year round to keep their rumens healthy and at a good pH level.

Illustration 52: The Author's livestock barn. Dairy animals and especially goats require good, easy to clean shelter.

    Protecting your livestock from bacteria and mites has to do mainly with keeping their shelter clean. While a concrete floor in a stall is a lot of work to build and maintain, it is highly recommended to help keep dairy animals clean and healthy. A concrete floor should have a drain to keep it dry, and it should be mucked out with a shovel every day. The best material to keep it dry is saw dust and also sand. This will absorb urine and wet manure, and it provides compost that is more valuable than gold. If you use straw as an absorbent, then you are inviting mites to nest in the straw and also to infest your livestock. We have a small home bandsaw that provides plenty of good sawdust for our barn. If you are unable to pour a concrete floor in your stall, then you will need to at least have well-drained gravel. You will need to shovel additional absorbent onto the floor daily, to keep it dry. This can be shoveled out weekly in the case of a gravel floor. If you keep your dairy animal's stall dry and clean, then bacteria and mites will not be a problem. One other preventative measure that you can take is to dust both the animal and the stall once per week with diatomaceous earth. This is a chalky rock powder that has been crushed into a substance that is actually sharp and deadly to microscopic organisms. It is harmless to the human touch, but you don't want to breathe it into your lungs. Animals can also eat it and it may kill harmful organisms in their digestive tracks, although this has not been scientifically proven. If this is not available, limestone and clay dust will also help tremendously.

These are some useful natural remedies and techniques that you can use to keep your dairy animals safe in the case of a long emergency. While there are plenty of chemicals and store-bought remedies, I have attempted to provide you with solutions that can be put into place without depending on modern supply chains. Some items that I have listed above will need to be stockpiled, such as vinegar, baking soda, and diatomaceous earth. The most important consideration for keeping your livestock healthy is you. The more experience that you have in raising livestock, the better they will fare if you are left on your own in a long-term disaster scenario. There is really no time to waste, if you wish to survive the coming dark age, then you need to begin the long learning process of mastering livestock husbandry immediately.

Figure 20: Milking Dairy Animals is a Daily Chore for the Whole Family

Harvesting and Processing Milk

Don't be surprised when you start milking your first dairy animal and your refrigerator is completely taken over by fresh milk. Our family of five milks just one dairy goat at a time, which produces just 2-3 quarts per day for 2 daily milkings. This doesn't sound like much, but it adds up to around 4 gallons per week. We don't drink that much milk so what can be done? If you stop milking your dairy animal, it will stop giving milk, or worse yet, it will get mastitis which can ruin the udder forever. Fortunately, you can turn that milk into cheese, butter, yogurt, ice cream, and even soap. Some of the recipes for doing so are surprisingly easy!

The biggest difference between store-bought milk and fresh farm milk is that store milk has been pasteurized and homogenized. Pasteurization is a process of heating followed by rapid cooling that is designed to kill any dangerous pathogens in the milk. At a large dairy, this is necessary as it is difficult to guarantee that all of the milk is safe. At a small homestead dairy, most people milk by hand and can take care to keep the milk clean and ensure that mastitis or other health issues are not occurring with the animal. To keep the milk clean, first clean the udder with soap and water, baby wipes, or special teat wipes. Next, direct the first two squirts of milk onto the ground. This ensures that any milk that is near the outside elements has been expelled. These are two easy steps that will help ensure the safety of your milk. For this reason, many homestead dairies do not pasteurize milk. This being said, you are responsible for ensuring the safety of your own milk, so choose wisely. At our house, we strain the milk through a cheese cloth, cool it in the refrigerator, and drink it as soon as possible.

Another difference between store-bought milk, and fresh milk, is that store-bought milk is homogenized. While fresh milk is uniform and consistent, after 1-7 days, it will separate into cream on the top and skimmed milk on the bottom. Cow milk takes less time and goat milk takes longer. In order for large dairies to sell their milk, they have to homogenize it to prevent the cream from separating. This is done by forcing the milk through small valves at very high pressure. This permanently breaks up the lipids in the cream so that the cream will not separate. This is a difficult process to achieve on a homestead, so the best solution is simply to drink your milk while it is fresh.

Butter

Many people don't consider butter-making to be a major survival or "prepper" skill, but the importance of fat in your diet and in daily life should not be underestimated. Currently about 40% of American adults are considered obese, and we consider fat to be in great surplus. In the old Dark Ages, however, fats and oils were considered high value barter items. They are needed to cook many recipes, and are also used in making soaps, ointments, and for food preservation. This is why substances such as olive oil were some of the most valued trading items of ancient civilizations. Olive oil was such an important trade good for the Roman and classical civilizations, that the signature egg-shaped oil jars, or "amphoras," are plentiful in the archaeological record all the way back to 2000 B.C.. When Roman civilization gave way to the dark ages, these jars almost disappeared. The reason is that during times of distress and violence, it is no longer easy to maintain groves of highly cultivated crops such as olive trees, and it is also difficult to maintain other crops that can be used to produce vegetable oils. The reason for this difficulty during the old Dark Ages was that raiders and war parties would regularly plunder the countryside, burning crops and orchards, and destroying infrastructure.

It was at this time that butter became an important source of fat and oil, used for cooking, soaps, skin care, and preservation. The reason for this is that butter comes from livestock, which are a mobile commodity. Try moving a crop field or an olive grove when bandits are spotted enroute to your location; it is impossible. But moving a dairy goat herd into the mountains... that is not so difficult to imagine. In the New Dark Ages, dairy animals will again become a prime source of fats. Butter is a delicious and easily obtainable fat. For years, my family has been harvesting both milk and butter from our small dairy goat herd, and our technique for harvesting butter is simple.

While the natural separation of the cream is not ideal for drinking milk, it is exactly what you want when you are making butter. As I mentioned, with cow milk, it does not take long for the cream to separate, no more than a day. But with a dairy goat, you should let the milk sit for 4-7 days in the refrigerator to allow the cream to separate. A wide mouth jar, or other container where you can scoop out the cream with a ladle or large spoon works fine. When the cream separates, you can see it at the top of the milk. This also helps give you an idea of what percentage milkfat you are producing. To make the butter, you want to scoop at the cream all by itself. About a quart of butter cream will make one commercial size stick of butter.

Illustration 53: Making Butter from Milk in a Hand Churn is simple and Relatively Easy.

Once you have your cream, it is important to make sure it is cool, down to 40-55 degrees Fahrenheit, and it helps to cool your butter churn or jar as well. Making butter requires agitating or mixing your cream for 15-45 minutes depending on what kind of cream, and what kind of technique you are using. Electric butter churns are faster but expensive. Hand butter churns are reliable, but an electric blender with a paddle works as well. If you don't have any of these, you can fill a jar ¾ full of cream and just shake it back and forth. This will wear you out as it takes at least 30 minutes. I prefer to use a heavy-duty standing blender because it is a multi-purpose tool and with solar power, it is off-grid capable. I also keep a backup hand churn in the case that my solar power eventually fails.

After you have your cool milk cream in your churn or blender, you want to start mixing at a medium speed. You can use the whisk for a few minutes until it becomes thick. It will turn into whip cream and look bubbly and thick. At some point, you will see little balls of fat forming and hitting the sides of your mixture. Just keep mixing these back in. When you see the balls of fat forming, put on your paddle, slow down, and pay attention. In sort of a magical process, the fat will suddenly bond together, and throw the watery buttermilk out and to the bottom of the bowl. You want to make sure that you don't burn up an electric mixer at this point, because it will get thick, so stay with it and keep it slow. Once you have separated the buttermilk from the butter, stop mixing and remove the buttermilk. You can then use a press or even just your hands, to ball up the butter and squeeze out any remaining liquid. You can discard the buttermilk or use it in baking. Don't keep it in your hands for too long because it will start to melt immediately. If you like salt, it only takes about ¼ tsp per 2 pounds of butter. You can mix the salt or other flavorings in with a mixing spoon. Goat butter is usually white, but some people put a dusting of annatto in it to make it look yellow like cow butter. I like the white color. Once you are done, shove the butter into a butter mold or dish and put it into the cool refrigerator to properly solidify. You have not really enjoyed butter until you make it yourself!

Making Cheese

Anyone who has raised dairy animals can tell you that there are times when milk is plentiful, and there are also times where milk production is slowed by the natural cycles of your livestock. In times of surplus, you can store this source of nutrition by making cheese. There are hundreds of ways to make cheese, and I am not going to turn this into a book about making cheese, but I want to make you think about how to make cheese in a self-sufficient way. What are the things that you would need to have on hand on your homestead if supply chains were suddenly cut off?

First, you will need some knowledge and practice. I highly encourage you to practice cheese-making and other survival skills before you are forced to do so because of food shortages. There are five basic steps to make cheese. The first is acidification, which is done by adding a cheese mold culture to the milk at a certain temperature. Different cultures require different temperatures and kinds of milk to survive. This turns the sugars in the milk into lactic acids. It will take you a couple of practice runs to become familiar with the acidification process. While I will not list all of the specific techniques, this often involves heating the milk to a certain temperature, adding the culture, and then waiting for a specified time for the milk to begin to solidify.

The second step in cheese making is coagulation, in which an enzyme called rennet is added to further solidify the cheese. Rennet is simply added and allowed to sit for various times depending on the cheese that you are making. Rennet speeds up the coagulation process and makes it easier to make cheese.

While rennet is usually made from a nursing calf stomach, it can also be made from stinging nettle (urtica dioica), a ubiquitous plant which might be easier to obtain than calf stomach. To make rennet from stinging nettle, start by gathering the leaves, but only well before the plant has gone to seed. If you do this after it has gone to seed, then you will poison yourself and never get the chance to make cheese! So, take two pounds of young tender leaves and bring them to a boil, then cover and let simmer for 30 minutes. For every two pounds of leaves, add one tablespoon of salt, and allow this to dissolve in the water. After that, you can strain the water into a stainless-steel bowl, and this water is now rennet that you can use in all your cheese recipes! Vegetable rennet usually stores refrigerated for 2-3 weeks.

The only way to completely avoid using rennet is to make ricotta cheese. Ricotta does not need any mold, culture, or rennet. Instead, you just need to heat 1 gallon of milk, ¼ cup of vinegar, 3 tsp of butter, and 1 tsp of baking soda up to 195 degrees Fahrenheit, then follow the steps of other cheeses below. This cheese tastes great but must be immediately refrigerated and doesn't store well like other cheeses.

The third step in the normal cheese-making process with rennet is to heat the cheese on very low temperature to about 90 degrees Fahrenheit, then add the rennet. Most cheese recipes call for about 1 cup of rennet liquid per 1 gallon of warm milk. Maintain this temperature in a stainless-steel saucepan until the curds and whey form and then you add salt. This process, ingredients, and temperatures vary for different types of cheeses, but in all cheese, there will be curds that solidify and are kept as cheese. The whey is liquid and will be discarded or used elsewhere, such as to feed pigs. To encourage the whey to separate, the curds are often cut apart by hand, releasing the whey. For soft cheeses such as gouda, ricotta, and brie, the curds are cut sparingly, allowing the moisture to be retained. For harder cheeses such as cheddar and asiago, the curds are cut into a fine texture. They can also be cooked further to keep the cheese homogeneous and soft rather than crumbly or grainy. There are many techniques for accomplishing this depending on the type of cheese that you are making. Salt is added early or late during this stage, also depending on cheese type. Salt can be added to the mixture of curds early on or it can be added to the outside of solidified cheese such as a cheese wheel. It can help form the rind on the cheese and is critical to help preserve the cheese. Salt is certainly something to stockpile in case of emergencies.

After separating the whey and retaining the solids, the fourth stage in cheese-making is to shape the cheese. For soft cheeses like chevre, or ricotta, we simply put the solid curds that become cheese into a plastic container in the refrigerator. For harder cheeses, it is helpful to form a wheel, or put the cheese in a mold. Some cheeses need to have weight placed on them for a specified amount of time to press on them and expel the excess water. These low-moisture cheeses are generally easier to preserve and store long term.

The fifth and final stage is ripening or "affinage", a highly variable stage, where temperature, humidity, mold, and other factors are monitored and controlled to create a specific flavor, texture, and type of cheese. A cave-like temperature and humidity are useful for some types of cheeses, such as gorgonzola or gruyere. At times, I have wished that we would have built our house near a cave, because of their usefulness of storing cheeses and other food. Still, you can make your own cheese cellar anywhere that you can dig below ground. Many cheeses also have surface treatments such as oil brushed on to them and other blue cheeses even have mold injected into the cheese.

As I mentioned, this is not a cheese-making book, but the above details should be enough to get you started and give you an idea of the basic knowledge, materials, and conditions that are necessary to make cheese. Just as they were in the old Dark Ages, cheeses are a great way to store the nutrition of milk during lean times. In order to do so, you will need to gain the knowledge to make cheese, stockpile the materials needed, and also build infrastructure like a cold storage room or cave where the cheese can be stored safely and hygienically. On your stockpile list, be sure to include plenty of stainless-steel pots and bowls, utensils, strainers, and cheesecloth, as well as cheese culture powders, molds, and presses. Infrastructure that you will need includes a good stove or heat source, a cold room or cellar, and a solar-powered refrigerator is also highly recommended. Most of all, you need practice, so get started and discover the joy of making cheeses! It was critical in surviving the old Dark Ages, and it will also help you and your loved ones thrive during the coming Dark Age!

Chapter 10: Preserving Food

In 1st world America, we have all but forgotten how to preserve food without the use of refrigerators and freezers. I have covered using solar freezers and refrigerators in the chapter on off-grid energy; now we will discuss alternatives or backups when refrigeration is not available. Backups are important because when it comes to backup plans, two is one and one is none, in other words, your primary often fails.

When I think of food preservation, I think of the remains of an old 19th century homestead that can be found on our property. Its most important features are made of stone and are all that remain of the homestead; the chimney and the root cellar. The root cellar was critical in preserving food for these early pioneers, keeping things cool and fresh long after the harvest. The root cellar in this old homestead was directly under the cabin. The fireplace was two-sided, indoors and outdoors, and was used to can food and even smoke food, on the outdoor side. It is important to know these techniques and others to keep your family fed and keep hunger at bay during hard times.

Building the Root Cellar

Using a root cellar is a simple concept. Storing items in a cool and dry environment discourages the growth of all types of microbes that will ruin your food. You simply need air-tight, mouse-proof containers, and a root cellar. The difficult part of this equation is the planning, design, and construction of the root cellar. I have built or helped build several of these and there are many tricks of the trade that you should know before undertaking the project. The design of a root cellar takes into account proper drainage, thermal mass, thermal gradient, excellent insulation, and if possible, active cooling via running water. It doesn't take an engineer to build a root cellar, but basic geotechnical engineering concepts are necessary to explain how all of these elements can help you build a root cellar as opposed to creating an unsanitary, unstable, nasty hole in the ground. Nobody wants that!

The first and most important part of a root cellar is excellent drainage. This is important for all construction, but it is often overlooked in small projects. Remember, anything worth doing, is worth doing right the first time. Even a small project is too much work to have to re-do it a second time.

Illustration 54: Cellar built by the author; a good cellar is drained well and takes advantage of the cool earth temperatures to preserve food.

The best way to set yourself up for excellent drainage is to put your root cellar in the side of a shallow incline or hill. If you have at least 4 feet of rise for 16 or less feet of horizontal run (1:4 ratio), then you have a steep enough location for easy drainage. If you have over 4 feet of rise for 4 or less feet of run (1:1 ratio), then your location is likely too steep and may lead to the collapse of your structure due to soil creep, or unstable rock. You want to be somewhere in between these two ratios. If you are in a very flat area and do not have such an incline, then I would encourage you to build an above-ground root cellar and cover it with dirt, in effect creating the slope that I have described, above ground level. The construction steps are the same for an above ground structure. If it is above ground, then you just have to cover it with enough soil to achieve good insulation and thermal mass, at least 3 feet, or below the depth of your local frost line. With added rigid insulation, you can bury it shallower.

After you locate your well-drained site, you need to dig your hole to the desired size of the cellar, plus a minimum of 4 feet extra on each side. The depth should be at least 2/3 the desired height of the root cellar. At this depth for a simple and small structure, most soils will not require compaction, but sandy or organic-rich soil should be removed beneath the location of the foundation and replaced with gravel. Soils that are mostly clay or gravel at this depth are ideal. At least 4 inches of clean gravel should be placed underneath the cellar to allow for proper drainage. You also need to dig your drain tile trench from the foundation of the cellar, out to "daylight," meaning out to the side of the hill where any excess water will flow out of. The trench should start at a level just below where the floor will be and slope away from your cellar at a decline of at least 1 inch per 10 feet. Use a level to make sure that it does not incline upwards at any point along the line, or else you will end up with a foul-smelling water pool in your drain tile or drainpipe. The trench should be wide enough to accommodate a 4-inch drainage tile. Do not fill it in until you have placed both the floor drainage pipe, and the exterior foundation perimeter pipe. After digging your hole and trench, and placing your gravel, you need to pour your foundation. Form it up with 2x4's and place rebar around the perimeter underneath where your walls will be built. The rebar will be 2 inches off the ground, held in place by rebar cradles or small bricks. The next step is to place the four-inch drainpipe in the gravel with a 90-degree elbow that goes up into the floor. The top of the elbow needs to be capped with a vent and be just below the level of the floor that you will pour, about 1 inch below level. The other part of the elbow will have your drainpipe attached and lead out of your concrete forms toward your declining slope, to carry water way.

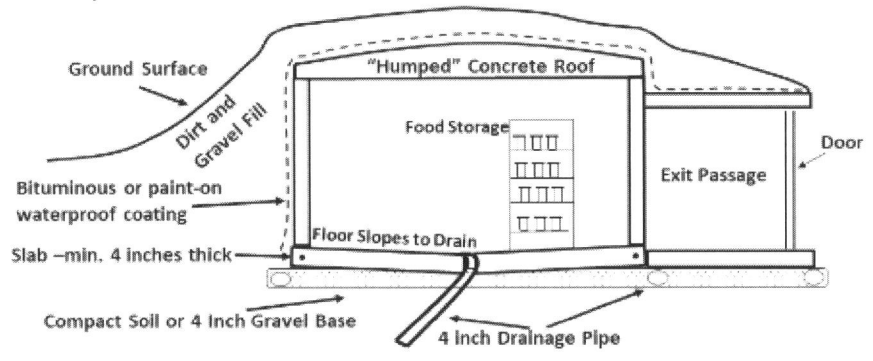

Figure 21: Root Cellar Cross-Section; this cellar opens to daylight, but you may just have a roof hatch

I once had a client that wanted a root cellar directly under his water-pumping windmill, allowing the water that passed through to cool the cellar. This is a great concept, but this particular client had a fairly flat site, and the hole was dug into clay. Drainage was even more important in this case because a windmill pump does spill a little bit of water. In this case, I had to dig a long drainage line, about 6 feet deep and 200 feet long until it came out the side of a ravine. I then installed a 4-inch PVC pipe, in order to allow the water to drain to the steeper area. I installed a vented cap on both ends to make sure that no critters crawled in to clog it up. This proves that as long as you are willing to dig far enough, you can drain any type of cellar.

After installing gravel, forms, rebar, and drainpipe, pour your concrete slab. When you screed (level) off your concrete, pivot around your drainpipe, so that the wood forms are higher, and the concrete slopes down from the wood, towards, the drain. Once the concrete is smooth and level, insert rebar into the wet concrete where the walls will be placed in order to keep the wall strongly fastened to the slab foundation. It should be placed so that rebar comes up through every other block, to ensure that the walls never collapse.

Walls can be made of formed concrete, but this requires a higher level of experience. For a novice, build your walls out of cinder blocks. You can use regular mortar, or you can stack the blocks without mortar, and then cover the outside with surface bonding cement. This is like stucco with small fibers inside. It will give your walls a high shear strength that will resist collapse from pressures to the sides as long as you have proper drainage. The surface bond is faster and stronger but also more expensive than regular mortar. When using surface bond, the first row of blocks on the bottom is still put in place with mortar and must be nice and level. Remember that the rebar should go vertically inside the core of the blocks, placing one half-inch rebar stick in every other block. Walls that are longer than 8 feet long need to have extra support in the middle, such as an extra concrete pilaster or column. Fill in all the hollow cores of your cinder block with concrete. This sounds excessive but it will greatly increase wall strength to prevent collapse from the sides. As mentioned, every other block also has a half-inch rebar in it. This rebar should stick out of the top, and be bent at a 90-degree angle, so that it can be part of the roof. At least one foot of rebar should remain after the 90-degree bend, to tie into the roof slab.

Illustration 55: The Walls of a Simple Root Cellar. This Cellar will have an entrance Hatch on the roof. It has Trenches for Drainage, and it also has a Water Well shaft in the middle which will help keep it Cool

After building your walls, it is time for the roof. The roof height depends on your comfort level, and the resources available. I have seen cellars that are only 5 feet tall, and they are uncomfortable to get into, but they do the job. Building a wood form for your concrete roof is simple, as long as it is not larger than about 6 feet wide by 6 feet long. Longer than this and you will need to seek help from someone with experience in pouring concrete roofs. The form will be removed 7 days after the concrete is poured.

The forms can be built using 2x4 lumber, and you simply build support walls inside the cellar, 2 feet apart and 16 inches on center. A plywood roof is then placed on top of this. It should extend onto the block wall no more than one inch, if at all so that it can be removed later and it holds concrete but does not prevent the concrete from covering and bonding with your blocks. Next you build a regular flatwork concrete form over your cellar using 2x4s. It should be placed on top of the outside of the concrete blocks, forming a lid. Don't forget to include a hatch to get down into your cellar. You do this by simply building a box and placing it on your form wherever you want the hatch to be so that the concrete does not get poured in that spot. The last step before pouring your concrete is to build your rebar grid above the plywood form. This grid can be made with ½ inch rebar wired together to form one-foot by one-foot squares across the entire roof. The rebar can then be attached to the 90-degree rebar that is coming out of the walls. Finally, you are ready to pour your concrete. Allow the concrete to flow all the way down into all of the cinder block holes so that the concrete is one continuous piece from the bottom of the cinder blocks all the way to the roof. When pouring concrete, you generally screed it off with a board, which removes excess concrete, making it level with the forms. After that, you float it all to make it smooth. When making your root cellar, you still need to float it smooth, but you don't screed it level. Instead, you pour extra concrete in the forms, so that the middle of the concrete is higher than the edges, making a slight hump in the middle. This will form a slope from the middle to the edges, so that the water can then run off without pooling up in the middle. Your slope should be at least one inch higher in the middle for every 4 feet to the edge. Use 5 bag concrete with 5-6 inch slump, reinforced with fibers to make a really strong concrete mix. While concrete is generally ready to walk on in 24 hours, I like to wait 48 hours before placing waterproofing, and 7 days before I place any dirt or serious weight on top. This allows for maximum strength. 7 Days is also a good time to remove the forms from underneath the pour. DO NOT GET IN THE CELLAR WHILE YOU ARE POURING CONCRETE ON THE ROOF OR BEFORE THE CONCRETE IS FULLY CURED. IT MAY COLLAPSE AND CRUSH YOU!

After all of the concrete is cured, you need to waterproof the root cellar. At a minimum, you can coat it with black bituminous tar or rubberized roofing products from your local building supply store. Rolled bituminous sheeting can be used for better protection. I recommend dimpled drain board as a final layer as well to further protect your root cellar from water that may accumulate around it.

After placing your foundation waterproofing products, it is time to backfill with gravel. Before placing the gravel, place your foundation perimeter drainpipe. This four-inch pipe goes just outside, and all the way around your foundation perimeter. It needs to be perforated pipe with the holes downward, and placed just below the foundation, sloping towards the drainage trench. The reason that the holes go downward in perforated pipe is because the pipe is not supposed to hold water. Instead, it simply is supposed to create a space where the water will flow into in the case of flooding. This pipe must slope downwards towards the drainage trench. Once it reaches the trench, hook it up to a solid four-inch pipe, and run that all the way to the end of the trench to "daylight."

Finally, it is time to backfill around your root cellar. You need to place gravel all around the root cellar, up to the top of the wall for a distance of at least 2 feet from the wall and 4 inches on top of the roof. For a 6-foot-wide wall section, 6 feet tall, this would take about 3 cubic yards of gravel. If you have followed all these instructions, and kept your walls no longer than 6 feet, then you should have no problem supporting 4 inches of soil, after the gravel. However, each situation is different based on soil conditions, type of concrete, etc. For such variations, and especially for large underground construction, it is necessary to consult a qualified engineer to evaluate your particular build.

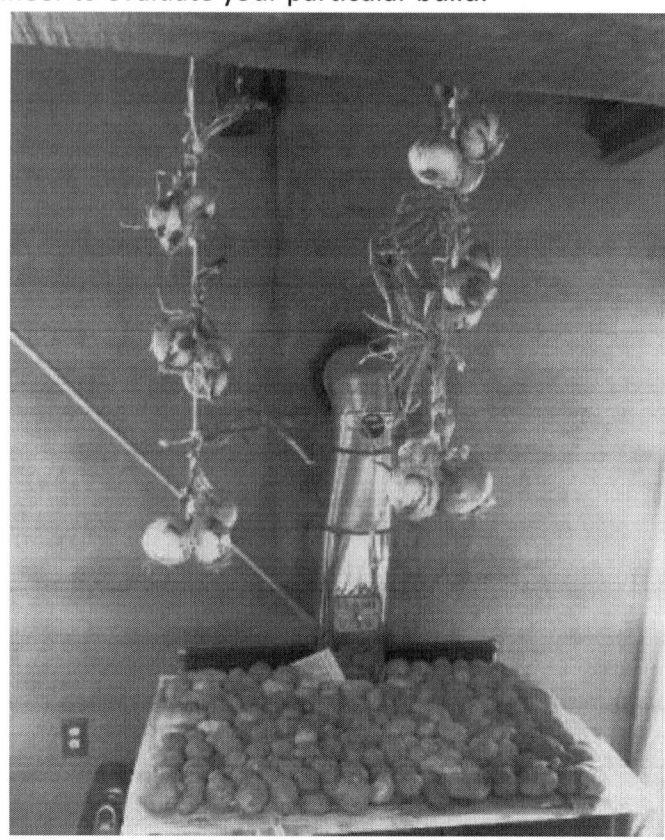

Illustration 56: Some Crops such as Onions and Potatoes should be Dried and Cured before being put in the Cellar

Stocking and Caring for a Root Cellar

A properly constructed root cellar that is kept closed will maintain a temperature of 45-55 degrees year-round. This is only slightly warmer than most refrigerators. This is a good temperature for storing potatoes, carrots, and other root crops, which should be kept in sawdust or newspapers, to keep them dry. These crops as well as apples and slightly under-ripe pears can generally be stored all winter in a root cellar, as long as you keep everything dark, dry, and free of mold. We also keep our jams, jellies, and veggies that have been canned in jars in the root cellar, just to extend their lifespan a little longer. Eggs that have not been washed can last up to 60 days in a root cellar because eggs that are not washed have a preservative coating. Milk can last two weeks at these temperatures, although raw milk will not last that long especially if it is even slightly contaminated.

Illustration 57:The key to preserving food in a root cellar is low humidity, cool temperature, cleanliness, and keeping out rats, mice, and insects.

    Just keep in mind that the cellar cannot continuously be opened and closed like a refrigerator, especially if you live in a humid environment. If too much humid air is allowed in during hot, humid weather, then it will condense on the walls and quickly cause mold. Insulating the walls with foam board can help alleviate this problem. Foam board on the inside and outside of the walls will do an excellent job of preventing mold. Insulated concrete forms, called ICF's, are Styrofoam blocks about 3 feet long, 16 inches tall, and 12 inches thick. They can be stacked together like Legos and then filled with rebar and concrete to form insulated concrete walls. ICF's are left in place after the concrete pour, providing excellent insulation and preventing condensation on the inside walls. Another technique to prevent mold on the walls is to wipe down the walls with a 10% bleach solution about every month during humid weather. This will help keep harmful mold from forming. Finally, you can also purchase a UV light and an ozone emitter, which are often combined in one device.

These will also kill harmful molds and bacteria in your root cellar, but they require a reliable source of electricity.

Canning Food

Not far from our home, there is a small, very traditional Amish community that survives without the use of electricity, motors, or even buttons on their shirts (buttons are too fancy). A friend of mine in that community, Emanuel, is the only Amish that I have ever met that seems to enjoy hosting non-Amish, and even has a great sense of humor. He has allowed me to take my students from my summer "Sustainable Living" course to see his farm. Every class seems to be most impressed by Emanuel's basement. Going down the stairs, they gasp when they find 2000 square feet of shelves stocked with full mason jars containing everything from cherries to artichokes to chicken to beef heart. In the case of a breakdown of society, Emanuel's family of 14 would barely notice. I have asked Emanuel about such an eventuality, and if he would use his hunting rifle to defend his family. He said that he is absolutely forbidden from doing so, but then again as he always tells me with a grin, "my in-laws that run this community always call me the outlaw." In Amish country it is apparently fine to tell the same joke over and over again.

Stocking your basement with canning jars is one of the easiest, least expensive ways to prepare for a food shortage. There are two types of canners that are commonly used: the boiling-water canner and the steam-pressure canner. The boiling-water canner is easier but it is only for high acid foods below a pH of 4.5 such as tomatoes, pickles, sauerkraut, and most fruits and berries. Pressure canning is more effective at preventing bacteria growth and botulism and this method is required for high pH, non-acidic foods above a pH of 4.5, such as carrots, okra, green beans, asparagus, peas, corn, beets, and lima beans. The Amish also pressure can meats, although I recommend waiting until you are an expert before trying this.

A boiling water canner, or water bath canner is simply a big pot that is deep enough to hold the jars being processed and still have enough room for one to two inches of water to cover the tops of the jars. It is also recommended to have enough room left for a short metal rack underneath your jars to keep the direct heat off the bottom, leaving about ¼ inch of space beneath. When preparing jars for canning, make sure that they are cleaned and thoroughly rinsed, along with the lids, and the bands. Make sure there are no cracks or defects in the jar, and especially the lid, that would let air in. The lids have a thin rubber seal that must be completely intact. As soon as the seal is even slightly damaged, it needs to be thrown away and replaced. It is a good idea to submerge the jars one last time in simmering or boiling water, before filling them with your recipe, to sanitize the jar with the heat.

When filling your jars, most foods should be heated to a simmer or boil before putting them into a jar. Delicate foods, such as peaches, can be put in the jars cold, but must be put in with a hot syrup, at least 180 degrees Fahrenheit, that should be poured in to fill the voids in the jar. This helps prevent the growth of bacteria, molds, or yeasts. It will make your life much easier and less messy if you buy a canning funnel to help you pour in your recipe without spilling it. When filling your jars, one inch of space should be left on the top for low-acid food, ½ inch of space should be left for high acid foods, and ¼ inch of space for jams, preserves, and pickles. Space is measured from the top of the glass on the jar. After filling, ensure that there are no remaining air bubbles, and then firmly place the lid and tighten the band, just fingertip tight.

For water bath canning, place the jar, completely submerged, into the water bath and bring to a boil. Most recipes call for boiling for 15 minutes. You must add 5 minutes when at 1000 feet above sea level, 10 minutes above 3000 feet, and 15 minutes above 6000 feet. Time doesn't start until the water starts to boil. Jar tongs are useful to remove the jars from the water after they boil unless you have a high tolerance for pain and burned hands. Once removed from the water, jars can be set to cool, and the lids will "pop" several minutes afterwards. This "pop" sucks the lids down tight and lets you know that you have a good seal. No "pop," no seal. The Amish remove the band after the lids are cooled and sealed. I'm not sure if this is because they are just being cheap, or maybe it prevents long-term rust around the band. Once the jars are cool, they are ready for your basement, pantry, or root cellar.

For steam-pressure processing, the method is similar. Because of the high pressure involved, it is important to examine your steam pressure canner and all of its parts and valves, to ensure that nothing is warped, cracked, clogged, or defective in any way. Don't use a defective pressure canner unless you want to get hurt very badly. Pressure dial gauges can be tested at your local ag extension office in most areas. Other canners come with a weighted gauge, which doesn't need to be tested.

To start pressure canning, you definitely want a rack inside of your canner base to keep the jars off of the bottom. Fill the canner with just 2-3 inches of water and simmer. Next fill, close, and place your jars immediately after being filled with your recipe. Seal the lid and leave the vent or petcock open for about 10 minutes, blowing off steam. Then close your vent or petcock and watch it pressurize. Yes, it's called a petcock. This should take about 5 minutes. Once it has pressurized leave it at that pressure for the time indicated by your recipe. Foods like beans are generally processed for 20 to 40 minutes while meats are processed for up to two hours. These low-acid foods need to be processed in your pressure canner at 240 degrees Fahrenheit to ensure that no harmful bacteria are present.

After your can has been pressurized for the proper amount of time, remove from heat, and allow to cool naturally, until the pressure gauge is back to zero. Next you can open the petcock and unlock it. Then safely remove the canner lid, ensuring that the steam is released away from your face to ensure that you don't look like a boiled lobster afterwards. These jars are very hot and will need to cool for 12 to 24 hours before checking a seal. They can be stored just like water bath jars.

Dry Curing Food

Every winter for 50 years, my father-in-law, who lives in the foothills of the Italian alps, butchers a hog to make countless treats including prosciutto, salami, sopresa, pancetta and other dry-cured pork treats. It always amazed me that he could hang pork from the rafters of the basement and create delicious, safe, well-preserved treats, many that are never cooked. The key to this skill is the use of salt and drawing the moisture out of the meat to create an environment that is inhospitable to bacteria or other pathogens. Eliminate the moisture and you eliminate the risk. Remember when salt curing food to use a reliable recipe and that too much salt is better than not enough. Too little salt and your meat will spoil and grow dangerous organisms. Salt treatments can include liquid brine, dry salt, or both. Nitrites and nitrates are curing agents that are also used very effectively, but they are not particularly healthy. My father-in-law uses a traditional technique using only salt that has worked for centuries and he has never even heard of nitrates.

Dry Curing a Ham

A well-trimmed ham for curing should not have any skin, deep cuts, nooks, or crannies that cannot be reached with salt. Measure out 1 ounce of finely ground salt for every pound of pork to be used. Divide the salt into three equal parts. The first third should be applied over the entire surface of the ham, paying particular attention to where the bone was cut out. Next, hang the ham in a cool area inside of a cloth bag. It needs to stay between 34- and 40-degrees Fahrenheit for an entire month. If your temperatures are not within this range, then you will spoil your ham and need to throw it away. You can do this in a refrigerator if you don't have the proper temperatures. Apply the second third of salt four days after the first one, and then the third salt rub goes on 2 weeks after the first one, then stays on for 2 more weeks, completing the initial cure. The ham should then be aged an additional 2 days for every pound of meat. So, for a 10 lb. ham, cure for the initial 30 days, then age for 20 more at the same temp. For additional flavor, you can also use a cold smoke, right after complete curing. Other types of meat can be cured in the same way, but ham is particularly tasty because of the high fat content. Leaner meats will cure in this way but will be particularly tough. Salami and sopressa are types of Italian sausages that are cured in the same way as the ham except that they have spices and salt integrated into a ground sausage mixture before curing. There are some great award-winning recipes out there, but the main ingredients are pork, lard, salt, pepper, spices, and garlic. Again, I want to stress that it is very important to maintain the right temperature and low humidity while curing meat, and always be aware of sources of contamination. This type of preservation really shows how important it is to stockpile salt for a long emergency. Finally, there is an inherent danger in raw meat so cure meat at your own risk.

Jerky

Deer or beef jerky is one of my favorite treats to enjoy all year round. My kids bug me for weeks prior to deer season because they can't wait to make and eat jerky. Making jerky is also one of the easiest and most enjoyable ways to cure meat. The first step in making deer jerky is to ensure that your meat is clean and free of any hair, dirt, or contaminants. This is not something that you want to do with your discarded trim, but instead use pieces like the hams or even the loins. Tough cuts of meat will make tough jerky. Tender cuts will make tender jerky.

Once you have suitable meat, cut it into very thin strips; this is critical!! It really needs to be cut into strips less than ¼ inch thick for safest preservation. While one person is slicing the meat, someone else can prepare the brine. Brine can be prepared by boiling one cup of sugar and one cup of salt in one half gallon of water until the salt and sugar melts into a thin brine. Next you can allow the water to cool and add spices, lots of black pepper (2 tablespoons), crushed red pepper (1 tablespoon), garlic powder (1 tablespoon), and turmeric (2 teaspoons). The types and amounts of spices are totally up to you. Some people just use teriyaki sauce, salt, and sugar. If you are working by yourself, make sure that you mix up your brine first, so that the deer meat does not spoil. Not letting your meat have time to spoil is critical for all methods of meat preservation.

Next you can mix up all your meat and brine in a very large bowl. The bowl for the above recipe should hold at least 1 gallon. The brine should be thoroughly mixed in, and the meat should be completely submerged, just under the surface of the brine. Then you leave it in the fridge or in a cool spot between 35 and 45 degrees overnight or for several hours.

Finally, the last step is to dry out, or dehydrate your meat. A dehydrator can be made or purchased and consists of several racks that can be stacked to allow air to freely flow through them. If you make your dehydrator, you should have an external source of heat. The heat is not to cook the meat, but just to slowly dry it out, but don't heat the air above 100-degrees Fahrenheit. The simplest way that I have found to do this is to place your metal racks about 30 inches above your woodstove with a small fire inside, when the temperature should be about -90 to 100-degrees. Another method is to build a dehydrator box outside with a south facing window on a sunny but non-humid day. You can then place a fan underneath the racks with a vent out the top of the dehydrator. Warm, dry air is the key. You should be able to finish in one day but need to be prepared to keep the dry air flow going for 12 to 18 hours. Commercially available dehydrators also work great, but they consume a considerable amount of electricity if you are off-grid. In any case, with 12 to 18 hours of warm, dry air flow, your jerky will be ready. Testing your jerky is easy. Good jerky can be snapped in half by bending it with your hands. As soon as it is this dry, it is ready to consume or put away for later. Keeping it in a cool, dry environment will help preserve it for extended periods. If you vacuum seal it immediately after preparing it, you can store it for up to 10 months. If you time it just right, you will run out just in time for the next deer season, and your family will start harassing you again to make more deer jerky.

Curing Fish

It was once quite common to find a barrel of dried fish right alongside a barrel of dried pork in every family larder or tavern basement. Unfortunately, this practice is no longer very popular, but dried fish can provide your diet with a high amount of lean protein and omega three that you will desperately need in hard times. While I love to hunt, our family goes fishing as often as possible mainly just to get the dietary benefits of fish meat. We have practiced dry curing fish mainly to keep the skill alive and be prepared for times when refrigeration may no longer be an option. Most people think that dry cured fish sounds nasty, but if done right, the taste just might pleasantly surprise you.

To dry cure 5-10 pounds of fish, first boil one gallon of water in a large stainless or enamel pot. Add one cup of sugar, two cups of salt, several dashes of pepper, and a few sprigs of oregano. Keep this at a boil until the sugar and salt have dissolved into the water, and then allow to cool to room temperature. Next, add your fish and allow it to soak and cool to between 35- and 45-degrees Fahrenheit. You want this to cool off and soak for 3 hours. After three hours, strain off the brine, and follow the directions below for smoking meat.

Smoking Meat

Meat can be either cold smoked or hot smoked, depending on your situation. Hot smoking is a way to quickly and safely preserve food at room temperature for up to a week. Cold smoking takes longer but if done properly, can dry out your meat so thoroughly that it will be safely preserved for two to three months at room temperature in dry conditions.

Hot Smoking

Any type of meat can be hot smoked but some of my favorites are venison, bear, and summer sausage. You will need a smoker, which can be purchased, but is also very easy to build. As a basic concept, a hot smoker is just a tall box, usually about 2 feet square, and 6 feet tall. It needs a fireproof section about 18 inches high on the bottom with a door on one side to add meat on the top shelf or shelves and smoky logs are placed on the bottom. There also needs to be a vent to allow just a little air to enter the bottom where the fire is burning. Meat can be hung in the top by cordage (rope), or you can place metal racks in the top. Do not place any meat within 3 feet of your flame. The last piece that you will need to build your smoker is a meat thermometer. This can be inserted into the wall of your smoker about 4 feet from the bottom, towards the bottom third of your meat shelves or hanging area. The thermometer will help you ensure that your meat gets smoked properly. I prefer to build a fire outside of the smoker, using several logs about 4 inches in diameter. Once these are red with embers on the outside, I move them into the smoker.

Next, I add damp or green wood chips that will flavor my meat. The bark should be removed from these woodchips as well. My local favorite woodchips are hickory or maple, but apple, mesquite, and alder are also great choices. Poisonous woods such as buckeye, mountain laurel, and black cherry should never be used, and evergreens don't give a pleasant result either, unless you like to chew on burnt pine tar. After loading the wood chips, the door is closed and there is very little ventilation, allowing the smoke to fill the box and fully penetrate the meat. The smoker needs to be brought up to a temperature of 160 to 190 degrees and maintained for the duration. Time cooking depends on the thickness of the meat being cooked. Thinner strips up to an inch thick work best and can be smoked in about 45 minutes. Summer sausage needs to be smoked for 2-3 hours. Internal temperatures of all hot smoked meats should reach 152 degrees Fahrenheit.

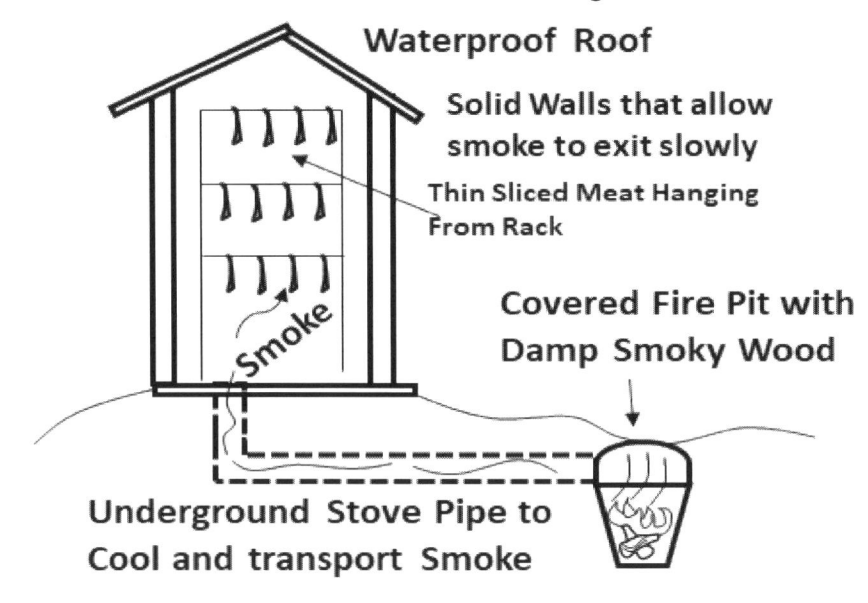

Figure 22: Cold Smoker

Cold Smoking

Cold Smoking is done in much the same way as Hot Smoking. In fact, the same apparatus can be modified and used for each. Meat is hung and prepared, usually using a brine, just like the one outlined above for making jerky. The main difference is that in cold smoking, the fire must be kept outside of the smoker completely, so that it does not heat the smoker directly. The way to achieve this is to build a fire pit on the outside of the apparatus. The fire pit should be buried about 2 feet deep and needs to be covered, with an exhaust pipe that goes into the smoker. The exhaust pipe should be at least 2 feet long before it gets to the smoker, to allow the smoke to cool. There also needs to be a vent to allow air to enter where the fire is burning. After the fire is burning with ample red coals, add your damp or green wood chips, as in hot smoking. Then cover the fire and ensure that the smoker fills with smoke. The temperature in the smoker should be kept under 100 degrees to ensure a true cold smoke. Keep in mind that the food is not actually being cooked, but instead it is being dried. This process often lasts for several days and is dependent upon keeping the meat free of bacteria and pathogens, and getting it completely dried. The process should definitely not be interrupted until it is complete, meaning that you should never start smoking meat and then let it stop for a few hours before starting again, you have to stay on it until it is done. You will know it is done when the meat is firm to the touch and very light weight. It should not feel at all like there is soft tissue like fat, live muscle, or jelly-like tissue inside the meat. While cold smoking is a time-honored and effective tradition, it should not be taken lightly. There is a high risk of bacteria developing in your meat at these temperatures, so make sure that you get an experienced and knowledgeable person to help you on your first attempt.

Chapter 11: Electricity

Our family sold farm products at the local farmers market for years and we came across all types of people, many of whom were just lonely and came to the market to talk someone's ear off. I remember two regular customers that were twin brothers, about 40 years old, that lived with their single mother, presumably in the basement of her home. They were supposedly nuclear technicians that traveled around the country, fixing controls on nuclear power plants and were big fans of that energy source. They would often tell you something clever, and then laugh by themselves for a seemingly long time, making everyone else feel uncomfortable. I was a vendor, so I would oblige them and listen long enough for them to make a purchase. Not knowing of my background, one of them once told me with a big grin, "you know, the problem with solar electricity is that it doesn't really work." I replied to him, "My family has actually been living off-grid with solar power for ten years now. Not only does it work reliably, but I have no utility bill." Then it was my turn to have about five minutes of uncontrollable laughter, all by myself, while he sat there feeling uncomfortable. He didn't buy anything from us that day. Oh well, it was worth it!

When designing your off-grid retreat, you should always keep in mind that technology is subject to failure, and you may be without electricity for an uncertain amount of time. It is for that reason that my previous chapters covered a multitude of off-grid adaptations that do not require electricity, to include passive solar design, wood heating, root cellars, etc. Nonetheless, producing your own electricity independent of the electrical grid gives you a survival advantage that most Americans currently lack. Imagine an economic or catastrophic setback to the United States that forces people to live as if it were the 17th century. Then imagine yourself, a 17th century pioneer with a set of solar-powered electric lights, a 12-volt fridge, and a freezer. That would be the cat's meow right? You would be the head honcho, the big cheese in your neighborhood! This is only the start of what becomes possible when you take control of your own electricity production. Other possibilities include food-processing accessories such as a meat grinder, security apparatus such as flood lights, and even transportation such as an electric utility vehicle. Welcome to the world of off-grid energy production!

Determining your Energy Needs

Any off-grid energy project must begin with an assessment of how much energy you will need and use. This consists of listing the electric features that you wish to take with you for your off-grid life. You then will calculate the number of watts that each of these features uses in 24 hours, and then total your electric consumption for a 24-hour period. This is the first and most crucial step in your energy planning because your entire electricity production system will be based upon these figures. Everything from your battery bank to your solar panels will be sized based upon this number. Be sure to include all the possible electric items that you want because it is easier to start with a surplus than try to enlarge your system after you realize that you don't have enough power. This is done by examining each electrical device, appliance, tool, light bulb, and fixture to determine the daily usage in your home. The best way to do this is to use the chart below. Take the hourly energy rating of each appliance, multiply by the number of hours of expected use, and then total all the results from each appliance. This is an important step because it will become the basis of your personal off-grid renewable energy system.

WATTAGE RATING FOR COMMON HOUSEHOLD APPLIANCES

APPLIANCE	AMPS	WATTS/HOUR
Blender	2 - 4	240 - 480
Can Opener	1.2	150
Ceiling Fan	.08 - 0.8	10 - 100
Ceiling Fan w/Light Kit (2-40watt bulbs)	1.5	180
Ceiling Light Fixture (2-60watt bulbs)	1.0	120
Clock Radio	0.83	100
Clothes Dryer (240v)	16.5 - 34	4,000 - 8,200
Clothes Iron	10	1,200
Clothes Washer	12.5	1,500
Coffeemaker	9.0	480 - 960
Dehumidifier	5.4 - 6.8	650 - 800
Desktop Computer	4 - 7	480 - 850
Dishwasher	8.5 - 12.5	1,000 - 1,500
Electric Range (240v)	5.5 - 10.8	1,320 - 2,600
Food Freezer	2 - 4	240 - 600
Garbage Disposal	3.5 - 7.5	420 - 900
Hair Dryer	5 - 10	600 - 1,200
Heater (portable ceramic)	7 - 12	840 - 1,440
Microwave Oven	4 - 10	480 - 1,200
Refrigerator	2 - 4	240 - 600
Stereo	2.5 - 4	300 - 480
Television	2.5	300
Three Way Lamp (30-70-100watt bulbs)	0.25 - 0.83	30 - 100
Toaster Oven	10 - 14	1,200 - 1,700
Vacuum Cleaner	6 - 11	720 - 1,320
Washing Machine	12.5	1,500
Water Heater (240v)	15.8 - 21	3,800 - 5,500
Window Air Conditioner	6 - 13	720 - 1,560

Figure 23: Chart for Doing a Home Power Audit to Determine Your Off-Grid Energy Needs, from:"theelectricenergy.com" - 07/03/23

Efficiency

Keep in mind that there are certain appliances that are just not feasible for the off-grid lifestyle. My family adapted well to living off-grid, but living without a hair dryer, curling iron, etc. was nearly a deal-breaker. No television, no problem. Small refrigerator, no problem. Hauling firewood, no problem. No hair appliances, now that was a big adjustment for the ladies in the family! It is not impossible to design an off-grid system that can handle hair dryers, but on a day with no solar or no wind power production, such appliances will drain your batteries in a hurry. The reason is that these items produce heat using electricity. Heating with electricity requires you to short circuit the electricity at a high amperage, thus creating heat and therefore quickly draining your electricity. Such appliances include electric hot water heaters, electric clothes dryers, toasters, electric stoves, electric space heaters, and yes, hair dryers. Some of these items are often most easily replaced by using propane as the heat source. In a situation where propane becomes unavailable, you must live without many of these items. I have discussed how to use a thermosiphon to heat your water with a wood stove in a previous chapter and the end of this chapter outlines how to heat water with a solar thermosiphon that you can easily build yourself.

Appliances

All lights on our homestead consist of 12-volt DC LED's, which are extremely reliable and here's why. LED's are extremely efficient and really the only logical choice when you are off-grid and trying to make the most of every watt because they consume less power. Most of the bulbs that we have use only between 3 to 5 watts per hour and take the place of halogens that would use between 45 and 75 watts per hour. Because our battery bank is nominally 12-volt, we found that the easiest, most efficient bulb to cheaply and easily find is the MR16 bi-pin bulb. These are readily available, affordable, and hold up well to the voltage range of any 12-volt system. You can find LED lighting in other DC voltages, but it may be a special order. Most of our lighting is track lighting or cable lighting but we have a few lamps that require a traditional screw-in adapter that converts a regular light into a bi-pin light socket. Most off-gridders that we have met convert their electricity from DC to AC with an inverter before doing anything with it. By using DC lighting, we are ensuring that if the inverter breaks, which sometimes happens, then our lights will still be on.

For the same reason, we have also chosen to use 12-volt nominal DC power to run our refrigerator and freezer. Again, if the inverter breaks, we will still be able to keep our food cool. Our refrigerator is a 7 cubic feet upright model, and we also have a 9 cubic feet chest freezer. Smaller than usual, but together they only consume about 800 watts per day. This is only about 10 percent of what the average fridge-freezer combo uses. This efficiency does come at a steep price, about $3000 total for both appliances. Sunfrost and Sundanzer are the top brands in this industry. Ours have lasted over a decade so far without a hitch.

This price would get you a very large and fancy traditional refrigerator, but when living off-grid, efficiency is what you are striving for, so it is well worth the money to buy a small, extremely efficient fridge.

Power tools are huge consumers of electricity while you are building an off-grid home. If you use power tools during a cloudy day without wind when you are on solar and wind power, then you will run down your batteries in a hurry. This does not mean that you cannot use them, on the contrary, most of our home was built while using power tools on solar power boosted to 120 volts by an inverter. Our system has a rated charging capacity of 3900 watts from solar panels and a storage of 1400-amp hours multiplied by a 12-volt battery bank. About half of our battery is usable so this gives us 8000 watts of stored power. Any 120-volt tool drawing less than 15 amps per hour is not too much of a stretch for us, as long as there is sunshine. 15 amps translates to 1800 watts per hour (15 times 120v), meaning that it would only use just under half of the 3900-watt charging capacity if left on constantly, but leaving it on for four hours without the sun would drain most of the stored power. Are you lost in the numbers yet? That's alright, we will discuss more about these calculations further along, and by the end of the chapter, you will be an expert. You just have to be smart about how and when you use power tools or other high draw electrical items. If you are going to need to use a circular saw or similar items, do it when you have a solar or wind charging source with surplus energy coming in. Even better, use battery-powered tools with a lithium battery pack. This works for most jobs and uses much less energy. You can also charge them when you have surplus power and a good lithium-ion battery will last a long time, making your life easier.

On our off-grid homestead, we use air conditioning not only to keep the house cool, but also to decrease humidity. That being said, we use it only when the sun is shining from about 10AM to 3PM on clear, hot, sunny days. Our house is very efficient, so we cool about 2000 square feet with a 10,000 BTU window unit. The unit uses about 800 watts per hour max and the solar panels provide over 3 kilowatts per hour, so the batteries can still get recharged while the AC is on. It also has a timer so that we don't have to turn it off manually. We just set it to turn off before the sun starts going down. This doesn't keep the house super cold but on the worst dog days of summer, we may hit up to 85 degrees for a few hours. This is just part of off grid living strategy.

Designing your Off-grid Power System

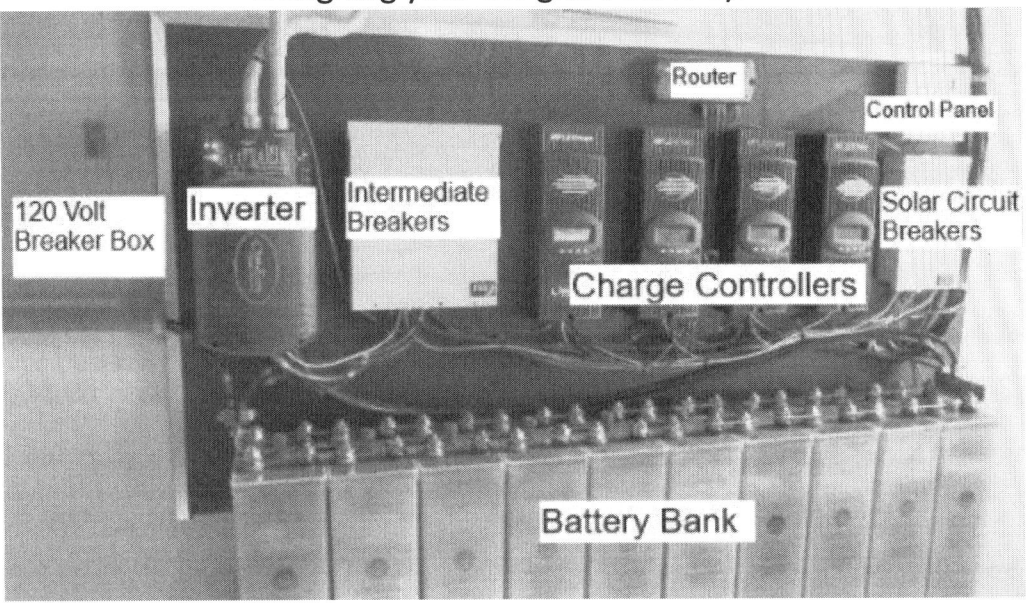

Illustration 58: Off-Grid Power System Designed and Installed by the Author

Batteries

Most people want to skip straight to talking about the energy source such as wind, solar, and hydro. BUT LISTEN UP, your first concern should be BATTERIES! While energy sources may change, you must first have batteries for almost all off grid systems. In fact, I have a relative who maintains the off-grid home of a wealthy real estate tycoon in Alaska. He has batteries that are charged up periodically by a generator, but no alternative energy source whatsoever. They will run the generator for a few hours per day to charge up the large battery bank, just like you would use solar or wind as a charging source. This is why, no matter what your charging source, the first step in going off-grid is to install batteries. No matter what your energy source, the batteries serve to bridge the gap between periods where energy is available, such as when the sun is not shining, or the wind is not blowing, or even when your diesel generator needs a rest.

Sizing and Choosing your Battery Bank

When choosing a battery bank, first consider the previous section on determining your energy needs. We discussed this first because your battery bank size is based on energy needs. When we first moved off-grid, my family and I were using only about 1.5 kw per day. This was enough for 12-volt LED lighting in our 750 square foot home (we added on later), 7 cubic feet 12-volt refrigerator, 9 cubic feet 12-volt chest freezer, and occasionally a fan, laptop computer, or washing machine. Over the years, we have expanded our home and our family and added over 1000 square feet along with an additional upright fridge/freezer combo. We also use about 3-4 hours of air conditioner (10,000 BTU) on hot sunny summer days. We can use power tools like drills, grinders, and saws when there is plenty of sunshine.

All of this has increased our usage to an average of 4kw daily in the winter, or 8kw when the air conditioner is in use. For a <u>very simple</u> off-grid lifestyle, try to plan for 3kw (3000 watts) minimum electricity use per day. We will use this figure in the following example calculations; so, let's say we need 3kw daily.

Next, think about the gap in energy that needs to be bridged when there is no sun. In our example, imagine that you rarely go three days without sun, and you rely 100% on PV solar electricity for your energy needs. This means that over three cloudy days you would need to have an available storage of 9 kilowatts of energy that you can use in those three days. If you plan for this amount of usable, stored battery power and you experience more than 3 days without sun or any other charging source, then you would need to rely on a fossil fuel-powered generator or some other source such as wind.

The reason that I specify that you need an **available** storage of 9 kilowatts of energy is because all of the energy contained in a battery bank is not available for use. In lead acid and AGM batteries, you start to seriously wear out your batteries when you use more than 45 percent of their total stored power. Just imagine letting your car battery die multiple times. It is a lead acid battery and would have to be replaced after this type of abuse. This means that if you want 9 kilowatts available, then you need to have a lead acid battery bank with a total rating of 20 kilowatts because 9 kilowatts is 45% of 20 kilowatts. In the case of Nickel Iron batteries, you can use at least 75% of the battery power without harming the batteries. This means that your Nickel Iron battery bank only needs to be about 12 kilowatts to provide the same amount of power as a 20-kilowatt lead acid bank. This is because 9 kilowatts equal 75% of 12 kilowatts. For lithium batteries, you can draw the battery down all the way to 90% depth of discharge, meaning that a 10-kilowatt lithium battery will suffice if you have 9 kilowatts of desired energy storage. As mentioned, this calculation is for a battery bank that may need to run without power for three days. If you have an additional energy source such as wind, and you think that the battery bank will get charged every single day, then you can get by with a battery bank approximately 1/3 this size.

Battery Type	Safe Depth of Discharge	Example: Usable Power Storage Requirement	Size of Battery Bank Needed
Lead Acid	45%	9 kilowatts	20 kilowatts
Nickel Iron	75%	9 kilowatts	12 kilowatts
Lithium Ion	90%	9 kilowatts	10 kilowatts

Table 4: How to determine size of battery needed based on type of battery and safe depth of discharge with an example requirement of 9 kilowatts of storage

When sizing a battery bank, they will often be labeled in amps, not in kilowatts. To determine kilowatts, you need to multiply the amps by the voltage of the bank. For example, a battery bank of 700 Amps and 12 Volts will contain (700 x 12) 8400 watts or 8.4 kilowatts of power. Again, don't think that you can discharge this battery bank fully or it will be damaged, especially in the case of Lead Acid batteries.

Types of Batteries

While the Nickel Iron batteries are almost three times as expensive as lead acid batteries, they can be discharged even more than 75% without damage, as long as they are charged up fully within a few days. In addition, Nickel Iron Batteries will last up to fifteen years with proper maintenance. At this time, you can then simply replace the electrolyte with new electrolyte and be good for another fifteen years. Another advantage is that you can store the electrolyte powder for the nickel iron battery and use it whenever it is needed. This potentially gives you many years of off-grid power in the case of a long grid-down emergency.

Lead acid batteries need to be completely replaced within 5 to 10 years, depending on how they were used. The one drawback is that Nickel Iron batteries must absolutely be refilled with distilled water every 1 to 2 months. Lead acid batteries must be watered about every 4-6 months, unless they are sealed, in which case they do not need additional water. All batteries need to be kept clean and the connections need to be kept free of corrosion. Convenient battery cleaner sprays can be found with automotive supplies and battery terminal protector spray is a waxy substance that also helps keep away corrosion.

Illustration 59: An Inexpensive Solar Electric System with Lead Acid Batteries Installed by the Author

Lithium batteries are slightly more expensive than nickel iron, but they are extremely light and convenient, and you never have to add water. They typically last between 8-12 years, and then can be recycled. While they perform better than nickel iron and have lower voltage fluctuation and loss, nickel iron can be reused instead of recycled. While I definitely do not recommend lead acid batteries for your off-grid system, lithium or nickel iron are both good options depending on your needs and your budget. Lead acid batteries should only be used if your budget absolutely cannot afford these other two options.

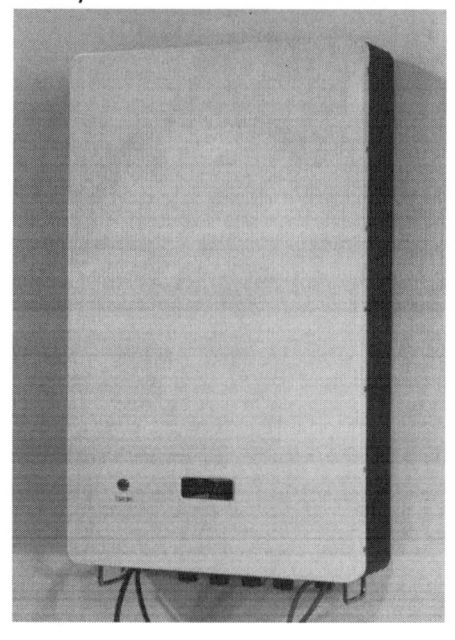

Illustration 60: Lithium Powerwall Batteries come in various brands and are very sleek and easy to hang on a wall. They sometimes come with smart features to ensure proper charging and efficiency.

    Batteries need to be kept in a controlled temperature environment, generally 20 degrees above or below room temperature, otherwise their performance will be seriously affected. All batteries that are not sealed will have some "off-gassing." This is when hydrogen gas escapes during the charging process. Hydrogen gas is hazardous and can catch fire, and other gases that come from large batteries may be hazardous to your health. For this reason, it is important to vent the batteries outdoors by keeping them in an enclosed room with a vent pipe. Since hydrogen is lighter than other gases, it will rise and so the vent should be located at the top of your battery enclosure. Some people choose to enclose their batteries in a box that has a ventilated tube leading outdoors. Alternatively, you may have an entire room or closet for your off-grid power center which can be ventilated with a fan or by using natural airflow. Often charge controllers, which we will discuss later, have an auxiliary power output for a vent fan attachment.

Solar

    I used to ask my Environmental Science students, "Wouldn't it be great if there was a fuel source for electricity that was absolutely free, like free coal, free natural gas, etc.? What if it didn't produce any pollution either?" They would always look at me with this dreamy stare, like, "oh yeah, that would be so unbelievably cool!" Then, I would tell them,

"Well actually, there is, it is called sunlight. In fact, fossil fuels were originally created by sunlight, which through photosynthesis, decomposition, heat, and pressure were transformed into liquid energy. Today, we can skip all of these steps and collect solar power directly through the use of photovoltaic panels, known as solar panels." Wow, what an enigma! Sunlight is one of those amazing creations in our universe that is hard to fathom. The way it works is that massive amounts of nuclear reactions on the sun create such an unimaginable quantity of energy that the energy is propelled through space at 300,000 kilometers per second. This means that the photons which make up this energy travel the 93 million miles between the Sun and the Earth in just under 8.5 minutes. The miraculous nature of photons is that they can travel such a huge distance and then effectively do work and move things, even creating electricity on our planet.

In the case of solar panels, a simplified description of what happens is that photons strike the surface, typically made of silicon, and then they excite or charge atoms which excite more electrons through to the other side of the panel. It is not the transfer of actual electrons but instead the motion of electrons like bumper cars or ocean waves that transfer energy, and this movement of electrons can then be routed via conductors (metal pathways) away from the panel and to electrical loads for our immediate use or storage in batteries. The movement of electrons that are not used or stored in battery (chemical) form are simply released as heat, and do not cause any problems if left unconsumed.

Solar panels are one of the most adaptable off-grid energy sources because they can be used almost anywhere where humans thrive. Exceptions would be near the North and South Pole or anywhere where sunshine is severely limited. Solar panels are still used in very cloudy, rainy places such as the pacific northwest and even Alaska, but you must plan for less daily hours of charging time during certain seasons, and you should have more battery storage capacity to deal with several days or even a couple of weeks without solar charging capabilities. Solar panels are also relatively easy to "plug and play," without requiring a lot of extra infrastructure such as towers or without exceptional natural features like rushing streams and waterfalls. In addition, they are relatively maintenance free. They do need to be reasonably clean, but rainfall has always done the job for me, and snow will occasionally need to be brushed off the panels depending on your climate. Solar panels are known for their longevity, with 20-year warranties being quite common, and reputable panels will be guaranteed against reasonably sized hail and ice. For these reasons, solar panels are the first off-grid power source that should be considered in most situations.

Illustration 61: Polycrystalline Panel Installation Managed by the Author; We have not had problem with hail damage, but you will have to clean off snow and ice or you will lose power.

There are three basic types of panels to choose from, polycrystalline, monocrystalline, and thin film. Polycrystalline solar panels are made up of dozens of small rectangular solar collectors. They are the cheapest and most used types of panels for off-grid applications. If a few of the collectors are broken, the panel will still have some limited output. Monocrystalline panels are composed of just one collector. They generally can be about 20% smaller than polycrystalline panels, and still have an equal energy output. If it is damaged at all, a monocrystalline panel will not work. Usually, the smaller size does not justify the additional cost and the susceptibility to damage. Thin film panels are mainly for specialized applications. They take up as much as twice the area of polycrystalline panels for the same energy output. They have the advantage of being very lightweight and can be made to be flexible or molded into irregular shapes. Thin film panels have been used to create solar collectors that double as roof shingles, but the cost is prohibitively expensive if you have any sort of limitations on your budget. I strongly recommend the polycrystalline panels at this time for both durability, practicality, and economy.

The orientation of solar panels varies based upon your geographic location. In the northern hemisphere, you will want to face the panels generally towards the south. Solar south is very close to magnetic south, but to reconfirm what your compass tells you, just wait for high noon and plant two vertical staffs in the ground. The shadows will form lines from the base of the staffs. If you extend these two shadow lines further until the point that they intersect, then you will have an arrow that points to solar south. At solar noon the lines will be near parallel so do this at least once in the morning and once in the evening to confirm. You can spray paint the lines on the ground so that you have a record confirmation. I cannot overemphasize the importance of proper panel orientation. A relative of mine works for an elderly billionaire land developer who wanted solar panels installed on his off-grid summer retreat. As they sometimes can be, this billionaire was very stubborn in demanding the panels be on the most visible side of the roof, which was the north side. He now has a very expensive roof ornament that produces no power but looks very eco-friendly.

Illustration 62: Installing rails for a Solar Roof Mount on a very Tall Building

Once you have determined the directional orientation or azimuth of your panels, you need to figure the angle of tilt upon which they will be mounted. This angle should correspond closely to the line of latitude where you are located. This means the further north you are, the steeper the angle of tilt. If you are located at 35 degrees latitude, then 35 degrees from horizontal is your ideal angle of tilt. If you are within 15 degrees of this number, then you are in good shape. It is also better to err on the side of being too steep, because in the wintertime the sun will be lower on the horizon, and steeper panels will catch more sun. If you mount your panels on a roof top, then this angle will be fixed and so it is important to get your angle right the first time, and it is helpful if your roof is oriented properly towards solar south to begin with. It is also very critical to avoid shading from trees or other objects. Do not underestimate the loss that you experience through shading. Twenty percent shade on a polycrystalline panel can lead to an eighty percent loss of power for the entire panel. I have seen this with my own chimney, and I have seen much worse loss from trees that shade some very expensive solar installations. If you can keep these angles in mind when building your home, then a roof mount might be right for you. Plan ahead to save yourself from huge disappointments!

Illustration 63: Ground Mount with 2kW Solar array, designed by the Author, Concrete base is a 6'x6'x4' reinforced solid Concrete cube designed to Resist Extremely High Winds

If you ground mount your panels, then you have the option of being able to adjust the tilt in order to follow the sun's track through the sky during different seasons. Alternatively, you may install your panels on a specialized sun-tracking mount with a photo-sensitive sensor to follow the sun. I have helped install these and they work quite well although they do tend to jump around a bit in cloudy conditions and during sunrise and sunset. I would advise against this type of setup because it is expensive and adds a layer of complexity to your energy production that may lead to a malfunction when you actually just need reliability. I would say that adding extra panels is cheaper and less complicated and will give you the same gain of power as a sun-tracking mount. This is especially true in the current era of cheap solar panel prices. A neighbor of mine that went off-grid in the 1970's paid 25 dollars per watt for a 200-watt solar panel. This panel would now go for around 1 dollar per watt, meaning that it was once $5000 but now costs only $200. This is why my solution for many solar limitations is simply to buy more panels!

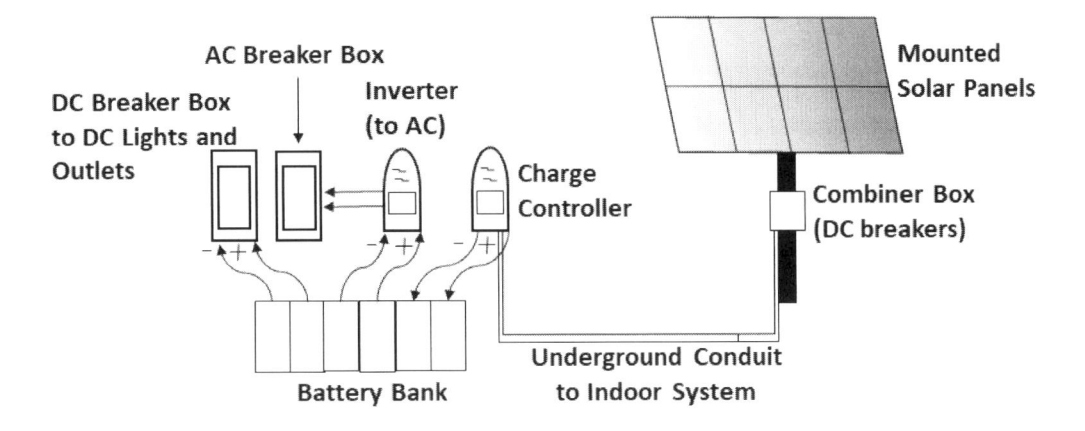

Figure 24: Basic Solar Power System Components

When planning for your projected electricity production, keep in mind that the watts for which the solar panels are rated for are not normally going to be that actual watts that they produce. This is because solar panels are given their rating based on ideal conditions, mild temperatures, low altitudes, clear skies, etc. In normal conditions, I like to plan for a solar output of 85% of the rated capacity. It will normally be more than this, but I do not like to set myself up for disappointment.

After this, consider the average number of good, direct sunlight hours that you will get each day. In my area, at about the 35th parallel of latitude, I plan for 5 hours of good sunlight daily, or about 4 hours winter and 6 hours summer. This is not precise, but a good planning factor for a stationary array. So, let us say that we have a panel rated for 200 watts. Eighty-Five percent of this gives us 170 watts and if I expect 5 hours of sunlight daily, then the panel should produce 850 watts daily (170 watts x 5 hours). In one week, let us say that we get on average 5 out of 7 days when there is good sun. The other two days in this hypothetical situation are cloudy. So, 5 days times 850 watts daily gives us 4200 watts weekly from this one panel. Since this needs to last us the entire week, take 4200 watts divided by seven days and we can plan on 600 watts to use daily from each 200-watt panel under these conditions. If we estimate that we will use no more than 3000 watts (3kw) daily, then we need 5 times this planning amount, or 5 x 200-watt panels. This scenario is designed for my geographical conditions. In the Pacific Northwest, you may plan for 6 out of 7 cloudy days, which will increase your panel needs and panel costs by a factor of 5 from the above formulation. The important thing is that you do the math prior to spending hard-earned money.

Wind Power

Location

A couple of years ago in January, I installed a pole-mounted solar array and system for a customer on one of the highest points in Missouri. While putting up the solar array, my crew and I felt like we were going to be blown off the grassy hilltop by a steady, bone-chilling wind. The wind kept up for the entire installation. I was so impressed by the wind, that I convinced the customer to install a wind turbine later that year. We installed a nice, 1kw turbine, that soon was producing twice as much power daily as the solar. If you live in such a location, then wind power is definitely for you, but the location means everything when planning for wind.

Your wind energy evaluation should start with terrain. Clear, flat terrain, or hilltops are ideal locations, while valleys or heavily forested areas won't work well at all. One mistake that is commonly made is to clear a small area within a forest for your wind project. This is ill-advised because of turbulence caused by nearby trees. As wind moves over and through trees, it swirls around making windspeeds highly variable. This type of turbulence will whip your wind turbine around, stopping and starting it chaotically. Not only will it not provide steady power, but it could also likely break the wind turbine or cause it to wear out in a short amount of time. Trees need to be a minimum of ½ mile away if they are near the height of the tower. In most large forests, a 60-foot tower will need to have ½ mile of cleared area around it to avoid turbulence. If you build a taller tower, for example 100-foot-high in an area with 60-foot-tall trees, you can decrease the distance to within 500 feet of the tower in order to avoid the turbulence. A clear hilltop that juts out above the forest will also work in the same way as a taller tower.

Illustration 64: A simple wind generator works just like an alternator and sends power down wires to a charge controller which is then plugged into batteries. Some have built in charge controllers in the turbine.

We learned all this the hard way on our homestead. Our first wind tower was only 50 feet high, with the generator barely rising above trees that were within 50 feet. It would spin, start, and stop constantly as the turbulence created by the trees wreaked havoc on the turbine. Fortunately, it was one of the cheapest models, and the tower was completely homemade. This was a good, cheap lesson on how wind power works. When it came time to spend money on a more serious tower, we moved the location to the top of the hill to a field with the nearest trees being over 500 feet away. Finally, a reliable, steady wind gave us the power that we had hoped for.

Besides terrain, it is also important to consider wind potential in your area. The Department of Energy publishes wind potential maps for the entire United States that will give you an idea of what to expect out of your wind energy investment. As a general rule, coastlines, high plains, and mountain ridges provide the best wind energy potential. But, again, the conditions around your homestead are the most critical factor to consider.

Choosing a wind Generator

When purchasing a wind generator, there are several important considerations to make. If you are already familiar with purchasing solar panels, then switching to wind will be somewhat confusing, as it is a different experience completely. First of all, prices for wind generators are highly variable. Most solar panels that are made for residential power applications are of similar price and quality. Wind generators, on the other hand, can be of very high quality, or they can be quite cheap. I have seen generators rated for 1 kilowatt that are sold for $900, and others with the same rating for $6000. Here, it is important to remember that quality is important. Our first wind generator was a cheap version, and it wore out in about 6 months. While we lost a couple of hundred dollars, it was actually worth it because we learned a lot about wind conditions and were able to choose a better site for a higher quality generator later on.

Several options are available when choosing a generator, so you must read the specs sheet. You will come across both vertical and horizontal axis wind turbines. Turbines with their blades on a vertical axis may look like an eggbeater (Darrieus type), or another type looks like an anemometer (Savonius type). These types of wind generators started to gain popularity in the 1990's but were generally inefficient and had a high number of maintenance issues. They are somewhat interesting to look at but from a practical standpoint, I recommend horizontal axis wind generators, which are more common to see and look somewhat like an old style western windmill.

While other types of motors exist, permanent magnet motors are definitely the best choice for small scale home power generation so look for this when you purchase. The key is that they start producing wind at fairly low wind speeds, as low as 6 mph. In simplified terms, the way a permanent magnet wind generator works is that when the wind turns the blades, the blades spin a series of magnets around a copper coil in the middle. This generates an electric current which then is transferred down your electric wires to your home.

It is also a great idea before purchasing, to examine the power curve rating of various wind turbines, to compare them and see which one meets your needs. This power curve will show the power output based on the wind speed for each generator. When examining this graph, you will notice that the "cut-in" speed, or the speed at which the generator starts producing power, is often around 8mph, but can be lower or higher than this. If you know you are in an area with low winds, then the cut-in speed is important, but you will also need to know at what speed you begin to produce significant power. This is also on the power curve chart. Beware of manufacturers that emphasize the start-up speed. This is insignificant because it is just the speed at which the blades start turning, without producing power. Don't even pay attention to start-up speed, instead, a low cut-in speed is what you want.

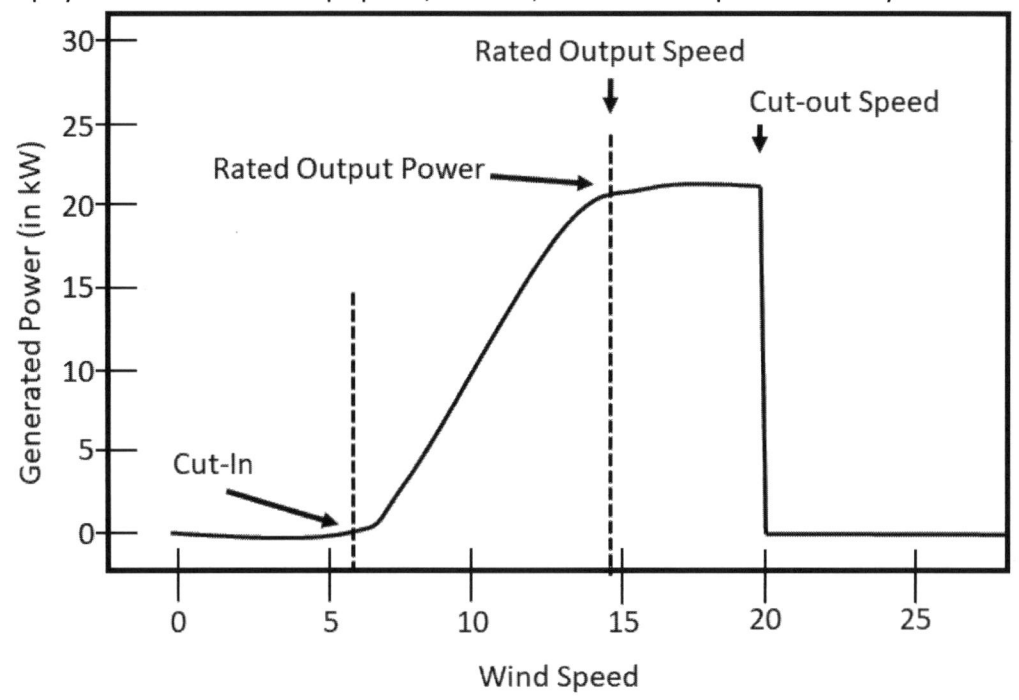

Figure 25: Wind Curve Power Chart

The power curve will also show the peak or maximum power, which is the top of the curve, where the most power is reached. In high-wind areas, it is fine if this peak is at a higher velocity, say 25-mph, because you might be interested in producing high amounts of power at or near the maximum wind speed. These are often between 20- and 40-mph. In areas with lower speed winds, you will want a low cut-in wind speed, and you want power to peak rapidly, at 20-mph or below. You will also want to make note of the rated speed on your power curve. The rated speed is the speed at which the turbine is advertised to produce at. For example, a 1 kw rated turbine will produce one kilowatt at a speed of 25-mph. Another manufacturer may also rate their machine at 1 kw, but at a speed of 30-mph. Obviously the 25-mph rating is going to produce more at lower air speeds. So, remember, when shopping for wind turbines, compare the power curve ratings! It is probably a good idea to print them out so that you can look at them side-by-side.

When choosing a generator, you should also know that, unlike solar panels, wind generators need to have somewhere to put the excess electricity that they generate. Once your batteries are full, you will need to have a "dump load," that takes over for excess energy. At our house, we simply use the hot water tank as a dump load, with excess current automatically going to heat the water. Some generators have a brake installed, just like the brake on your car. In the case that your batteries are full, the wind generator automatically applies the brake, and then you no longer need the dump load. I would strongly recommend against purchasing one of these models because the brake will eventually wear out and it is nearly impossible to replace. When this happens, the excess electricity will then burn out the motor in your generator or cook your batteries. One advantage to wind generators with such a brake is that they often can be used to charge your batteries without an additional charge controller, because the brake and the generator control the voltage. Without a brake, a charge controller will add to your upfront cost, but it will likely save you money in the long run when you don't have to replace the brake. Other wind turbines have a "yaw" or tail that automatically furls, preventing the turbine from catching too much wind, meaning that it folds to protect the turbine. This type of setup will still often rely on a charge controller and is much less likely to break. The charge controller is just like the charge controller for solar, which is discussed a few sections below.

Towers

One way to compensate for trees or less than ideal terrain is to build a taller tower. The type and height of a tower can make a big difference on the price, performance, and ease of maintenance of your wind generator. Residential size wind towers range from 60 to 120 feet tall. Anything less than this and you may find yourself with an expensive lawn ornament. This is an area where many people try to cut corners but building the proper-sized tower will make the difference between the success or failure of your wind generator. Some homeowners will attempt to save power by mounting the tower to their roof or the side of the house. This almost never works because the high amount of torque and movement on your tower can cause damage to the home over time, and also can create strange vibrating and buzzing sounds in your home, like, "did a helicopter just land on the house or is Sasquatch eating the roof shingles?"

While it is tempting to save money simply by building a shorter tower, a taller tower will pay you back with higher production. In general, compared to a 60-foot tower, an 80-foot tower will give you 20% more electricity, and a 100-foot tower will produce 30% more electricity. That 20 or 30 percent increase may not sound like a big deal, but it can make the difference between year-round refrigeration capability, or intermittent refrigeration and spoiled food. In areas where there are trees or other obstructions, then a 100-foot tower may be necessary just to get the blades to start turning smoothly.

There are two main types of towers, free-standing and guy wired. Free standing towers are much more expensive, difficult to maintain, and more difficult to install. For homesteaders, I strongly recommend a guy-wired tower. A guy wired tower can have a pipe in the center, or a lattice. A pipe center is fine for smaller turbines, under 1kw. Anything over 1kw will mean added weight, and so a lattice tower is recommended for these. You will need to pour concrete under the base of your tower to support the weight and three more pads for the three anchor points of your guy wires. As a general rule, I recommend a 3x3 foot cube of concrete from ground level down 3 feet deep below a tower that is 1-kw or less. A 4-kw turbine and above, or a tower over 70 feet tall will need to have a 4x4x4 feet foundation, and a 10kw turbine or a tower over 90 feet tall should have 6x6x6 feet foundation. Similarly, all three of the guy wires for your towers will need to be anchored in concrete. For a 60-foot wind turbine, your anchor should be 2x2x2 feet of concrete. An 80-foot tower should use a 3x3x3 anchor, and a 100 foot tower should use a 4x4x4 concrete foundation. In loose sandy or gravelly soil, add 50% to all these measurements. A cage made of rebar spaced at 1-foot intervals will ensure that the anchors hold in even the worst weather. I have used a jackhammer to create these anchor holes in rocky areas and while difficult, it is absolutely necessary. Nothing could be deadlier and harder on your wallet than a 100-foot tower with a wind turbine crashing to the ground, or worse, on top of your home.

Guy Wires and Erecting the Tower

Guy wires should be a minimum of ¼ inch thick EHS (extra high strength) steel cable for a tower up to 100 feet and a turbine rated for up to 3 kw. A high strength turnbuckle should be fastened at the end of every cable near ground level so minor adjustments can be made to tighten the cable. The anchor should also be made of EHS steel embedded in the concrete.

When erecting the tower, consider how you will conduct maintenance later. It is possible to erect a tower using a crane, which can cost between $500 and $2000 for the day. This is safer and easier, but you should also consider maintenance. If you are using a guyed lattice tower, it is possible to climb the tower, albeit with considerable effort, in order to service the turbine. With a pipe tower, you will not be able to climb up the pole to conduct maintenance, unless you are an exceptionally talented acrobat, or some kind of gifted dancer. But for the rest of us, I highly recommend a tilt up tower. These types of towers are fitted with a hinge, at or close to ground level, that allows you to tilt the tower up or down for maintenance, with the use of a hand-cranked winch.

Tilt-up tower kits are readily available, and I do not recommend trying to fabricate one yourself. To erect the tower, you will just need to pour the concrete pad according to the previously mentioned specifications and use the recommended anchor bolts to affix your tilt-up kit to the pad. Guy wires on two sides need to be measured and attached to the pole or lattice prior to tilting the tower up. The wind turbine will then need to be attached, making sure not to damage the blades while it is on the ground. The best way to do this is to have a permanent on-ground mount in place in the spot where the turbine will rest every time that it is lowered. This mount should be in the form of two U-shaped brackets upon which the pole can rest, right below the turbine. Finally, with all wires attached, the turbine is lifted in to place by tightening the cables on the third side by using a hand-crank or motorized winch. A hand-crank winch sounds simple enough, but a tower over 40 feet tall requires a large amount of force to be erected, making a motorized winch a good idea. Alternatively, a tractor or even draft horses can be used to pull the tower up but be ready to affix a cable loop to your anchor immediately so that you don't lose control of the tower after it is erected. This can kill you faster than almost anything in this book, so do this job at your own risk.

In the case that you choose to erect a lattice tower that is not tilt-up, then you will need a crane for the initial installation and erection of the turbine and the tower. It is not possible to get a larger-sized turbine to the top of a tower without the use of a crane. While you can perform routine checks and maintenance by climbing such a tower, you will have to have the assistance of a crane to replace or to do serious repairs on the wind turbine. I know, many of you are probably thinking, "Yeah right, I'm smart enough to figure out how to get that thing down without a crane." Well, go for it! It is going to burn in like a Blackhawk helicopter going down, so stay safe and don't end up as chopped suey! Once you have installed your wind turbine, check out the charge controller section of the book.

Hydro-Electricity and Micro-Hydro

While wind and solar power are great, I always tell people that are thinking of purchasing an off grid homesite to consider making clean, flowing water their number one priority. Because of the mass and flowing nature of water, there is more potential energy in water than in wind, and unlike solar or wind power, many water sources flow 24/7, 365 days per year. Micro-hydroelectricity systems not only produce dependable power, but they do so at a lower cost than other renewable energy sources. While most wind turbines have blades that are measured in feet, micro-hydro blades are generally just a few inches long. In addition, a 200-watt micro-hydro generator in 24 hours will produce the same amount that it takes a 200-watt solar panel to produce in 4 or 5 days of average sun with no cloudy days! The key to proper development of a hydroelectric water source includes maximizing the head, or elevation of your water source, protecting your system from floods, and preventing debris from clogging your system.

Maximizing the head for your water source means that you want to utilize a combination of water flow (volume over time) with head (elevation of water column) to maximize your power production. A micro-hydro system will be rated for a certain flow, which is measured in gallons per minute, and it should have a power curve chart, just like a wind generator. The power curve chart for a micro-hydro system will be based on head (in feet or meters), and flow (in gallons per minute). It is important to analyze this chart and compare it to your specific situation before purchasing a micro-hydro generator.

Analyzing your Water Energy Potential

Water energy potential is a result of multiplying head times flow. Head is simply the difference in height between where your water where it enters the flow pipe and where your hydro generator is. It only includes the closed pipe distance, not any open water or waterfalls above the pipe. Flow is simply a measure of water in gallons per minute. To find the flow, just put a 5-gallon bucket at the bottom of your flow pipe. If it takes one minute to fill, then the flow is 5 gallons per minute (gpm). If it takes 10 seconds, then you have a flow of 30 gallons per minute. (60 seconds per minute divided by 10 seconds multiplied by 5 gallons equals 30 gallons per minute)

Once you have this information, you can plug it into this simple equation: [head (feet) × flow (gpm)] ÷ 10 = Watts per hour. This simple calculation is for a basic micro-hydro generator with a 53% energy efficiency, which is about average. There is also some friction loss from the pipe that is not in the calculation, but this will not be significant as long as you don't use a tiny pipe that restricts the flow too much. I recommend using at least a 2-inch pipe for most single residence applications with over 10 feet of head.

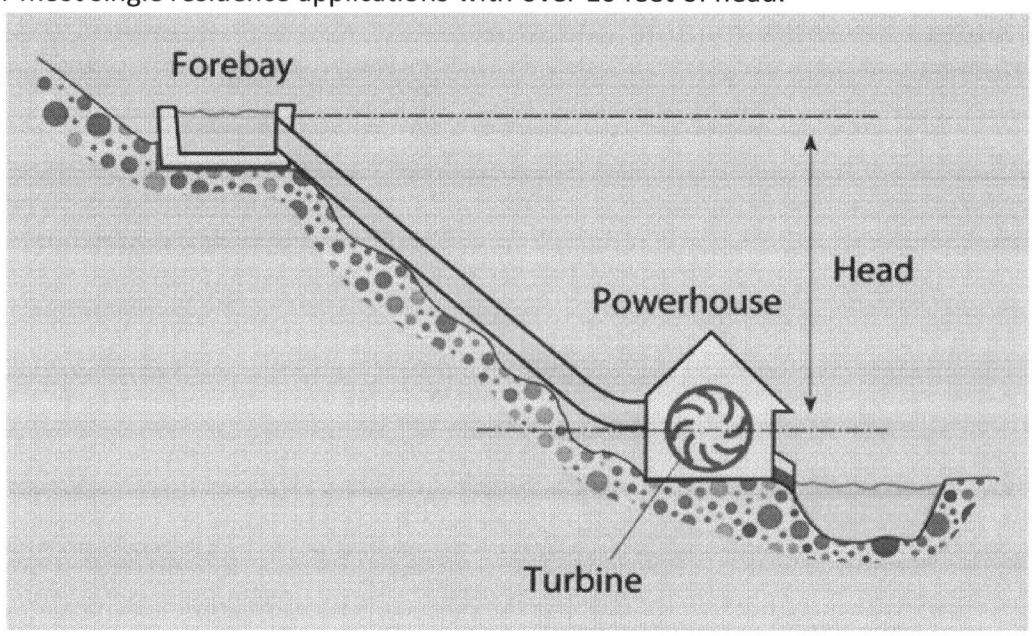

Figure 26: Simplified Hydro Setup, the pipe from the Forebay can also be Vertical and the Turbine in the Powerhouse can be turned Horizontal, and many more configurations are possible, this one from: www.energy.gov/energysaver/planning-microhydropower-system

When evaluating the energy-production potential at your micro-hydro site, keep in mind that the greater the head, the less flow of water you need. This lower flow of water is the reason that a smaller, less expensive micro-hydro generator can be used on a site with greater head. Any site that has less than 10 feet of head is considered a "low head, low energy" site, and may not be suitable to provide all the energy requirements for a single home.

To determine the head on your site, there are three basic methods that can be used. On a site where there is a great distance between your water intake and your generator, you can get a rough idea of the head by looking at the elevation lines on a USGS map. You can also use an aircraft altimeter to measure head by taking a reading both at the top and the bottom of your potential micro-hydro site. Finally, if you are not measuring over great distances, you can also use the hose method. You will need two people and a 30-foot length of hose with a funnel on one end. Have one person stand upstream to funnel the water into the hose. The other person will stand downstream and lift the other end of the hose up in the air. Then measure the height above the stream where the downstream end starts to overflow. This height is your head. You can then repeat the process with the upstream funnel now being located where the downstream measurement was taken. Measure the head again and again and add up the total head until you reach your hydro generator site downstream.

Once you have determined your head, then you can also take your flow in gallons per minute that you learned by doing the bucket test. So, if you have a head of 50 feet times a flow of 200 gallons per minute, that is 10,000, then divide by the constant of 10 and you come up with 1000 watts in an hour, which will produce 24,000 watts in 24 hours. This is a very sizeable amount of electricity that should be sufficient for any individual homestead. 300 watts of power per hour for 24 hours a day is about the minimum required to run an extremely efficient single family off-grid home. These parameters should give you an idea of the size of the Micro-Hydro generator that you should purchase.

Choosing a Micro-Hydro System

When selecting a Micro-hydro power generator, you need to already have surveyed the site where it will be located, and you need to know the flow, the head, and the distance that the water will travel as well as what obstacles might be in the path. Some generators are designed for low head with high flow, while others are more ideal for high head with low flow. There are still other "mini" hydro setups that are more designed just to charge your computer or turn on a light bulb. You will need to be sure to match your choice with the proper rate of flow and head that applies to your situation.

Once you have determined the above size specifications that you need, you then need to match the voltage of the hydro generator with the battery bank that you will be using. The battery bank specifications have already been discussed in the preceding section on batteries. A good micro-hydro generator will not need a charge controller but will instead automatically come with an output to charge 12-, 24-, or 48-volt batteries. This way you can just hook directly into batteries, with proper fuse protection of course. After the batteries, an inverter will still be needed as outlined two sections below, to convert the DC power into AC power.

Finally, when considering which generator to purchase, you need to check the durability and size of the nozzles and fittings that come with your prospective micro hydro generators. I recommend stainless steel turbine wheels and brass nozzle inserts for your water connections.

Installation Basics

While there are many types of micro-hydro systems, I will describe installation for one of the most basic, which is also likely the most practical for the majority of homesteads. This is a simple horizontal turbine style, which can normally be placed in a box no more than 2 feet square and coupled with 2-inch pipe. For this size example this type of system will comprise of a water line that drops 150 feet and fills 20 gallons per minute, all through the 2-inch pipe, producing 300 watts per hour. (150x20÷10=300)(head x flow divided by 10 equals watts produced)

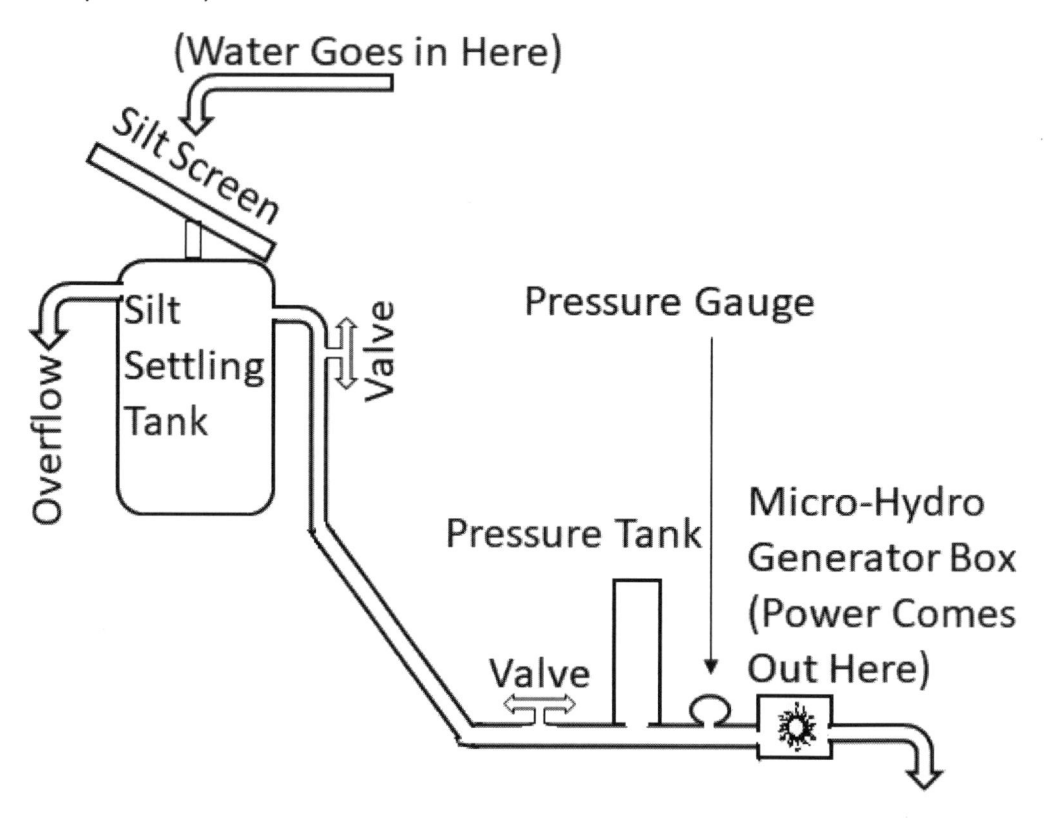

Figure 27: Example Micro-Hydro System

1. Starting from the water source and moving downward, the first step in building a basic micro hydro system is to build the screen box. This is simply a sifting box with a screen in the bottom, usually made of rot resistant wood (cedar is great). The screen is angled so that water will pass through to enter the system, but debris is caught by the screen and will be washed off to the ground.
2. Next the water goes into a silt settling tank, typically a 5-gallon plastic drum, that allows any silt that passed through the screen to settle out. You can't have it go to your turbine because it will get jammed up and break if it gets full of silt. Checking

the 5-gallon barrel annually and after big storms to make sure it gets emptied of sediment from time to time will be necessary.
3. Finally, a 2-inch pipe will be attached to the side of the barrel, about 6 inches from the top, so that it is high above the silt, but also below any floating things (like a dead rat that floats), so that it will only allow clean water to pass down the two-inch pipe.
4. Next the penstock pipe, the pipe going from the silt tank to the micro-hydro turbine, can be emplaced. Remember if you are going for 150 feet of head, this is only the vertical drop that you need to achieve. Unless you are going straight down, you will need much more than 150 feet of pipe to go down a long slope until it drops by 150 feet of elevation as measured by an altimeter or your chosen method of measurement. This long distance is why I recommend using HDPE (poly-pipe), which comes in long rolls that are more economical than most other types of pipes, and because it comes in a roll, you minimize the couplings that are needed. This pipe does come in 2-inch diameter as well which is good for the volume of water in this example. Remember that for every foot of drop, you are adding 2.31 pounds of pressure so a drop of 150 feet means that your pipe should be rated for at least 350 PSI.
5. Before you run your pipes into your micro-hydro generator box, you need to install a pressure relief tank, and a pressure gauge, which both T off from the main penstock line. The pressure gauge needs to be able to measure at least 20% above the head of your system. These water pressure gauges can simply be screwed into the main line and are useful for diagnosing any malfunctions or power outages. In fact, it should help you calculate the height of the water in your penstock, if you divide it by 2.31. This way you don't have to run all the way to the top of the mountain to check water. The Pressure relief tank should also T-off from the penstock. This tank just consists of a 4 inch PVC pipe that is capped off. It is important and serves as a buffer to prevent the water hammer effect that can shock and break your micro-hydro generator.

Illustration 65: Micro-Hydro Generator Box

6. Finally, after the penstock goes past the T's for the pressure relief tank and the pressure gauge, it is ready to go into your micro-hydro generator. Some of these are "plug and play," and you just connect the fittings to the entrance and also an exit pipe to get the exiting water a safe distance away so as not to cause erosion of the surrounding soil or corrosion of the metal parts of your system. Others may require you to plumb the entrance pipes with a nozzle spraying on to one or more sides of the turbine. In this case, the turbine will be mounted in a box that you may be required to build if not supplied, with an exit hole and fitting for water to go down the exit pipe a safe distance away.
7. Some micro-hydro are "plug and play" and have a built in charge controller so that the wires can go directly to your batteries (through fuses), but if the wires need to go to a charge controller, this is the same as for solar power and the rest of the system is described below.

Charge Controllers

Now that you have planned for your power source, it is time to discuss charge controllers. When electricity comes from a source such as solar panels, wind generators, or a micro-hydro generator, the voltages will not normally be conducive to charging your battery bank, or even to use on your household lights and appliances. Even a wind turbine or solar panel that is meant to be directly connected to your batteries must have a built-in charge controller. In order to properly maintain a battery bank and prevent appliance melt-down, it is very important to invest in a quality charge controller, or even multiple charge controllers if your off-grid system is large.

This is also the time to decide what voltage your off-grid system should be, so that you will be able to set up your charge controllers properly. Battery banks are generally set up with a nominal voltage of 12, 24, 48, 60, or 72 volts. Anything higher than this can get very dangerous. DC power will not shock you at low voltages, but at higher voltages, it will grab onto you harder than AC current. The higher the voltage of your battery bank, the more charge you can achieve with just one charge controller, meaning that you can use fewer charge controllers. A lower voltage bank will take more charge controllers to charge an equal amount of watts, because each charge controller is limited by amps (volts x amps = watts). Again, remember that charge controllers as well as associated wiring, circuits, and other components, are limited by amps, but not volts. The higher the volts, the lower the amps given the same power in watts. For example, it is common for a charge controller to be limited to a 30-amp charge but to be capable of charging a battery bank of anywhere from 12 to 72 volts. Remember again, that your total power (watts) is found by multiplying amps times volts (amps x volts = watts); this is all on a "per-hour" basis. This means that the above charge controller can put only 360 watts (12 volts x 30 amps) into a nominal 12-volt battery bank, but it can put 1800 watts (60 volts x 30 amps) into a nominal 60-volt battery bank, which is 5 times as much power for the exact same charge controller. A good charge controller will run you in excess of $300 so it seems that it would make sense to use as few as possible and therefore go with a high voltage battery bank, however this is not always the right choice.

Voltage of Battery Bank	Desired Watts of Charging Power per hour	Amp Capacity of Charge Controller	Number of Charge Controllers Required
12	1800	30	5
24	1800	30	3
48	1800	30	2
72	1800	30	1

Table 5: How Many Charge Controllers do you need? This is found by Dividing Desired Watts by amps and by voltage, then rounding up to the nearest whole number.

While you save money on charge controllers by going with a higher voltage battery bank, there is a big downside. Remember, in my discussion of batteries, that I mentioned using 12-volt lighting, refrigeration, fans, etc. There are many, many 12-volt appliances and there are also some appliance options for a 24-volt battery bank, but very little above that voltage. So, if you are like me and want to run a bunch of low voltage DC appliances, then you can simply achieve the same charging potential as a higher voltage system by buying more charge controllers. In the above example, if you wanted to stay with a 12-volt system, where each charge controller is limited to 30 amps, you would need 5 charge controllers to achieve the 1800 watts that could be achieved with just one charge controller in a 60 volt system (12 volts x 30 amps x 5 controllers = 1800 watts). Why on Earth would anyone want to spend $1500 on 5 charge controllers when you could just buy one charge controller for $300? The reason is that it is desirable to use low voltage DC appliances due to the inefficient and high maintenance nature of power inversion. Next, I will elaborate on this and explain how inverters and power inversion work.

Inverters

"What is power inversion?" you ask. Power inversion is a process necessary to convert battery power, which is direct current (DC), into alternating current (AC). Direct current gives a one-directional flow of electron activity at a steady rate, where alternating current provides a flow which switches polarity 120 times per second at 60-hertz, creating a charge which resembles a sign wave. In the United States, AC currents are around 115 volts. Converting DC battery power to AC power is not a simple process, and it has to be done while electrical loads shift and change as you use appliances, turn up the power, turn it off and constantly change the demand placed on your inverter. For this reason, you may easily expect to lose about 10% of your electrical production, just through the inefficiency of power inversion. This inefficiency is the first reason to run important lighting and appliances on DC power.

The second reason is that power inverters are perhaps the most temperamental of all the components in your off-grid electrical system. This is because they work so hard trying to keep shifting to accommodate the varying electrical needs in the average home. If your inverter breaks and you have no DC power back-up, then you are out of luck until you can get it fixed. If replacement or repair is not possible, then instead of solar panels, you just have some shiny roof ornaments. While I would expect a charge controller and other components to last over 10 years, and solar panels to last a lifetime, I really am happy to get 5 years out of a power inverter, because they are more temperamental and usually overworked.

Therefore, if really preparing for long term disasters is your goal, I recommend running as many lights, appliances, and other necessities off of your DC battery power, without a temperamental inverter in the middle. Twelve-volt lighting is readily available in any hardware or home improvement store, and there are many practical and attractive choices. Fans and other things like 12-volt laptop adapters are also available. There are some excellent 12-volt refrigerators and freezers on the market, which meet very high standards of efficiency as well. Many of these can be found at RV stores or outlets that sell appliances for marine applications. While there are slightly fewer options available for 24-volt lighting and appliances, this is an option that can cut the number of charge controllers needed in half.

Illustration 66: An inverter converts DC battery power to standard AC power for your normal outlets. This one has DC wires coming in from the batteries, AC going out to the home outlets, and there is another AC wire going into the top so you can use it as a charger to charge batteries as needed. Fuses are also needed.

It is still nice to have a power inverter for power tools, washing machines, and kitchen appliances that only come in 115-volt AC power. Just keep in mind that when, not if your inverter breaks, you will either rely on a generator, or be out of luck with these modern conveniences until you can replace or repair the inverter. Purchasing at least one back up inverter is also an option. Being off-grid, I do not aspire to own anything that consumes 220-volts at a time, although a more robust and expensive inverter can do that too.

It is now very common to find an inverter that will also charge your batteries when you need to use a fossil-fuel-based electrical generator to make-up for too many cloudy days (solar) or days without wind (wind power). You simply hook the AC wires from your generator into the AC input terminals of your power inverter and the inverter will automatically sense the incoming power and use it to charge your batteries. Some generators even come with a sensor that will turn the generator on automatically when batteries are low. My recommendation is to not spend too much on a generator, but instead use that money to buy more solar panels or invest in wind power. This way you don't become overly reliant on fossil fuels, a commodity that can suffer from supply shortages.

Solar Hot Water Heating

There are few luxuries in off-grid life that are as easily attained as hot water. In modern life, we look at hot water as a human right, but the cost in terms of energy can be incredibly high. Typical electric coil water heaters with large tanks often consume 1/3 of the total electricity used by most households. This translates into anywhere from 10kw to 30kw per day depending on your tank size and usage. Tankless water heaters typically use only 10-20 percent of this amount, making them an incredibly efficient alternative. But living off-grid means that you must really think outside of the box when designing your homestead and its energy sources. Tankless water heaters are a great alternative, but they still use either large boosts of electricity or some amount of propane for their heat source. I have visited many other countries that lack these resources and have seen some incredible and ingenious alternatives.

This reminds me of a fun story that I promise will lead back to hot water, so bear with me. I was stationed in Italy when I met my beautiful Italian wife, and we thought, why not honeymoon in the neighboring country of Greece! We found a great deal on a honeymoon package to the island of Crete, and we were on our way. Before I left, I called the CQ (admin) desk at my company headquarters in Italy. My good friend Jimenez was manning the CQ desk, and I asked him to sign me out on leave. I had pulled him out of hot water a few times, so he was happy to sign me out and save me from having to make another trip back on to base. But before I could hang up, Jimenez, in his thick Puerto Rican accent, says, "Wait just a secon' you sonabeech! I'n going to pay you back for the last time jou help me out. I'n going to reep up this damn leave form so jou don't geet charged any leave. Hoppy honeymoon!" " Wait a second," I protested "you are going to get me in hot water and I won't have a…" "Too late!" yelled Jimenez over the phone "Deed you hear that noise, I yust reeped it in half, have a great tine wit your new wifey!"

I was always nervous about breaking rules and risking getting into "hot water", but in just 3 hours, we had taken a quick flight across the Adriatic Sea, and we were checking in to the Royal Knossos Village in Crete. It was awesome, with a view of the Mediterranean, two pools out front, slippers, bathrobes, and our own balcony. This brings me back to the point of my long drawn-out story, hot water. As I prepared for my long hot shower to get relaxed after being stressed out by the situation with Jimenez, from my balcony, I noticed a large tank on top of every bungalow in the village. "What the heck? What are all those ridiculous black tanks on top of the bungalows?" My new wife was like, "Really, here we are at the Knossos Royal Village, with our beautiful view, plush slippers, embroidered robes, big bed, etc., and there you are wondering about the plumbing on the roof tops!" Okay, so I didn't want to get in hot water with the new wifey, so I put it aside for the rest of the day.

But the next day, riding in a tour bus through the hot dry countryside of Crete, I noticed that every single household had a black tank on the roof. I couldn't wait to get back to the hotel to investigate our own rooftop. My new wife just stared in awe as I ran around the back of our vacation bungalow and climbed straight up the roof access ladder with the sign that said, "authorized personnel only." When I got to the top, I walked straight across the flat roof and put my hand on the black surface of the 55-gallon drum. "Ouch!" It was about 225 degrees! Just as I suspected, at the bottom of the tank was a copper inlet tube and at the top of the tank an outlet tube. The bottom tube was cool to the touch because it was the cold water while the tube coming out the top was hot water and was hot enough to burn your skin. I realized that the entire island of Crete was not paying 1/3 of their electricity costs towards the hot water tank, like Americans do. Pretty smart Cretans! In fact, they were not even burning fossil fuels. In Crete, this is easy, because the temperature is never low enough to freeze the plumbing. They can directly heat the water and with their flat roofs, they can use gravity to run the water into their homes. After this realization, I was finally able to get back to our honeymoon vacation and stay out of hot water for the rest of the trip.

     Several years later, my wife and I were still in the honeymoon phase of our marriage, of course, but we had decided to move off-grid. I remembered the hot water lesson that I had learned in Crete. Unfortunately, we had not chosen a tropical or Mediterranean paradise to build our off-grid homestead, so freezing temps would have to be a consideration. I was on a budget, so I quickly eliminated the idea of spending $8,000 on an evacuated tube system. These types of systems use a form of alcohol that is run through the outdoor tubes and cannot freeze. Heat from this alcohol is piped inside to a tank that has a heat exchanger attached to it. The heat exchanger transfers the heat to the water tank and then it is usable. For me, a simpler system is more desirable. The $8,000 system is not only pricey, but there are several things that can break; the glass vacuum tubes, the water pump, and the heat transfer device. Instead, I set out to design a tank that was more like the Cretan system.

     It only took me a couple of days to install an outdoor thermosiphon solar water heater with a cold weather drain valve. In my chapter on heating the home and wood stoves, I discussed our wood stove thermosiphon system for heating water during cold weather. This thermosiphon is similar, but because the water pipe goes directly outside, you must have a valve to shut the water flow off from the inside, and another valve to drain the water out from the very bottom pipe in your outdoor system. This thermosiphon, just like the one for the woodstove, has a pipe that comes out of the bottom of your indoor tank, goes through the wall and into the solar water heater. The hot water then rises to the top of the solar water heater and goes through another pipe and then through the wall and into the top of your hot water tank. It is important that your solar heater be at about the same height or slightly lower than your indoor water tank so that the hot water will naturally flow to the right spot when it is heated, thus avoiding the need for a pump. The solar water heater itself is simply a series of dark-colored pipes that collect solar heat and allow the hot water to rise and go back into the water tank. These pipes should be placed in a flat box of some sort that is closed by plexi-glass which will allow the sun to shine in but does not allow the heat to escape.

This system works great for temperate climates as long as you install a good drain valve that is at the lowest point in the system and therefore allows all of the water to be drained before any freezing weather strikes. At our homestead, we use it with the same tank as our woodstove thermosiphon water heater; two systems, two sets of pipes, one tank. The tank that we use is an old used propane water heater that was cheap to buy and already comes with the inlet and outlet threaded pipe fittings that we needed to put in the pipes from the new systems. You can also use propane on this type of tank for a backup and a third option. With propane you have one tank with three sources of heat for your hot water. If you install shut off valves for your stove water and your solar water, and one heat source breaks, then you can easily switch to an alternate source. With a solar water heater, you can ensure that your family always has free hot water in any emergency or grid-down situation, and this will surely keep you out of hot water with the wifey!

Chapter 12: Transportation

      During the Global War on Terrorism, the United States Military found that we were no longer conducting training missions where there was a ready supply of fuel, electricity, or maintenance parts. Surviving amidst chaos often requires transportation, and the military had to sometimes learn very quickly how to achieve transportation, off-grid style. One of the earliest images that news reports fed back to the American public was that of special operators on horseback or even using mules to transport people, food, water, and equipment through the rugged mountains of Afghanistan. I personally have logged hundreds of miles carrying loads often in excess of 100 lbs. while serving in such "light" Infantry units. They should call it heavy AF Infantry instead of light. As resources become scarce in our world and we find ourselves without cheap fuel and readily available repair parts, our need for transportation will not go away. Those who wish to survive will need to adapt and get by just as humans have in the past, and the way that they still do in many third world countries.

      When I think about third world transportation, I think about a boy named Ahmed that I once met in Iraq. For several days, my scout team was assigned to an observation post not far from an important airfield in our sector, on the outskirts of Kirkuk. Many people think of Iraq as a big sandy desert, but the area around Kirkuk is not like this at all. While there are no forests, there are abundant grasslands, and fields of grains such as wheat that reminded me of the American Midwest. At this particular observation post these dry, grassy fields gently descended from a low but sharp and rocky mountain ridge, that cut towards the sky like a jagged knife blade. A paved but heavily potholed road also wove down from the direction of the ridge, with several clusters of cinder block walls and tin shacks along the way. Many of the walls were patched with cardboard and scraps of plastic. Trash blew across the fields and dirty kids played in drainage ditches, sometimes climbing on a rusting burnt-out tank hulk to our flank. This is where I first laid eyes on Ahmed, driving a donkey that pulled his two-wheeled wooden cart to the city every morning, returning towards the ridge, normally with an empty cart in the early afternoons.

      On the sixth day of our uneventful mission, we were to extract via helicopter as potential IED's made a ground extract an undesirable choice. That morning a yellow haze hung heavy on the western horizon, and gusty winds began to kick up dust and blow all the random trash from its resting places. By early afternoon, the yellow haze had enveloped us, and we were squinting and spitting the sand grains out of our mouths. Worst of all, we received a call from HQ that helicopters were grounded and we were to exfiltrate 10 miles on foot with 500 lbs. of gear between the four of us. Just then, here comes Ahmed and his donkey cart, braving the dust storm that kept everyone else behind closed doors. Ready to go home and knowing the value of American dollars, I took a gamble and emerged from our hide to make Ahmed an offer. At first, he was not just surprised, but deathly afraid and he may even have pooped his pants a little. This quickly turned to elation when I offered him two American twenty-dollar bills for a ride on his jackass and cart. "Tank you, Tank You!," he said, even throwing in "Good Bush, Good Bush!" I tried to explain to him that it was Andrew Jackson on the Twenty-dollar bills, not George Bush, but it was lost in translation. No matter, Ahmed was grinning so hard with his new $40 smile that he must have packed 10 lbs. of sandstorm grit into the spaces between his jagged yellow teeth before we got back to base.

I expected praise for arriving back at HQ in such a timely manner but instead was told that exfiltration was to be by foot. Being naturally insubordinate, I unsuccessfully tried to convince my superiors that a jackass does indeed have feet. Despite my exasperation at the time, the lesson to be learned here is that a jackass is by far a superior mode of transportation for heavy loads than your own human feet. Evidently, it is also more dependable than a helicopter and other mechanically vulnerable means of transportation, especially in a sandstorm. In this chapter, we will discuss the merits of pack animals as transportation, as well as other grid-down carriages such as solar-powered vehicles. The importance of these survival tools cannot be overstated as hard times threaten your survival. Even if you plan to hunker down, there will come a time when you need to resupply. When this happens, the difference between an individual who thrives and one who barely survives is how fast you can move and how much your ass can carry.

Illustration 67: I'm not a fan of camels but when you need a ride you need a ride.

Pack Animals

One of the greatest things about living next to the Amish is the experience of witnessing their daily mastery of horsemanship. One of the most surreal experiences that I have experienced with the Amish was watching them mow their fields with horse-drawn sickle bars. I had taken one of my environmental science classes from the university to one of the Amish farms for a field trip. We were discussing pasture management when the Amish mowers appeared from the top of a grassy hill. The sickle bar mowers were being towed behind four teams of horses online, with four drivers. They were able to mow a swath about 35 feet wide with one pass. As they drove their teams past us, all we could hear was the hooves and heavy breathing of the horses, as well as the mowers that sounded like 4 thousand pairs of tiny scissors clipping smoothly in unison at 155 clips per minute. It has never ceased to amaze me that these Amish were using just 4 horses and 4 drivers to mow an area in the same amount of time that it would take two 125 horsepower diesel powered tractors, each with huge 16 foot mowers attached. The whole Amish setup was powered by horses, which were powered by oats and hay, created by earth, water, and sunlight. In a way, the Amish were using solar power. What a great system!

Over the years, I have picked up some knowledge of horses from the Amish, and have found that for some, horses and pack animals are a great mode of post-collapse, New Dark Age transportation. The most important lesson that I have learned is that work horses are not just a pet or a hobby, but horse living is a way of life. A horse that will work for you to plow your fields, cut your hay, and transport you and your family must be part of the family and needs to be worked with and well-cared for every day. I have seen many of our non-Amish neighbors attempt to juggle caring for horses with working a 9 to 5 job, playing sports, going on vacations, and more. To top it off, they have to then pay for expensive feed and buy expensive high-quality hay from people like me. Some of these people in my area have then had to pay the Amish to re-train their horses so that they can be manageable again. The key to the success of the Amish horse whispering is consistency. They do not have fancy vacations and hobbies and there is always someone there to get up early, feed the horses quality feed, ensure that they have good shelter, and most of all, work with them every day.

Providing high quality feed for your work animals is not easy. This is a huge task as the average size horse can easily consume 1000 lbs. of oats and 6000 lbs. of hay annually, not to mention the need for at least 3 acres of good pasture in a favorable climate. I have seen horses that were not provided adequate nutrition and believe me, it is not worth it. They become skinny, lethargic, and will certainly develop many health issues associated with poor nutrition. To raise 1000 lbs. of oats, you need to have at least ½ acre that is cultivated, fertilized, watered, and cared for. You also need the proper equipment for harvest and an adequate storage area. To Harvest 6000 lbs. of hay, I recommend allowing a minimum of 3 acres of high quality grass and legumes, that are set aside and not grazed or used for anything else. Again, you need tools for harvesting and a space to store all this hay. The Amish often hire me and other local "English" to bale hay in their fields, but almost all of them have a hay loft in their barn to put up loose hay. The loft is the ideal location because as long as they have a good roof, then the loft will keep the hay dry and way off the moist ground.

If you do not have the time to work consistently with your pack animals or if providing feed seems too daunting a task, then you may want to look into solar powered utility vehicles.

Figure 28: Electric UTV's are not your Granny's golf cart, they are 4-wheel drive and with Lithium Batteries can go 8 miles or more on a charge.   Best of all, no one will hear you coming.

Solar-Powered Utility Vehicles

A common sight in many chaotic third world countries is a young man standing on the side of the road with a jerry can of fuel for sale. This makeshift gas station seems odd to many Americans, but if you believe that you will never see a fuel shortage in your lifetime, then you may not have considered the complex process that has to occur to allow you to consume your share of America's 50 million barrel per day habit. Hydrocarbons formed over millions of years must be extracted from thousands of feet beneath the Earth's surface or the ocean, then transported to refineries that are often in areas often under threat by hurricanes, social unrest, war, or earthquakes. Then this goes on to a long and complex distribution network and pumping stations in a process that consumes as much as 50% of the energy that it produces. The idea that ethanol or biofuels are a solution to this problem is pure fantasy. There is no way we will continue to make fuel from food sources in a world of 8 billion souls going on 10 billion by the middle of this century. So, if not fossil fuel or ethanol, then what is the best mode of off-grid transport if I don't want the hassle of pack animals?

Friend, what you need is a solar-powered utility vehicle. But isn't a solar-powered vehicle a futuristic experiment still in the design stage? Not at all! On the contrary, it is a daily necessity on my farm that is even simpler and easier to maintain than a gas or diesel-powered vehicle. All you need to create such a "work horse" is an electric UTV such as the Polaris EV, a few Solar panels, a charge controller, and some basic electrical components.

The Polaris EV or similar UTV uses a 150-amp, 48-volt battery bank that is mounted beneath the seat. By taking amps x volts, we know that this gives us a 7200 watt or 7.2-kilowatt capacity. Daily, we can discharge or use 40% of these batteries, which comes to almost 3 kilowatts of usable power. To refill this in 4 hours, we need an array of solar panels to charge at 0.75 kilowatts per hour for 4 hours. Add 20% of this amount for reasonable system inefficiencies, and your solar panel array need rises to 0.90 kilowatts or 900 watts per hour. You can achieve this by adding just three x 300-watt solar panels!

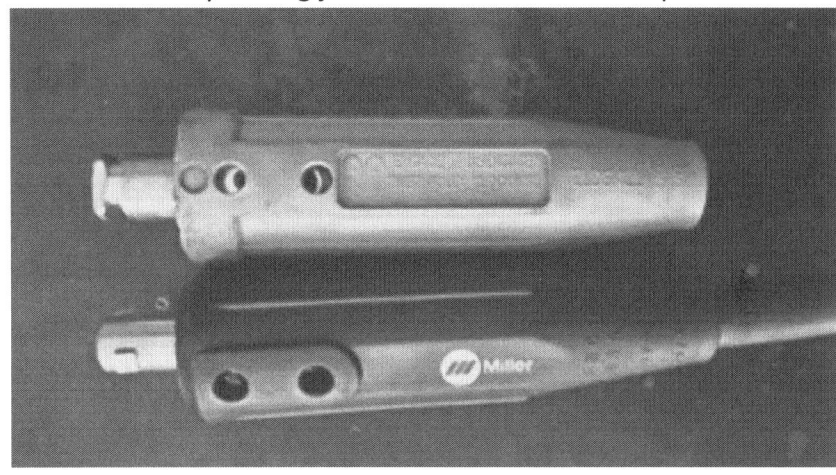

Illustration 68: Welding Cables are robust enough and can be quickly attached from the proper charge controller to the terminals of your Electric UTV batteries. It is dangerous to attach a negative to a positive!

The solar panels are simply fed into a circuit breaker box known as a combiner box. From there the wire goes into the charge controller through a final circuit breaker and on to the batteries in the UTV. There are several types of quick connects/disconnects that will work here so that you can disconnect the UTV and drive without taking the solar array with you. I like to use Welding cables because they can support a large amperage. Keep in mind that the positive and negative cables coming out of the battery bank of your vehicle must never touch each other. If they do, such a large battery bank can produce a huge arc and start a fire or burn someone severely, so do this at your own peril. I like to tape the cables together at an offset so that they cannot touch each other without removing the tape.

This way of charging your UTV batteries is actually simpler than plugging the UTV into a wall outlet. The reason is that solar panels produce the same type of direct current that batteries use for charging. When you plug a UTV into a wall outlet, the wall outlet carries alternating current, which must be transformed into direct current by the battery charger in the UTV. This process often causes the UTV charger to wear out and does not do a great job charging your batteries in comparison to a quality solar-powered charge controller.

When using a solar-powered utility vehicle, it is important to remember that the myth of unlimited resources will get you in trouble. You are now in the limited world of zero fossil fuel usage. I typically can go 5 miles on one charge, but I try to keep the speed low to save battery. There are lithium battery replacements that are made specifically for these EV's, which will get you closer to 10 miles between charges. I try to get my work done in the morning and the evening so that the vehicle can recharge through the middle of the day during peak sun hours. Also keep in mind that on cloudy, rainy days, you will just have to do your job on foot or in a gas-powered vehicle. Alternatively, you can use multiple vehicles and switch to a fresh vehicle on a cloudy day. Do not try to discharge lead acid batteries below 50% or you will damage them permanently. Lithium batteries will last longer, even from 10-15 years and they require much less maintenance.

Battery care is the most important maintenance feature of the electric utility vehicle. Many people that purchase these electric vehicles do not like them because they do not like or do not understand how to take care of the $1500 battery bank. These batteries should be checked monthly with heavy usage, and bimonthly with light usage. If using lead acid, the batteries should be topped off to the recommended fill level at this time and the water should never reach below the lead plates on the top part of the battery. Only distilled water should be used to top off your batteries, never use a highly mineralized water source such as well water as it will cause the batteries to wear out much faster than normal. If you take good care of lead acid batteries, they should last for at least 5 years. It is also important to clean the batteries when they are inspected to prevent corrosion or other electrical shorts. Battery cleaner spray as well as battery protectant sprays can normally be found at your local auto parts store.

Chapter 13: Security

Normal people do not consider security when purchasing or building a house. They are relying on the rule of law to protect them forever, and I hope it does. But if you are reading this book, you are probably not one of those normal people. You have come to realize that even security cannot be taken for granted. An appreciation of history or some global awareness is all one really needs to realize that good law enforcement is a luxury that we have come to take for granted. Individuals are ultimately responsible for their own security, which is one reason why in the U.S. we have the second amendment. Self-protection and security were critical for three hundred years on the American frontier and it is still like that in many parts of the world.

I remember standing by without adequate orders after the invasion of Iraq in 2003. Truckloads of armed men were looting and stealing everything that wasn't tied down, even toilets. Scores of families were evicted from their homes by force, and for revenge. After seeing this, if normal means leaving security completely up to someone else, then I want no part of normal. Humans can be totally wretched; it is a fact of human nature.

Normalcy bias occurs when we are limited in our view of what is normal by relying solely upon our own experience. Normal Americans or Western Europeans have grown up in prosperous times, where there were enough resources to go around for everyone. It has been seen as unfair that anyone should go unfed, or even without a cell phone. We think it's normal. In my military experience serving in undeveloped countries on four different continents, I have seen perspectives which change my view of what normal is. I've seen African children beaten for trying to shine a foreigner's boots, Iraqi women smacked in the head for looking up at a convoy of trucks, and entire families in the Balkans evicted from their homes because their side lost. Force in many countries is not wielded by those with the law on their side; the powers in control have no interest in moral superiority or standing up for what is right. Instead, these countries are ruled by those who have the might, the will, and the cruelty to dominate others by force, and those at the bottom get little pity and no help. This is not just a story or a legend from the past, it is a reality in many countries around the world.

With the current deterioration of morality, disdain for western values, logic, and economic freefall, it seems clear that the American normal will soon give way to a different kind of normal, the kind that is now only seen in the undeveloped world. Victims will no longer get help and protection, and instead those who victimize others will benefit the most. This will put Americans into one of three categories; the victims, the victimizers, and the self-sufficient.

Those that are self-sufficient will need a security plan to keep themselves out of the victim category. If this seems strange to you, go visit Mali, Burma, Syria, Kosovo, El Salvador, or any other poor third world country. If it can happen to them, then it can happen to you, so prepare yourself now. I've been there and I can show you how it's done.

Rules of Engagement and When to Shoot
A Few Scenarios

In a military conflict, commanders try to make it easy for military personnel to decide when to pull the trigger. They use rules of engagement to make it known that you may shoot anyone with a certain uniform, anyone that is dressed as an armed civilian, or on the other extreme, the rules may state that you may only shoot after being shot at. Things are far murkier when it comes to dealing with an insurgency, surviving in a failed state, or even in a dysfunctional country. In these types of situations, you can count on civilians being armed, loyalties are often unknown, and people purposefully hide their intentions from one another. It is a shadowy world and there are several scenarios to consider.

All these problems are compounded by a failing or ineffective state apparatus. At times, it would be better to be in a totally failed state because a totally failed state will not send corrupt law enforcement or para-military forces to extort money or lock you and your loved ones up for attempting to defend yourself. I often stop law enforcement to thank them and let them know that they are actually what is keeping our country in the first world, the thin blue line between us and chaos. It is real and it is important. As soon a country's law enforcement begins to ask for bribes, exact vengeance, become partisan, or become otherwise corrupt, then this country has begun to slip into a failing state. Time spent in a failed state is much like being in purgatory; you think you don't care which way you are going; you just want to get out. Even going from a failing state to a completely failed state is better because in a completely failed state, even though the bad guys can still get you, at least you won't be locked up for trying to defend yourself. In a failed state, the original hierarchy has fallen away to expose the underlying order at the small community and neighborhood level. This implies that a failed state will not necessarily lead to anarchy. Instead, it will lead to a hierarchy that is much closer to home. In this type of hierarchy, for better or for worse, you may be just a few doors down from your new leader. This is what I have seen in failed states around the world; the person in charge is a local power broker, a warlord, a gang leader, or a tribal elder, and they are always backed up by armed young men.

An important right is the ability to defend oneself, to bear arms for the specified purpose of self-defense. One sure sign of a failing, or dysfunctional state is the mass confiscation of firearms. Most successful states do not feel threatened enough to spontaneously round up arms and armed citizens because they are secure in their authority and ability to deal with crime. I'm specifically referring to mass round-ups, not introducing reasonable regulation. A failing state is almost like an insecure person, thrashing about at suspected and unseen enemies. Unfortunately, it is also in such a dysfunctional state that arming oneself becomes very necessary, often when it becomes illegal at the same time. The problem is that the state apparatus, law enforcement, etc., generally lacks the intelligence to distinguish between armed citizens that wish to defend themselves, and those that wish to prey upon others, and this can be a difficult distinction to make.

I witnessed just such an example while serving in northern Iraq, in an area where Kurds, Sunni Arabs, Turkmen, and Assyrian Christians all co-existed, in a situation that could never be called "harmony." Everyone was armed, and the highly dysfunctional new Iraqi government was attempting to re-assert itself. We had been operating around a medium sized town where Kurdish fighters known as Peshmerga (translates to "those who face death") had whipped other ethnic groups into submission. Their leadership had even managed to stop the fighters from stealing, extorting money, and most types of intimidation. As I mentioned, the Iraqi government was trying to re-assert itself, and decided to setup a government checkpoint just north of our town, manned by soldiers from the southern, Shiite areas. Naturally, one of the first orders of business was to conduct a raid on the Kurdish base of operations, to disarm the Peshmerga. With American mediation, it went off fairly peacefully, with just a small amount of gunfire.

But, as I mentioned, this was in a dysfunctional state. Resources and prerogatives dictated that the Iraqi Army would move on. As soon as the Army was gone, Kurdish Peshmerga were immediately attacked, and several individuals were murdered by Sunnis seeking vengeance. The Peshmerga were run out of town along with several large Kurdish families. Assyrian Christians and Turkmen were the next targets to be murdered and run out of town. The area later became a base of operations for insurgents and Ansar al Islam, the predecessor to Al Qaeda in Iraq, even later becoming ISIS. This example demonstrates the mechanics of why a failing state continues to fail. Local hierarchies are often undermined and even disarmed for the sake of asserting higher government power. When the higher government fails to deliver security or anything else, a dark, shadowy power apparatus often emerges. Unfortunately, this more sinister apparatus is often very adept at concealing and smuggling their weapons, so they don't care about government efforts to disarm them. A dysfunctional government will often fail to disarm the most dangerous elements in society, while the more benign or even benevolent local forces will be forced to submit and disarm at the government's request, leaving them to easily fall prey to or join the shadow powers.

So, the lesson to be learned is that when you find yourself in a country which is becoming a failing state remember the scripture, "the meek shall inherit the Earth." This does not mean to be a big meek bunny rabbit. That would be pathetic. Instead, be a quiet, powerful, but meek Grizzly bear, quietly going about his business. Do not roar and loudly proclaim that you are the new "big man on campus," because at this point, even a failing state is more powerful than you. By all means, arm yourself, protect yourself, and build friends and allies in your neighborhood and local area. But you need to be discreet above all else, and do not make yourself a target. If you hang a big flag that says, "Come and Take It!"

for all to see, then it is likely that someone tougher than you will actually come and take your stuff. Instead, let's discuss some rules for discreet behavior, keeping a low profile, and your rules of engagement that tell you when to use deadly force.

Escalation of Force Starts with Discreet Behavior

Rules of engagement are often centered on escalation of force. As a soldier, I remember being told how to escalate force properly. If you get a hard stare, stare back even harder. If someone throws a rock, you may throw a rock back, and put a round in your chamber. If someone points a weapon, put them down. I like to have an escalation of force plan, but I like to back it up a few steps. I think that real escalation of force starts with discreet behavior. If you are very discreet, and no one notices you in the first place, then you will not have to use force.

First, be Invisible

This is the real first step in the "escalation of force." In some parts of the United States, or the world for that matter, it is quite easy to get off the beaten path. In the Yukon, in the Mojave Desert, or in Greenland, it is quite easy to find a place where you are extremely unlikely to be found. The question then becomes, "How long can you survive in such a place?" With an unlimited budget, you can certainly put away years of food in a bunker in one of these locations. You might even develop a unique set of survival skills to survive in such a location. But the fact remains, these are desolate locations, where survival is difficult, and most people are not cut out for such an existence.

In other areas of the world, mainly in rural mountainous areas such as the Southern Rocky Mountains, the Ozarks, or even the elevations of the Andes Mountains, cultures have survived and even thrived, for centuries. The Anasazi, the Inca, and the ancient mound-builders flourished in areas that are now considered remote. These are the general type of "off-the-beaten path" locations that will allow you to produce food as well as blend into your surroundings and avoid confrontation. More specifically, your homestead location should be located, in military terminology, away from "Avenues of Approach," and "Key Terrain." If you can see a road from your homestead, people on that road can see you too. If you build your homestead within view of a river, expect visitors. In desperate times, expect hungry and even uncivilized visitors. Other key terrain would include bridges, important food sources, or a key mountain pass. Stay away from all of these places, and anywhere that attracts other people.

Shaping Your Homestead Location

The security plan starts when choosing a location or terrain for your homestead. My time as a Ranger Instructor was a great lesson in examining terrain for security purposes. As a mountain phase instructor, we devoted a lot of time to analyzing all types of complex terrain for offensive, defensive, and reconnaissance purposes. Your homestead retreat is where you plan to provide for the needs of those you love and care for. It is many things but above all it must be safe in all kinds of scenarios. It can be treated much like a defense. One of the best methods of defense is concealment. Finding that hidden hilltop or knoll within a fertile, hidden valley is like finding a gold mine, or almost a pearl of great price.

I remember going on patrol in Kosovo, and every major street and valley seemed to have been wrecked by violence. Buildings were smashed, streets had been cratered, and people looked desperate. Every wall was full of bullet holes. However, every once in a while, we would come across a lone farmstead in a hidden fold in the mountains. It was always in a place "back in the holler" as you would say in the U.S. There, livestock grazed, a garden grew, life continued and people seemed somewhat content. They had survived the descent into chaos and come through the other side to see a better day.

Given the opportunity to choose your homestead location, think about that hidden hamlet, holler, or nook. You need to be away from avenues of approach that are well-traveled or important such as an interstate or highway. You also need to be away from key terrain, such as communication towers, important infrastructure like a grocery store, water treatment plant, or oil refinery. These types of places are often the site of intense struggle or troublesome mischief. Your ideal location should not be visible from a great distance away, but it is good to be able to see visitors approaching before they are right on top of you, at least 100 yards out is preferable.

The Double Line in the Sand Technique

My favorite technique when choosing a base of operations in hostile country, or even your personal homestead is to first draw a "line in the sand" that you will defend, giving your home security plan focus. To be clear, I am not some kind of insurrectionist or whatever label you might choose. My point is simply to prepare for security contingencies, as security should never be taken for granted. In 1995, did anyone think Russia would invade the Ukraine? Well surprise, here we are, the future happens, and you need to prepare, now! The contingency works like this:

The outer line is a rough circle around your homestead and should be visible from your homestead which is your observation point and your defensive position. This outer line is simply as far as you can see on property that you can expect to control. Do not draw a line in the sand across a public right of way or your neighbor's property that you do not control. The purpose of the line is to give you early warning of intruders in your own space. It is basically where you can post no trespassing signs and you can also be sure that if someone is there, then they are intentionally violating your space. In an ideal situation, this line would be 300 yards from your point of observation, which is typically your home.   This distance should keep you safe from most small arms fire. Because of property lines, it may have to be 25 yards away based on your situation. It may not be a neat circle because if you live in uneven or complex terrain, then your visibility will be limited by terrain and property features around you. For example, let's say a ridge in front of your house blocks your view, and the top of that ridge may likely be the farthest you can see and so that is a good place for the first line in the sand. A cliff presents the same limitation as a ridge, and both are excellent "lines in the sand."

Those with military tactics training may recall that the military crest is not the highest point of a hill. Instead, it is just downhill from the crest, so that you can engage the enemy at the maximum effective range of your weapons, but your rear is not on top of the hill, so that you cannot be fired on from behind without the enemy approaching within close range. This way, you also do not silhouette yourself at the top of the hill. In other words, you can engage targets to your front at long range, but the actual geographical hilltop is to your rear, shielding you from behind. Defensive positions can then be dug into the hill so that you can fire but still be protected from all directions by your fortifications. So, by utilizing the military crest of the hill, your outer line in the sand stretches far to your front, to the max effective range of your weapons but to your rear it is closer, only stretching to the nearby top of the hill. You want to be able to see fairly unobstructed all the way to this outer line in the sand, so, if possible, clear vegetation and trees that would obstruct your view. Vegetation or objects that are within 50 feet of your home and do not obstruct your view from your observation point or potential firing points can serve as concealment and do not need to be removed. As long as vegetation does not greatly obstruct your view, then it will help to camouflage your own location and movements.

Many of us cannot simply clear all of the trees around us because of property rights, or we may have valuable trees, buildings, etc., that cannot be moved. That is acceptable, but just remember that your outer line in the sand is only as far as you can see. If you can only see 25 yards in one area, then that is your outer line, and you will have little advance warning of intruders. If this is the case, pay close attention to the obstacles section in this book, so that you can slow and hinder intruders that will be in close proximity to your homestead.

Apart from clearing vegetation and improving your field of view of this outer line, it is helpful to at least mark the boundary with no trespassing signs. If at all possible, a fence can be erected as well. There is often a fixation on making such a perimeter fence solid, like a solid rock wall in medieval times, or like the great wall of China. The problem with such a solid fence or wall is that it gives intruders concealment from your view, and cover from fire, should you be forced to engage them. If the wall or fence is directly next to your home, it gives you cover and concealment, but the outer line in the sand should instead be something that you can see through like chain-link or barbed wire so that intruders cannot hide and conceal their movement around your property.

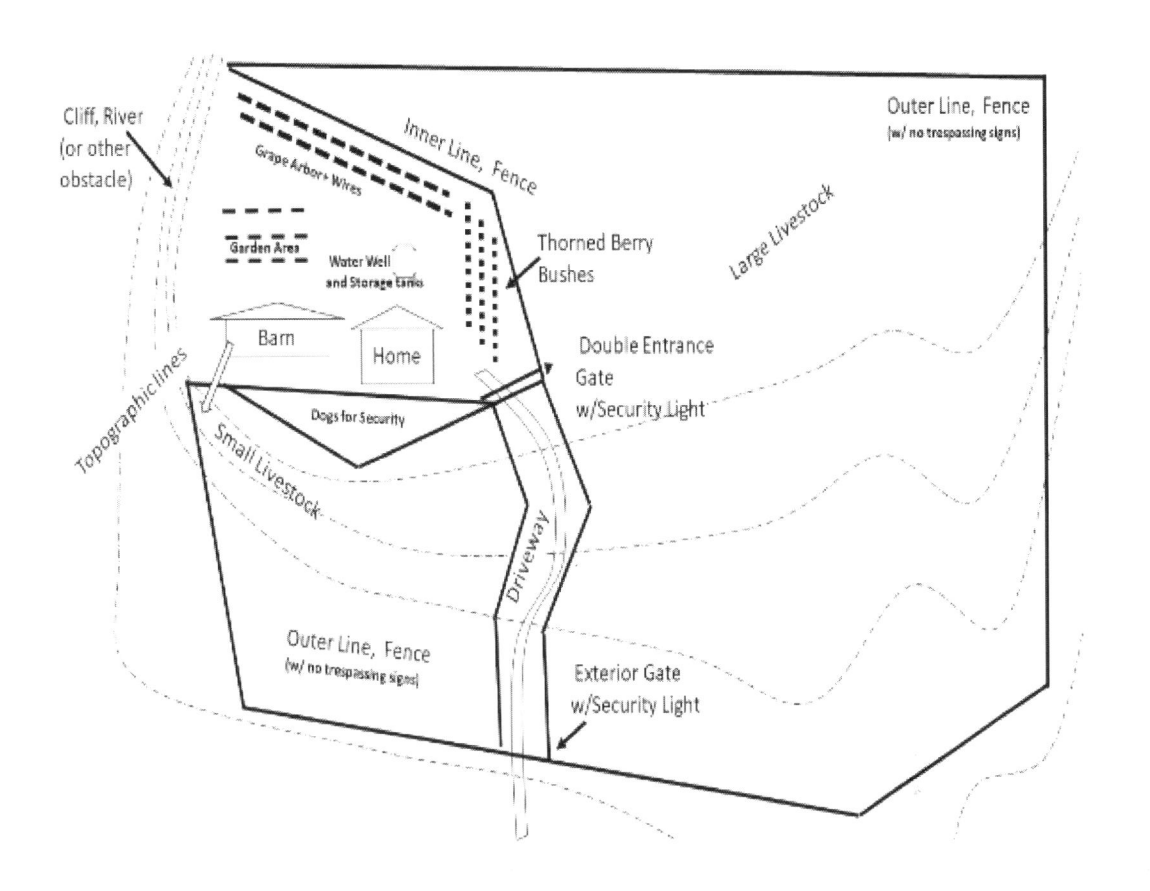

Figure 29: Example of a Homestead Layout with Security Considerations

Hurricane fence is excellent, but unnecessarily expensive. A less expensive fence that is fairly difficult to cross is a woven wire fence with at least one strand of barbed wire on top. The taller the woven wire and the more strands of barbed wire, the better. The barbed wire should be spaced no more than 9 inches apart, so that individuals cannot slip between the wires. This type of fence is also excellent for all classes of livestock, so it is useful even if you never have to use it to defend your property. If you can afford razor wire and concertina wire without angering your neighbors, that is great too, but don't build something that will injure livestock or innocent bystanders. One of my neighbors actually put up razor wire along the public road. Other neighbors don't like it and his miniature goats manage to get through it and eat everyone else's flowers and gardens. Making everyone hate you is not a good survival strategy. (Talking to you Richard.) A well-installed livestock fence would have been more effective. If the situation only allows for a few strands of barbed wire for your fence, that is better than nothing.

Now let us discuss your inner line in the sand. While the outer line in the sand is meant to give you early warning, the second line in the sand is one that should never be crossed by intruders. The first line may or may not have a fence or obstacle, but the second line in the sand should absolutely have an excellent fence that is very difficult to cross. The first line was at or around your maximum effective engagement range with your weapons.

The second line should be at a range at which you are sure not to miss, anywhere from 25 to 100 yards depending on your situation and skill. Again, a solid medieval-type wall looks very impressive, but this is a great place for an intruder to hide. Save that for the walls of your own home or bunker. For the inner line, consider a very substantial wire fence that hooligans cannot hide behind. Because the inner line is obviously smaller, it may be affordable to construct a hurricane fence here. A woven wire fence topped with barbed wire is also an excellent option. If you are able to construct your inner and outer lines in the sand of these fences, then you have also created an excellent grazing space between the two where you can raise livestock as discussed earlier in this book.

The inner line is a great place for additional obstacles that will trip up anyone that is lurking around. Some examples include beehives, grape arbors that have integrated wires, low vines and plants for intruders to trip on, guard dog kennels, guard donkeys or geese, sewage lagoons, ponds, and other obstacles that are not easy to hide behind, and that slow down movement.

Now imagine yourself looking out from your windows or the porch of your homestead, but you live in a war-torn country. This is not modern America, but it could be the future, a scenario where law and order has broken down completely. When anyone crosses that first line in the sand, that is posted with no trespassing signs, then they most likely know that they are wrong, and this gives you an idea of their intentions. In war torn countries, these people are confirmed as hostile and then taken out by snipers. If for whatever reason there is no way to confirm hostile intent, or you don't catch them, then the second line in the sand is designed to effectively slow down and temporarily stop hostiles before they actually get to your home. This is where dogs should be barking, security lights should turn on, and you prepare to use deadly force while the hostiles get caught on your fence wire, trip over your beehive, fall in your sewage lagoon, and get attacked by that mean and nasty pet goose that you were saving for Christmas dinner. On small properties, the outer line might be just a big suburban yard, and the inner line might be a raised porch railing. Consider making your porch railing more difficult to climb in this scenario, or screening in your porch. That way if an intruder tries to get on your porch, you have bought more time to arm yourself.

One trick for early warning is to locate your homestead in a concealed valley or small draw and have a point of observation on a hill just above the homestead where you can post someone to observe your surroundings. In desperate times, you must be aware of thieves, looters, and those just looking to feed themselves at your expense. If you don't have enough manpower to post someone in an observation position, then a second story on your home or an elevated point such as a deer stand is a good place to post a sentry when you feel danger is lurking. Don't forget, concealment can also help you avoid many unpleasant encounters.

To ensure that your homestead is concealed, consider both winter and summer vegetation. A good friend of mine hastily chose his retreat in the middle of the summer in the Appalachian Mountains and immediately began construction. By late fall he had made great progress and it seemed the location was perfect. As the leaves fell, he realized that his excellent vantage point included a two-lane highway in the distance, from which travelers or potential marauders would certainly never fail to miss the newly constructed homestead in the nearby hills. Also consider that after building your homestead you may need to clear vegetation for solar energy or for agricultural purposes. Make sure that this isn't going to reveal your private retreat to passers-by.

It is very difficult to conceal your retreat if it is in plain view. In some circumstances, a large camouflage net can be purchased. I purchased a 45-foot diameter net for $300 several years ago. These can provide aerial concealment as well, even concealing you from satellite imagery such as Google Earth. Flat paint can also be used but is not as effective as a net due to the sharp angles and regular shapes that catch the human eye.

Obstacles

Rather than have to fight off unwanted guests to your homestead, it may be worth the effort to create obstacles to discourage them from visiting in the first place. Obstacles can be used to block access completely, to slow progress, or to channel movement in a certain direction. The idea is not only to block access as much as possible, but always leave one route of access a little easier to penetrate. That way if someone does get into your space, you know from what direction they are most likely coming.

Normally, an obstacle that you are not able to overwatch is not very effective. This is because an individual that is given plenty of time can dismantle just about any obstacle. Therefore, it is best to have a clear a line of sight to your obstacles so that you can observe, and if your life is threatened, fire upon intruders. The distance to the obstacles depends on how far away you are able to effectively engage targets. I like to say that you should keep your friends close and keep your enemies no closer than 800 yards, which was the range of the M24 (Remington 700 in .308) that my team carried during the invasion of Iraq.

In addition to obstacles that are within firing range, I like to have an external obstacle beyond that one, so I know if they show up at the inner perimeter (line in the sand), then they deliberately breached the outer perimeter (line in the sand) and ignored the no trespassing signs. This gives you a better idea of their intent.

Obstacles can consist of anything, but it is useful if you can locate your homestead where it is partially protected by natural obstacles. Cliffs, thick brush, swamps, and waterways are all excellent barriers between your fortified home and unwelcome visitors. These are most readily substituted by livestock fences, which are most inconspicuous and serve a dual purpose in the country. Electricity is very difficult to maintain because if it is grounded out in 1 spot, then the whole fence is down. Barbed wire is very simple to cross by pushing wires up or down. A 4-foot-high woven wire fence with at least one strand of barbed wire that is 6 inches above the top of the woven wire is much more difficult to cross. They also make a 6-foot-high woven wire deer fence which is even better. Taller fences than this become extremely cost prohibitive, or are made of cheap, easier to cut materials. I would not go smaller than 16 gauge for any fencing thickness.

Key Terrain

When I was a newly minted Infantry officer at the Infantry School in Ft. Benning, Georgia, I remember our instructors, all hardened combat veterans, spending days demonstrating the importance of key terrain and how it so often determines the outcome of a battle or operation. Battles are generally fought, and lives are sacrificed over key terrain, that when controlled can be used by artillery, heavy machine guns, and air assets to dominate the battlefield, like pieces on a chess board. Key terrain is a piece of ground that has characteristics which make it easier to survive, defend, and dominate the battlefield. If you control key terrain, then you control the security and the resources in a larger area around the key terrain. It is the same concept when choosing a location for a homestead that is meant to withstand turbulent times where your security is your own responsibility. Some desirable characteristics that enable survival have already been covered in choosing your homestead location. They include an area with water, a south-facing slope, food-production potential, and at least partially protected by natural obstacles. These are important in terms of long-term survival, but it is also important to think about the possibility of having to defend your homestead, in the case of a breakdown of law and order or an uptick in crime and thievery in your area.

Many individuals believe that simply occupying the top of a hill can give you a big advantage as a defender. This is not necessarily the case. Being at the top of the hill means that you are silhouetted against the sky, making your shape stand out easily to anyone coming up the hill. To review, a military crest of the hill is a location just off the highest point, a slight spur off of a ridge or hilltop can serve the purpose. At the military crest, you can observe anyone coming up one side from a distance and you have a higher vantage point, but you are not silhouetted, and do not stand out against the sky behind you, as there is still a taller hill or ridge to your rear. Anyone who approaches you from the crest of the hill will be closer and higher, but they silhouette themselves against the backdrop of the hill as soon as they are close enough to see you, making themselves an easier target. The military crest is a great place for a sniper team because it allows the sniper to observe and engage at long distances in one direction, while the spotter can easily detect and engage anyone silhouetting themselves from the other direction towards the top of the hill. In this way, the spotter easily covers the rear.

Improving your Key Terrain

In a homesteading situation, your occupation of the land is long term, and so you may spend a lifetime improving your land, including making your key terrain work for you, protecting you and your loved ones. The first step to improving your key terrain is to improve your field of view. Obviously, it is best to leave your immediate location more concealed, but you still want to be able to clearly see the areas where individuals may want to approach your homestead. In a sniper team, the spotter is often covering the crest of a hill, which is generally to your rear. The crest of the hill is a great place to clear first because if you are approached from this direction, you do not want your attackers to have the opportunity to take cover or conceal themselves. Instead, you want to engage them from a covered and concealed position while they are in the open. On a homestead, this is often facilitated by clearing pastures for livestock at the top of the hill that you are defending.

In the other direction, downhill, a sniper also needs to be able to see his or her field of fire while maintaining cover and concealment. One way to do this is to clear the underbrush nearby. A canopy of trees benefits a defender by providing enough concealment to obscure a stationary defender, but not enough for a moving attacker. On the other hand, an attacker can move easily concealed by the underbrush, and so this must be removed first, as far out from the homestead as possible. Once you are around 100 yards from the homestead, it can be helpful to completely clear additional areas. These are good areas to turn into pastures or crop production as they will be easily observed and protected because they are in view of your homestead. This is one way that homesteading combines with tactics to create the ultimate survival homestead. If you do not own these areas, and cannot clear them, then you must work with what is there. At a minimum, try to make sure that you can at least observe key avenues of approach from your defender location. These include not only roads and trails but also streams and gentle ridge lines and spurs that are easy to travel upon. Sometimes just clearing a few branches can mean the difference between a surprise visitor or a prepared and ready homestead defender.

Illustration 69: Some of the Young Men I Trained;
My Goal was to Give them the Tools to Come Home Alive

Chapter 14: The Gear Locker

A gear locker is important on your homestead because it contains those items that you need in order to defend your loved ones and your property when a security threat arises. As a soldier deployed down range, I would generally have my gear just stacked beside my bunk, and it would go with me wherever I went, or it would be otherwise left under guard. For a citizen in a county gone awry, you may not be able to take all of your kit or gear with you everywhere, so you need to have a gear locker that you can secure your weapons and other security items in. It should be able to be locked, it would be great if it is hidden, and it will probably need off-grid electricity to charge your radios and/or optics. Americans often do not think that their weapons lockers or safes need to be hidden, but when your country becomes third world, you will likely get a third world strongman or woman that wants to confiscate your gear. The second amendment and even the Bill of Rights ceases to exist in the third world. This is not a lament or a celebratory statement, just a pragmatic observation, and a heads up.

We all love our gear, our toys, and our gadgets, so why am I not putting this section right up front? The reason is that your gear locker needs to be designed based on your circumstances, your terrain, and scenarios by which you defend yourself, and so we discuss gear, after things like key terrain. For example, based on your terrain and vegetation, you may only normally engage targets at 300 yards or less in your area, or you may have vantage points to engage from over 800 yards away. Defending your home after an intruder is already inside your walls also requires different equipment than dealing with an unwanted camp of post-apocalyptic marauders on your land at night. These factors drastically alter the type of kit that you may need.

Illustration 70: Author with M24 Sniper Rifle in Iraq. This Rifle is basically a Remington 700 in .308.

Firearms

When planning for purchases of defensive gear or kit, it is important to prioritize, and acquire items that you need the most first, buying more in order of priority as funds become available. So of course, first things being first, let's talk guns. The firearm that you need first doesn't depend on how cool you think it looks, how popular it is, or even what you are comfortable shooting. Instead, like any tool, it depends on the task that you need to accomplish.

For example, I have an ex-military neighbor, Mike, who lives close to me and runs cattle on expansive pastures surrounding his ranch home. There is little cover to be had near this home, so he is rather exposed. His advantage is that he has visibility for 800 to 1000 yards in every direction, and he has multiple fence lines and gates to slow down potential intruders and thieves. Unfortunately, Mike is convinced that he is so familiar with the AR-15 due to his military background, that it is always going to be his weapon of choice. What Mike needs to realize, is that his main advantage is standoff, meaning that he needs a weapon with 800-to-1000-yard range, not the 300 to 400 yard range that an AR-15 has. With his AR-15, Mike just has the ability to make a lot of noise while bandits with a bolt action Remington 700 in .308 keep him pinned down and steal his cattle. Many Americans who haven't deployed overseas may snicker when they hear the word bandits, like we are in some old western movie. But let me tell you, when a country descends into chaos and hunger, it becomes the wild west, and you don't want to be outgunned by the bad guys, Ali-baba, pirates, or yes, bandits.

Having longer range does not always mean outgunning your adversary. When I was a Ranger Instructor living in Dahlonega, GA, I could barely see 100 yards in any direction from my house, or in the nearby forest areas, and I never took a shot while deer hunting more than 75 yards away. It was just thick vegetation everywhere, mountain laurel up and down the steep ridges. Clearings were just places where kudzu could grow. On one occasion while training Ranger students, we had given the students the mission to conduct an ambush, and I witnessed just how important it is to consider range, and field of view when engaging a tactical target. First, consider that Ranger students are always tired and hungry, on the verge of starvation, and they make obvious mistakes for this reason. Often while on patrol, they will go night after night, finishing up their mission late, only to get to sleep by 2 or 3 in the morning, but waking up at 5. One out of three also must stay awake at all times to pull security, meaning that they get 1 ½ to 2 hours of sleep per night, turning them basically into zombies. At that time, when I was an instructor, they also had two military rations to eat, one when they woke up, and the other before they went to sleep. A lot of very tough men quit or are broken in Ranger school. At Ranger school they say, "We build Warriors," but to be more accurate, they should also say, "but we sometimes break hard men like popsicle sticks, snap!"

Let's get back to the ambush: In this situation, the terrain was rough, and getting to the trail where the ambush was conducted meant climbing over mountain laurel infested hillsides, grabbing roots as handholds, and slipping on the mossy, loose rocks up the steep slopes. It was also midsummer in the southern Appalachian Mountains, which I can tell you, are just as hot as the Panamanian jungle. The platoon leadership team was being graded and it is up to them to scout and select the ambush location. When the platoon student leadership finally got the assault, support-by-fire, and security elements into the selected locations, the men were so exhausted that half of them just flopped down on their asses, and some were inadvertently dozing off, even though that risks severe punishment. They were absolutely smoked out of their gourds! Unfortunately for the platoon leadership who was being graded, the vegetation at their chosen location was so thick that the trail was not visible from the assault or support positions that were only 15 yards away. So even though the weapons on hand could have easily been within range of a 200-yard ambush site, this ambush could have been conducted with pistols and tomahawks at this close range. Nonetheless, the positions were setup, camouflaged, and the claymore mine simulated-demolition-charge was installed, just a stone's throw from the trail. All this accomplished, many of the students fell asleep. The location was so terrible that instructors couldn't even crawl through the brush to check on students positions or wake them up. It was what we call a shit-show in progress. The mission and the leadership grades would be a failure. The one thing the students appeared to do correctly was to be silent, but it was just because they were asleep. Sometimes when this happens, the instructors will just let it happen just to teach a hard lesson in failure during training, to avoid the same failure later in actual combat.

Illustration 71: The Author with an M240 Machine Gun with Camouflage Face Paint

On this particular occasion, the opposition forces that were supposed to be ambushed by the Ranger students were still about 45 minutes away. Instead, a female deer and her two fawns were browsing along the trail. The students were so stealthy, because they were dead-ass asleep, that the deer did not even notice 30 Rangers passed out less than 45 feet away, with machine guns, explosives, and thousands of rounds of ammunition. There was one student, however, that was so hardcore, so keen, that he still had his eyes open, probably because he put his MRE tabasco sauce on his eyelids, being the hard MF that he was. This machine gunner, Ranger Duffie, had been pushing the other students all day to keep up, stay awake, and don't screw over the platoon leadership that was getting graded. Nonetheless, he was the lone survivor, still awake, and peering down the sights of his machine gun at some sort of movement indiscernible through the thickets. To him, it must have been the opposition forces. Duffie pulled the trigger, letting off a long rapid burst from his M240 belt-fed machine gun. This set off a chain reaction where instinctively the student platoon leader squeezed the clacker for the claymore mine, "boooom!," and all of the machine guns and small arms opened fire as the sleeping Ranger students who could only see the leaves two feet in front of their faces jerked their triggers lighting up the darkening sky with flashes and bangs. The mama deer jumped 6 feet into the air straight down the steep slope, and after prancing left, then right, and tripping on each other, the 2 fawns disappeared from sight as well. From my position, I was startled as the guns opened up and the claymore simulator exploded sending a terrified squirrel tumbling down from a tree branch and onto the back of a machine gunner. Unhurt, the squirrel scampered off and lived to tell the tale. While this was all an impressive display of firepower, it resulted in a straight flush of "No-Go" failing grades for the platoon leadership. The important lesson to take away is number one, identify your targets. Number two, your weapon systems need to fit the scenario that you expect to fight in. I say again, **your weapon systems need to fit the scenario that you expect to fight in.**

In this type of environment, you don't need range, but instead you need rapid fire. A lot of ex-military personnel scoff at the inaccuracy of an AK-47, but at ranges less than 100 yards, a fully auto AK is a great way to keep your enemies' heads in the dirt. It also provides great suppression out to 350 yards, but I would argue that most old run-of-the-mill AK's don't fire accurately past 200 meters. An AK is more rugged and can handle more rounds at a faster rate of fire without overheating than an AR-15. AK's often have over 122 grains of powder while a military 5.56 round (military M-4/civilian AR-15) has only 62 grains, resulting in a more frightening crack of nearby rounds from an AK, and more impact on things like cinder block walls, trees, and sandbags on the receiving end. I can tell you that there is nothing more unnerving than taking cover behind a cinder block wall while some Holy Rolling Jihadi hammers away at the disintegrating wall with his AK.

Illustration 72: An AR-10 shoots a .308 round that will put the hammer down on any opponent out to 600 yards out.

Still, the small but extremely high velocity AR-15 round tends to tumble and bounce inside the tissue of the human body, resulting in some atrocious, hard to treat, and usually fatal wounds. An AR-10 is much more intimidating and has even more impact than an AK, because of the larger size of the round, the noise, and the power. It also has typically around 180 grains of powder on the civilian side, three times the typical 5.56 (AR-15 round) giving it greater ranges than both the AK-47 or AR-15. With practice and proper ammunition, a standard AR-10 chambered in .308 will help you reach out and touch targets up to 600 meters away. The one drawback is that unless you have the special heavy-barreled version, then you will overheat and ruin the barrel at a rapid rate of fire. Instead, it is meant for medium to long-range, steady, well-aimed, sustained (slow) rates of fire. In summary, choose an AR-15 for light but well-aimed sustained fire, an AK-47 for less accurate, but more rapid and heavy fire, and an AR-10 for very accurate, heavy impact, and slow controlled fire.

Type of Rifle	Max Effective Range	Grains Powder per Round	Length of Round millimeters	Diam. of Round millimeters	Rate of Fire Standard Barrel
AR-15	300 meters	62	45	5.56	Rapid
AR-10 with scope	600 meters	180	51	7.62	Sustained
AK-47 (standard)	200 meters	122	39	7.62	Rapid /Cyclic
Remington 700 in .308 with minimum 12x scope scope	800 meters	180	51	7.62	Bolt Action

Table 6: Typical Combat Rifle Characteristics: many will argue with this description because of variable models available and skill level differences, but this is what you typically see in practical application of these weapons

Many of us in forested locations live in areas with moderate visibility, 300 yards may be the view on one side of your homestead, but on the other side, a hidden ravine might allow the enemy to sneak up to within 50 yards of your location. Versatility is what you need in this scenario, and with broad scenarios without long-range engagements, the AR-15 style weapon is the real ticket. It allows you to take that shot out to 300 yards, but also to rapidly engage closer locations as well.

With two to four defenders on your team, it is highly advantageous to leverage multiple types of weapon systems in order to engage targets at varying ranges, and at different rates of fire, depending on location, concealment, and the number of attackers. Realistically, on a homestead, you might be equipped with kit similar to my scout sniper team in Iraq. We typically had one man with a bolt-action sniper rifle, for long range, highly accurate fire out to 800 meters. It's basically considered an accurate deer rifle in civilian life. If we had to enter a room, to establish or change positions, we typically had two or three men with M-4's (military version of the AR-15), and the sniper would carry a Beretta 9mm pistol. For firefights within 300 meters or less, the M-4 was also appropriate. At one point, we also had a captured AK-47 which was also handy to suppress enemy fire, better used just to keep their heads down, such as when you need to move or break contact and avoid being engaged by accurate enemy fire. We also had light anti-tank weapons, grenades, and claymore mines, but you won't likely get your hands on any of those, and I want to encourage you to stay legal while using weapons only in self-defense. I say again, stay legal y'all.

Zeroing your rifle

When U.S. forces squared off against religious zealots and inbred mountain men posing as terrorists in the middle east, it soon became obvious that their marksmanship program was pure crap, at best, nonexistent at worst. Worst of all, they seemed to have never zeroed their weapons, and instead would rely on prayer to hit their targets.

I highly discourage you from using prayer to zero your weapons, instead, you should find a comfortable and legal firing range, and zero your weapon. Do this by firing 3 rounds at a time at a fixed-distance bullseye target, and after each three rounds, adjust your sights until you are hitting the bullseye. Always aim at the bullseye and do not aim off center to compensate for the last rounds that you have shot. In other words, do not use "Kentucky Windage." Once you have adjusted your sites enough to the point that your rounds are hitting center mass, then your weapon is zeroed. An important question to ask yourself is, "how far away should my zero target be." In military basic rifle marksmanship, 25 meters is the typical zeroing distance, and this is a good starting point. However, in advanced rifle marksmanship, you need to understand the distance that a round drops as it travels from your rifle and towards the target. The below diagrams demonstrate this round drop.

ACTUAL DROP	RANGE	200M ZERO
-0.66"	50M	0.46"
-2.74"	100M	1.99"
-11.96"	200M	-0.0"
-29.52"	300M	-10.33"
-57.99"	400M	-31.56"
-100.91"	500M	-67.25"

Table 7: Drop in inches of a 62 grain 5.56 round at various ranges with a 25 meter zero and a 200 meter zero

In this example, we are using the typical drop of a 62 grain 5.56 round, as when firing an AR-15. As you can see, the actual drop is quite significant at long ranges, and this is what you experience with a 25 meter zero. For this reason, it is highly recommended that you zero your AR-15 out to 200 meters, so that you can hit further targets without aiming extremely high. Of course, this requires a lot of walking, but it will make your aim much, much better than someone that is only trained in basic rifle marksmanship. In this example, you can see that with a 200 meter zero, a 50-meter shot will only be ½ inch high, and for a 300-meter shot, you will only have to aim 10.33 inches higher than the center mass of your target. Aiming holdoffs for different distances with a typical AR-15 zeroed out to 200 meters are demonstrated below:

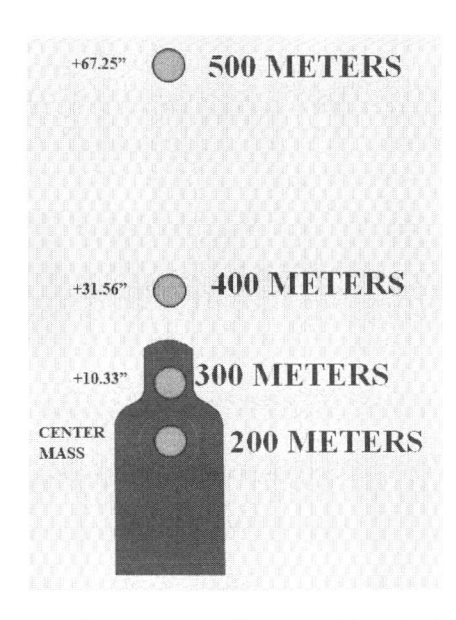

Figure 30: Hold off distances for a man-size silhouette with an AR-15 zeroed at 200 meters.

By properly zeroing your rifle, you will have a huge advantage over any criminal or illegal threat to your homestead, and you will also be a better hunter. As you can see, it is important to understand the drop of the round as it relates to the trajectory of your rifle. In this way, you can more rapidly engage targets out to 300 meters without a huge adjustment or aim "holdoff." Ranges beyond 300 meters are always difficult with an AR-15, but they are more achievable with a 200 meter zero, as this requires less compensation for round drop. Remember with rifle marksmanship, that you need to understand your rifle, zero your rifle, and pick the correct rifle for the job that needs to be done.

Optics and Lasers

Just like choosing the right tool for the job, you need to also choose the right sight or scope for the job. I once was part of an experimental test / vendor event of multiple high-tech and high dollar military grade scopes that were designed to be used on the Carl Gustaf 84-mm recoilless rifle. It shoots anti-tank, bunker-buster, and large area anti-personnel rounds that are 3.3 inches wide and 2-3 feet long; small missiles that are shot at targets up to a mile away. It is also the loudest shoulder-fired weapon on the planet and when you pull the trigger, the noise and the concussion feel like you just got punched from the inside of your skull. The trick to shooting the "Goose," as we called it, was to pretend that you didn't know you were about to get punched. It's a hard trick to pull. Choosing optics rugged enough for this weapon that also can engage targets a mile away is no easy task. For the vendor event / experiment, the Department of Defense had invited some Army Rangers, some Navy Seals, some Marine Recon, and some Air Force TACP's. Before the shoot, we had the opportunity to ask questions to the vendors, defense contractors who had flown in from all over the world to sell their products to the U.S. Military. The Rangers asked primarily how far you could see and engage targets with the different scopes, and if they could be used at night. The Marines were more concerned with if it would break if you smashed it with a rock, and the Navy Seals only ever had one question for each vendor, "Will it malfunction in the bath tub?" The Air Force wanted to know if it would get damaged if you spilled taco or pizza sauce on it. Just kidding, why would anyone invite the Air Force??!!

When you are selecting optics for your rifles, you should ask these same types of questions. Think about what targets and distance you will be shooting at, if you are shooting at night, how your optics will be used and abused, oh, and if you are a frogman, maybe even how water resistant it is.

Iron sights are quite sufficient for most short-range hunting needs, and they hold up well while using an assault rifle in rugged conditions. More advanced scopes and sights serve three purposes:

1) Magnification to see distant targets.
2) Faster target acquisition (red dot or holographic scopes).
3) Allows the shooter to see targets in the dark or unclear conditions (night vison or thermal).

For many assault rifles and for self-defense, many people opt for an aim point sight or a holographic sight with a floating dot in your scope and no magnification. First, I must say that I love holographic sights. It makes it easy to aim without worrying about your cheek-to-stock weld. This means that when shooting iron sights, you keep your head in the same position relative to the weapon (cheek-to-stock weld). Floating dot scopes are supposed to compensate for slight variations in head position, so you just raise your weapon and fire as soon as you can put the dot on the target. When I was serving in the military, I loved the floating dot. But, then again, I was part of an army with vast supplies of batteries and a good supply chain. Nowadays, I am not in the military, and I worry more about future resupply. For this reason, I now prefer a simple reticle in a scope that does not require batteries.

A reticle scope, one that has simple crosshairs, often comes with variable magnification options. Many of these start at 4 or 5 power and they typically go up to 9 or 15 power, giving you an advantage that is similar to looking through binoculars. A 10-power scope will magnify an object to 10 times the actual size. With a variable magnification scope, you can turn up the magnification when needed. Turning up the magnification does have one drawback, however, which is that it also decreases the field of view. Field of view is the width of the target that you can see in the scope. So, with higher magnification, you will lose some width left to right and top to bottom, from what you can see in your scope. If you want to engage close targets rapidly, it is better to adjust to a low magnification so that you can see a larger area through the scope, and therefore see more and acquire your target more rapidly. When shooting multiple targets at close range rapidly, you need to have a maximum sized field of view, meaning that magnification does not help. When you have plenty of time to acquire and engage a target at a far range, then you want to turn up that magnification higher so that you can see the distant targets better, even if you sacrifice field of view and speed.

I have found that for variable range shooting such as deer hunting, a variable range scope is a great option. While I am walking in the forest to hunt, or in a thick brush area, where I cannot see far, then I will turn the magnification all the way down. This way, if I see a deer, then I can acquire and engage the target quickly. If I am set up in a position where I can see for a long distance and I can take my time, then I will scan my target area on low magnification, and then turn up the magnification when I find a target to engage. This is how you properly use a variable-powered scope. I have a Burris scope that is variable range from 4.5 to 15 power for hunting deer. It set me back about $1000, which is a good mid-range glass price.

In the Army, our sniper rifles would typically have Leupold daytime scopes that cost about $10,000 and went up to 15 power magnification; probably the best glass made in the U.S. at the time. Average shooters with a little training can easily see, engage, and often hit targets out to 800 meters with this type of scope. Compare this with iron sights shooting where 300 meters is about as far as you can see and hit a man-sized target.

When purchasing glass, pay close attention to clarity ratings. The clarity rating of your glass will determine not only the price of your scope but also how well you can see targets at long range. Some manufacturers such as Swarovski and Leupold have excellent clarity in their glass, meaning that you can engage targets at great distances of a half mile or more. Buying cheaper scopes with cheaper glass will mean that you cannot see or engage targets that far out. Most high clarity glass is manufactured in Europe, Japan, and sometimes in the U.S.. Chinese Glass has been known for low clarity for years.

Recently, I have found that for generic, everyday rifle needs, I prefer daytime scopes that have a variable power scope that starts low, at about 1.5 magnification, and goes up to 4 power. This is great as you get older, lazier, and cheaper and you don't want to put as much time and money into marksmanship. The 1.5 power makes a target just a little larger, without sacrificing your field of view. In a good scope with a wide field of view, you don't hardly notice the size difference of the target, but you will shoot more accurately than with no magnification. You can easily see and engage targets even in the same room with you at 1.5 power. At the same time, turning this up to 4 or 4.5 magnification will allow you to accurately shoot man-sized targets outdoors up to 300 meters with an AR style rifle. In my area, we have some invasive species and pests such as armadillos that harm our native species. These cat-sized animals can easily be acquired and shot at 100 meters on the 4.5 magnification setting, with an AR-15.

Finally, when purchasing a daytime scope, pay attention to what the advertiser and reviewers say about durability and the caliber of rifle that it is rated for. If you put a scope that is made for a .22 varmint on a bushmaster AR that shoots .308, then it will break on the first shot. If you plan on using it in the rain, make sure that it is water resistant. There are also a lot of off-brand and knockoffs out there so beware. Buy from a reputable source or a knowledgeable dealer, preferably one that will accept a return if something goes wrong.

In summary, when choosing optics for your rifle, think about what you will be using it for, and keep in mind that you will get what you pay for. A cheap scope will definitely break if you use it with a high caliber weapon. It will also be ruined by infiltrating moisture if it gets wet. I generally spend as much on a scope as I spend on the rifle with which it is used. Don't forget to match your scope up with what it will be used for; aim point dots are good for close range, fast target acquisition while high magnification scopes with good clarity will do the job at long ranges. There are scopes with low and variable magnification power that will serve as good multi-purpose scopes as well. Like many other survival items, buying a good rifle scope is all about choosing the right tool for the job.

Night Vision and Thermals

When I was in the Ranger regiment and also serving as a Ranger instructor, we did as much training at nighttime as we did during the day. We were all very good at using night vision while running, shooting, driving, and more. Well, most of us were good at it except for the old farts. I remember an old crusty Sergeant First Class, who would run around tripping on everyone behind the support by fire line with machine guns roaring, yelling, "Ranger, who is this??!! Ranger, rapid rate of fire, 12 o'clock, on my tracers!! Ranger, who is this??" But pretty much everyone else was proficient. For a time, I served in a bike squad, and our job was to use Kawasaki dirt bikes and undisclosed tactics, in order to conduct rapid combat deployments of our forces. This meant a lot of training with night vision while riding dirt bikes, which was extremely dangerous.

Illustration 73: Ranger Special Operations Vehicle; You can do anything with night vision that you can do in the day, with practice.

I was stationed with 1st Ranger Battalion, in Savannah, Georgia, and we would ride along the loose, sandy trails of our local "Back 40" training area along with the "RSOV's," the ranger special operations vehicles. On one particular evening, I was moving back from a security position, when I inadvertently came upon an RSOV that was on the wrong trail and attempting a five-point U-turn. You can't see nearly as far with night vision as you can with visible light, so I only had time to lay the bike down on its side and skid to a halt, bailing out just in time, with my bike ending up under the RSOV. One of my colleagues was not so lucky a year later and suffered serious permanent and total brain damage from a similar collision. It's a very dangerous job, while deployed and even while training.

Many people might wonder why I place night vision as a second priority for gear purchases, and the reason is simple. Darkness can take up half of your life, and if you can't see in the dark, you are as helpless as an old lady with dark sunglasses in a movie theater. "Give me your wallet, Granny!! That's Why!" Just kidding, but really think about it, most criminals love to work at night. The good news is that with the proper investment and training, you can turn this into a big advantage for yourself. If you have ever worn night vision and watched people without it stumble around in the dark, you know what I mean, it is hilarious! It's like watching a bunch of lost and blind little puppies.

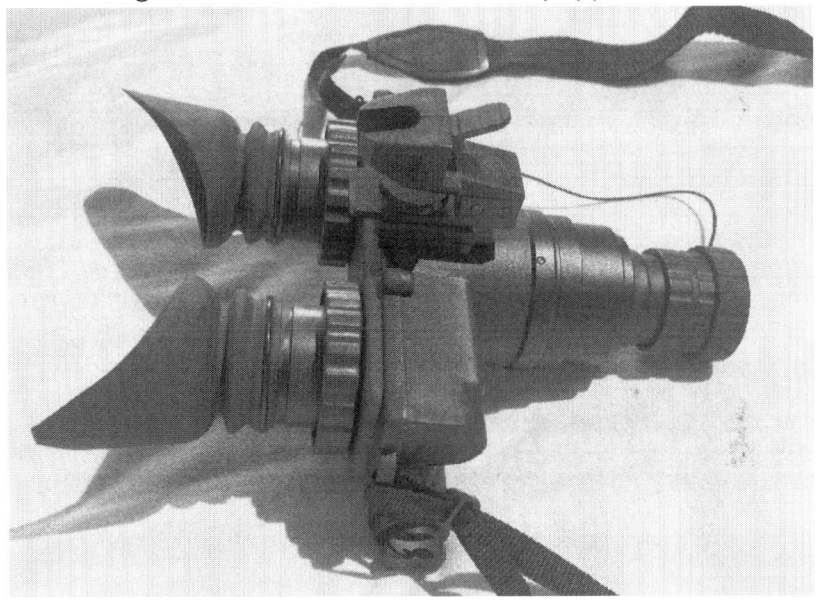

Illustration 74: PVS-7 Style Night Vision Goggles are Available Commercially but be sure to get a mount.

Remember that night vision, also called starlight scopes, enhances the light that is available, allowing you to see objects in low light conditions or with infrared illumination, but not with zero light such as in a cave. Thermal on the other hand, allows you to see objects that are emitting heat, and they stand out like beacons against a cool background, even in total darkness. The advantages of regular night vision are that a night vision scope is generally cheaper and more rugged than thermals, uses less battery power, and can see IR lasers or floodlights. Disadvantages are that it is easy to hide from someone using night vision with the use of camouflage, by remaining motionless, and by not using any light sources. While starlight scopes enhance the ambient light from the stars, the moon, distant streetlights, etc., you do not want to use starlight scopes or night vision in front of bright lights or especially sunlight. This will hurt your eyes or damage the scope. This type of night vision often comes with a cap that has a pinhole in it so that you can test out the functionality in full daylight without damaging it or hurting your eye. Just put the cap on and turn it on and it will work the same as if it were nighttime. With an IR laser mounted on your rifle you can engage targets almost better than if you were in broad daylight. You just have to make sure that the laser is zeroed and put it on the target, then pull the trigger. An Infrared laser is like an invisible laser pointer that you can only see with starlight scopes and night vision.

The main advantage of thermal optics is that it makes a warm target standout easily, though some optics are much better than others. It is very hard to hide from thermals, even if you remain motionless and camouflaged. Disadvantages to using thermals include that they are very expensive, especially if they are rugged and therefore designed to be mounted as a weapons scope. They also have difficulty in warm temperatures, such as when the hot summer sun heats up the landscape, or even in rocky terrain after the sun goes down and the rocks remain warm. Finally, thermals do not pick up infrared light or lasers, so you cannot use them to spot a weapons-mounted aiming device.

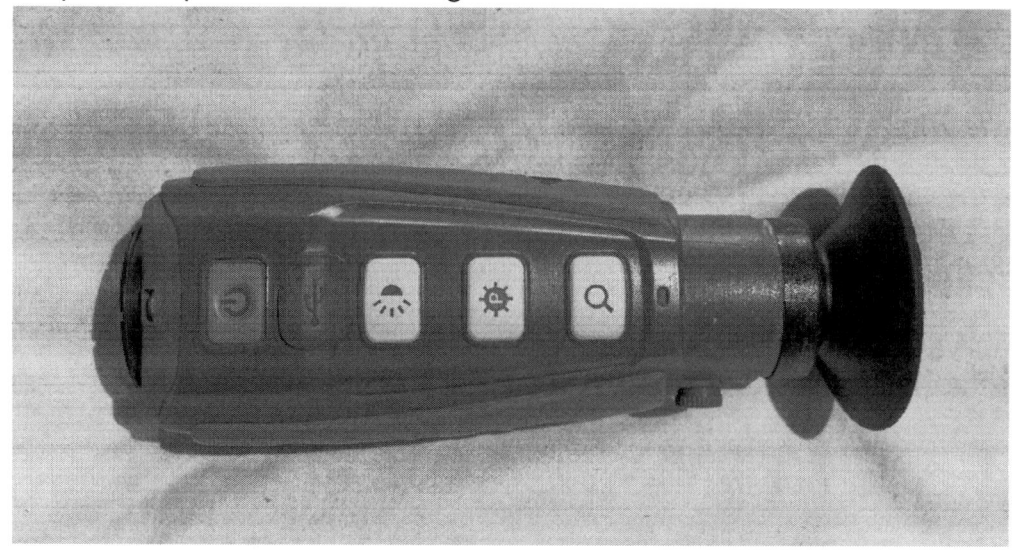

Illustration 75: Handheld Thermal Scopes are commercially available and relatively inexpensive; I highly recommend models that outline heat signatures in red or orange.

The only real economical solution that gives you the best of both worlds without buying an expensive thermal rifle scope is to use a handheld thermal scope to pick out targets, but then to use a night vision or starlight scope to fire at the targets. This works in a defensive position because you can set the thermals down easily and pick up your starlight device to fire. In the offense, I have found a creative solution. I have experimented and found that it actually works to mount a thermal device in front of one eye and regular night vision on the other eye. This takes some ingenuity to create the proper mounts, but you can actually see the thermal image and the starlight image together, even though you have one in each eye. It takes some getting used to, but it allows you to use an IR aiming laser mounted on your weapon, while you see thermal signatures. A cheaper technique is to mount the thermal device on a head mount but then use a visible aiming laser on your weapon. The fatal flaw here is that a visible laser easily allows your opponent to find your location, but that is what you get for being a cheapo.

Now, for those big spenders, you can get a high-quality thermal scope that is rugged enough to mount on any rifle, for around $10,000. The price on some of these has gotten more reasonable, but quality goes down with price. You can get another version with a little less optical clarity for $3000, but at this price you have to hope that it is rugged enough to withstand the recoil of your chosen rifle. Also, it is more difficult to scan for targets with thermals mounted on your rifle than when they are mounted on your head or helmet.

Illustration 76: It is very difficult to hide from a thermal scope on a rifle, like this one mounted on an AR-15, but they can be pricey.

Better yet, if you are really loaded, and can figure out how to legally do it, buy one of the new military hybrid night vision thermal goggle sets. These, "ENVG's" or enhanced night vision goggles, will run you over $20,000 but you will absolutely own the night. These systems allow you to see starlight images but added thermal highlights make warm bodies stand out like a sore thumb. The way that this works starts with a regular starlight scope, that is mounted to your helmet or head mount. This makes it easy to see objects around you, walk, and with practice, you can even drive. The thermal enhancement to this night vision means that anything that is warmer than its surroundings will be outlined in orange or red, things like humans, animals, or vehicles. Best of all you can still use your IR laser on your weapon while you have the goggles strapped to your face, meaning that you can still fire accurately, even from the hip.

Illustration 77: It is easy to Aim with Night Vision and an IR Laser, this one also has an IR spotlight which helps when no ambient light is available.

IR lasers

The main concern when purchasing an IR laser is ruggedness. You need to ensure that your laser is designed to take the shock from firing the rifle on which it is mounted. I have tested many IR lasers that were mounted on rifles and found that some of them break after firing only a few rounds through the rifle. I once was part of a small pilot program at the Infantry School in Fort Benning, Georgia, where we tested various night sights that were being marketed to the Department of Defense. We were tasked to not only fire with the lasers mounted, but we also had to drag them through a field exercise to include a parachute operation. We had our chance to test each sight. To the dismay and embarrassment of the manufactures, we broke 9 out of 12 of their high-tech weapons sights. For this reason, I will never forget that all the fancy options that are advertised for various laser weapons sights need to take a backseat to ruggedness. It doesn't matter if an IR laser has an attached flashlight, spotlight, or disco ball option. It only matters that it doesn't break when you fire with it mounted. This means that you need to be prepared to spend more on a laser sight that doesn't necessarily have a bunch of added options. Many of the cheap sights are smaller, because they don't have internal shock absorbers, or adequately robust wiring, so keep this in mind. Also, always shop for a sight that has a number of great reviews and be prepared to spend at least a couple of hundred dollars on a respected name brand. If you buy a $30 sight from China, it is guaranteed to break when you need it the most, just ask the Russians in Ukraine.

Zeroing your IR laser is also a very important skill. It starts with mounting the laser on your rail. Most popular AR style rifles can be mounted with a rail system that makes the mounting of your IR laser easy. I normally put some lock-tite on the threads of the mounting screws to ensure that they don't come loose later. Nothing will loosen a bolt like the repeated firing of a rifle. It is also a good idea to tie and tape your weapons sight down to your rifle, with something that will not melt on the barrel. Every infantry soldier has spent days in the field searching for lasers, optics, or weapons that have been lost on field exercises. These are sensitive items that you don't want to fall into the wrong hands or to be lost. When I was completing Officer Candidate School to become an Army Officer, we had to delay our graduation because Major Aziz, one of our international students from Jordan, had lost his laser that was supposed to be tied down. I was always very polite to Major Aziz; his manners were excellent, and I remember that he was extremely offended when anyone passed gas in his presence. Unfortunately, everyone else was also extremely offended by his loss of a sensitive item of equipment because instead of spending the weekend with our family members, we had to walk online for miles through the pine forests of South Georgia as it rained on us. We finally found it, and it had been run over, and smashed on a small dirt road. We still had to spend that last extra night in our sleeping bags, which is when I learned why the sleeping bag is sometimes called a fart sack. Poor major Aziz had a very smelly night, and was deeply offended (No, not by me.) The moral of the story is to find a way to tie down your optics and lasers to your rifle. My preferred technique is to put a zip tie around the laser or optic, then tight 550 cord (para-cord) around that, and to the stock of your rifle, using an end of the line bowline on each end. Then you burn the ends of the 550 cord so that they don't fray. You can also use 100-mph (duct tape) around each knot to ensure that it does not come untied or slip off the optic or rifle. You must also ensure that this does not interfere with the functioning of the rifle.

 Once you have secured your laser, a boresight zero is helpful. To zero an infrared laser you have to wait until dusk or nightfall when your night vision will function clearly. For an AR style rifle, you can take out the back pin of your rifle so that the upper receiver is separate. Then you take out the bolt. This will allow you to look down the inside of your barrel. Propping the weapon up horizontally and looking down the inside of the barrel, focus on a target that is at least 25 meters away, and strap your rifle down to a fixed object so that it stays focused on that target. A 25-meter zero works quite well for most gunfights that take place after dark. In some circumstances, a 200 meter zero will be more accurate and give you an advantage. This target obviously must be visible to the naked eye, so if it is dark outside, using a chem-lite, small flashlight, or other very dim light source will work well. Then, taking care not to move the rifle, turn the laser on. The laser will have a knob on the top and somewhere on the side that adjusts the aim of the laser. Adjust those knobs so that the laser points to the same spot that the barrel is focused on. Reconfirm that the barrel is sighted on the same point as the laser. Once you have done so, then your boresight is complete.

 You can then reconfirm your zero by shooting at a target 25 meters away, and then working your way out to 200 meters away. Your laser may be just a little off from your boresight and that is not unusual, just make minor adjustments as you go along to get the laser back on the target. Keep in mind that when you shoot with an IR laser, you are looking through your night vision, not looking down the barrel of your rifle. In fact, this is the only time that it is okay to shoot from the hip, as long as you can keep the butt of your rifle stable. Keeping your head and night vision away from the rifle will prevent you from damaging your night vision with recoil or powder burns. IR flashlights or good moonlit nights will help you get your laser zeroed out to 200 meters or so. Many head-mounted night vision optics are compatible with a 3-power magnifying attachment that can help you get that far zero nailed down with your night vision.

With a good tight zero, your rifle mounted laser with head mounted night vision is a serious force multiplier. As the U.S. military has repeatedly demonstrated multiple times in modern history, night vision allows one man to fight like 10. It will allow you to shoot, move, communicate, acquire targets, and re-engage in a flexible and rapid manner.

Radios

Many people would argue that cellphones have made things like walkie-talkies and even wristwatches obsolete. I love to wear a wristwatch because it helps me avoid staring at my phone all day, and helps keep me from being late, but my teenager gives me a lot of grief over it. She says that I am outdated and look ridiculous with a wristwatch. But what does she know, can you imagine James Bond without a watch? Most teens don't even know what a walkie-talkie is. If all cellular phone service suddenly failed, then suddenly there would be a huge shortage of wristwatches and walkie talkies. The point is that certain things that are obsolete and outdated right here and now in the United States are actually very necessary in third world countries and they will make a comeback once again in modern countries as the dark age chaos ensues.

Many people missed it because they live in a sheltered social media bubble, but when Covid-19 broke out globally, there were people in South Asia that went and cut tall 5G cellular communications towers with metal cutting torches, because they were convinced that the 5G was causing or exacerbating the virus. One of my farm customers is a holistic medical doctor that agrees that the relatively high frequency of the 5G ways do have a harmful effect on the human body. This is a whole different ball of wax that we are not going to dive into. But the point is that we live in a rapidly changing world, where new and complex technologies can be invented, installed, and wiped out in rapid succession. Sometimes to prepare for the collapse of complex but fragile new technologies, it is good to use an old, self-supporting back-up in order to preserve a semblance of self-reliance. During an outbreak of civil unrest, cell phones can be rendered useless by destructive mobs or even by a government crackdown. In such cases, a walkie talkie is a great backup plan so that you can communicate with neighbors, loved ones, and allies.

While the primary advantage of a walkie talkie is that it doesn't require a cell-phone signal, it also can be more cost effective, because there is no monthly cost or usage charge. Once you buy the radio, you are free to use it as much as you like. Also, walkie talkies work in areas regardless of the strength of a cell phone signal. In some remote areas, this can be absolutely critical. You can also use walkie talkies in a group or with a push of a button, you can just talk to one individual. They have the ability to stay on one channel, or in many cases, you can scan multiple channels. Secure channels are possible with added cost, and with a license you can increase the range of walkie-talkies.

First, know that a walkie-talkie is simply a two-way radio that is portable. While a regular radio can only receive, a two-way radio can both transmit and receive. There are two main frequency categories for two-way radios, UHF or VHF, meaning ultra-high frequency or very high frequency. UHF has a low band from 378-512 MHz and a high band from 764-870 MHz. VHF has a low band from 49-108 MHz and a high band from 169-216 MHz.

Lower frequencies, namely VHF, can transmit longer distances, while high frequencies, UHF, will have greater penetration ability through things like buildings, dense trees, and even into caves. Al Qaeda was known to use UHF radios to communicate in the cave networks in the Tora Bora region of Afghanistan and later in the Bajaur Agency of Pakistan. The reason has to do with the way that high frequency waves have shorter, more compact wavelengths that will bounce around corners, crevices, and through microscopic holes. Meanwhile low frequency waves are also longer and are easily blocked, but they require less energy to project long distances when unobstructed.

In the United States, all the legal frequencies are called FRS frequencies. FRS stands for Family Radio Service, and off-the-shelf walkie talkies will be FRS. They can only communicate with a maximum power of 2-watts, which restricts their range to under two kilometers or 1 mile under good conditions. These walkie-talkies are between 462 and 467 MHz, which is a good happy medium for communications, but the low legal power threshold of 2-watts severely limits you from communicating long range or from penetrating through barriers such as cave walls.

Technically you need a license to operate a GMRS or General Mobile Radio Service device. At the time of this writing, this is not being enforced and you can still purchase and use a GMRS radio. This allows you to go above the 2-watt threshold, all the way up to a 50-watt base station or repeater. A typical 5-watt handheld GMRS will reach out to 20-35 miles and with GMRS, you can also use external antennas and repeaters, further increasing your range. As I mentioned, you technically need a license, and this may start being enforced at any time. Power and battery requirements are higher for higher power GMRS radios.

Radio Type	Range	Typical Power of Handheld Model	Frequency	Characteristics
GMRS	20-35 miles	5 Watts	462-467 MHz	Happy Medium; Range and Penetration
FRS	0.3 to 1 mile	2 Watts (*Limited by Regulation)	462-467 MHz	Totally Legal, Short Range
VHF	Up to 20 miles	6 Watts	30-300 MHz	Can Travel up to 20 miles handheld, but easy to block
UHF	4-6 miles, 1.5-3 in urban terrain	4 Watts	300-3000MHz	Greater Penetration of Concrete, Steel, and wood

Table 8: Characteristics of Different Handheld two-way radios

Like other items, you get what you pay for when it comes to two-way radios. A pair of cheaper walkie talkies with a 1-to-4-mile range, a charger, and no special features typically will run you about $40 per pair (2023 dollars). If you bump up to a 35-mile range hand-held GMRS water-proof radio with a high durable rating, they will often be around $150 per pair. As I mentioned earlier, these GMRS radios currently require a license, but it has not yet been enforced. Many preppers will try to save and go with the cheaper radios, but these will generally break in short order, and have to be replaced. One hundred and fifty dollars is not a high price to pay for long range and dependability.

The batteries that your walkie talkie will accept are another important consideration. In the military, I preferred radios that accepted replaceable, disposable batteries, because I would go long periods without access to a charging station, or without time to charge for that matter. The military was buying the expensive replacement batteries anyway. On a homestead, where you pay for your own batteries, it is probably better to have the ability to charge your own batteries. When choosing a rechargeable battery, lithium-ion batteries will give you the longest battery life, hands down. There is also the option of getting a radio where the battery can be recharged, but you can also put in AAA batteries in the case that the rechargeable battery goes dead.

Whichever walkie talkie you decide to go with, remember that once the cell tower goes down, it will probably be too late to buy a two-way radio. We have become so accustomed to hearing from and keeping tabs on our loved ones that a two-way radio back up to your cell phone is a must for any survival situation in which modern technology and cell communications are no longer available.

Body Armor

When I first joined the Ranger battalion, I was sent to a platoon that had just lost soldiers to disciplinary action due to hazing activities. I was a replacement for those losses and when I arrived, I found that the disciplinary action had not stopped the hazing. It was like a fraternity on steroids with cool guns and gear. I experienced unlimited "smoke sessions," and I even saw one new private stuffed in a sleeping bag and then hung out of a third story window. I still have a picture of a new arrival taped to the wall with 100 mph tape (army duct tape). One of the most memorable sights was when I came home to the barracks one weekend to witness two drunk Rangers with their Ranger body armor on and a 9mm pistol. They were flipping a coin to see who would go first to get shot at. Private Snuffy shot first at Private Bootlace, hitting him square in the Kevlar plate. He was shaken up, but the light caliber round had just embedded itself in the plate without even cracking it. They were able to pry the perfectly formed round out with a knife. Next, Private Bootlace, who was more drunk, took a turn to shoot at Private Snuffy. Unfortunately, he missed the Kevlar plate but instead hit the outer tactical vest, which is finely woven, "bullet resistant" Kevlar. This part of the vest is designed to stop exactly what they were shooting, a 9mm round (with 50% probability of success). Private Snuffy doubled over with pain, then crumpled to the floor, seemingly dying, the wind knocked out of him. I rushed over to help, afraid at what I might find as I ripped off his vest. Oddly enough, the round was poking out from the inside of the vest, but barely stuck with the rear end still in the vest. The front portion had pierced the soldier's skin down to the top layer of meat, leaving a dry, dark red burn circled by brown, looking much like a bullseye. Lucky, lucky Private Snuffy.

From that day forward, I have taken a keen interest in learning the characteristics of the various types of body armor, and especially what type of rounds the body armor is designed to stop. Besides stopping power, the coverage area is also important; does the plate cover your entire torso? Are your sides vulnerable? Your groin? The final consideration, especially for someone like me with an Infantry background, is how heavy is your body armor? Is it light enough for you to shoot and maneuver? There are many variations of body armor, and many choices to examine.

Back in the 1990's when I first joined the military, effective body armor use was limited to special purpose units. Common units had "flak" vests, but these were heavy, cumbersome, and designed to protect you from shrapnel and casing fragments. They were also known as PASGT or Personnel Armor System for Ground Troops. These could stop a 9mm going no faster than 1400 feet per second (426 m/s).

Illustration 78: Author with the Original "Ranger Body Armor"

Back in the 1990's, in special operations units such as the Ranger battalion, we were issued RBA, or "Ranger Body Armor," which had Kevlar plates in the front and the back. Like a flak jacket, the base vest could protect from shrapnel, but the plates in Ranger body armor were also designed to protect from direct rifle fire, including Ak-47 and most 7.62 rounds, but only on the plates. These were some of the first "Level III" protective plates, but they were heavy, with the entire vest weighing in excess of 25 lbs., but they were still just about the best protection available at the time.

With the invention of ceramic ballistic plates, Ranger body armor was soon replaced by IBA, Interceptor Body Armor in the year 2000, weighing in at a much lighter at 16.4 lbs., and still giving protection against direct rifle fire to the ceramic plate area, and small caliber protection to the softer areas. As a light Infantry soldier at the time, I was thrilled to have a light but effective body armor option. The accompanying SAPI (small arms protective insert) plates were designed to protect up to 7.62 ammunition. Areas without plates still give protection from shrapnel and up to 9-mm. The interceptor body armor also came with add-on groin and neck protection from shrapnel, giving just a little more peace-of-mind to the wearer. Neck, throat, and groin protectors bring the weight of this body armor up to 33.1 pounds, doubling the weight and making this armor much more cumbersome. I never served in a unit that wore the additional protectors.

Illustration 79:The Author Wearing Interceptor Body Armor, So Light Compared to Ranger Body Armor

The Interceptor Body Armor has carried various types of plates throughout the years, as the U.S. government worked to provide greater protection to troops in conflict zones. The original SAPI plates (Small Arms Protective Inserts) gave level III protection. Later, in 2006, the enhanced version (ESAPI) gave level IV protection, meaning that they were more resistant to 30-06 armor piercing rounds with a steel penetrator. ESBI (Enhanced Side Ballistic Insert) provides the same protection but for the side of the body, basically in between the other two front and back plates. Finally, the military came out with the XSAPI, X-Threat Small Arms Protective Insert, which is heavier than the ESAPI, and provides slightly enhanced protection from M993 armor piercing sniper rounds, deemed a level 4+. This XSAPI has not been widely used because such a threat has not been prominent and the added weight for these plates was not seen as a good tradeoff for the slightly added protection.

Body Armor Type	Protects Against	Weight
PASGT Vest only	Fragmentation and 9mm round	12 lbs.
Ranger Body Armor	AK-47 (plate) 9mm (vest)	25 lbs.
Interceptor Body Armor with SAPI Plates	AK-47 (plate) 9mm (vest)	16.4 lbs. (without groin protectors)
Interceptor Body Armor with ESAPI plates	Armor Piercing 30-06 (plates)	18 lbs. (without side protectors)
Small Plate Carrier with ESAPI plates	Armor Piercing 30-06 (plates)	12 lbs.

Table 9:Modern Body Armor Characteristics; price goes up as weight goes Down and protection goes up.

Many special operators during the war on terror started to just wear plate carriers with the ceramic (usually ESAPI Plates). The reason is that the plates generally protect the vital organs, and the plate carriers are very light weight. While this gives you no protection to some of the less vital or flank shots, it does bring the weight of your body armor down to an amazing 12 lbs. Finding the right balance between enough protection and too much weight is a common theme when choosing the right body armor for you.

The only way to find maximum protective body armor at a relatively light weight is to spend more money. By spending more, you don't only gain a higher level of protection, but you can also bring the weight of the armor down. To make this choice, it is essential to understand the different levels of body armor, the weapon systems that they protect against, and the materials and weights of materials that they are made of. The protection levels are designed to counter the force of rounds, which is a combination of the mass of the round times the velocity ($F=M \times V$). Basically, levels I and II are like the old Army flak vests, and they will protect against most low caliber and low velocity rounds, namely, less powerful handguns. Level III protects against either a low velocity and high mass, or a high mass and low velocity round. These include 7.62 rifle rounds and .308 Winchester, full metal jacket. Level III-A starts to give you some protection against more powerful rounds, such up to 44-magnum lead rounds and most common AR-15 rounds. Level IV will protect against 30-06 armor-piercing rifle rounds, which are relatively high mass and high velocity rounds. I say relatively high because there are limits, meaning that no body armor will protect you against a fifty-caliber machine gun. The mass and velocity of that type of round will kill you through blunt or crushing force, even if you could hypothetically stop it from piercing body armor. You can start to see some manufacturers talking about level V body armor, but I do not believe that they intend to protect against larger, faster, or more powerful ammunition and weapons. Instead, level V body armor is a claim that has more to do with covering more of the body or giving the wearer greater dexterity by adding hinge points, or greater flexibility of the body armor.

When choosing body armor, there are three manufacturing materials that you will find. First, woven Kevlar is flexible and light, but generally provides only up to level II protection against small pistols, shotguns, and shrapnel. Steel can provide up to level IV protection, but it is so extremely heavy, that it normally renders a rifleman combat ineffective and you can't carry it far or move quickly without wearing yourself out. The one advantage that steel body armor has is that it is relatively cheap and can take more direct hits than ceramic body armor without being ruined. If you do get steel, make sure that you get steel with an anti-spall coating, otherwise you will just be creating shrapnel that can kill you just as easily as a bullet. Don't expect to walk around with steel body armor, it is so heavy that you will mainly be able to just sit there on your butt.

There has been no material more advanced than ceramics for creating body armor. Ceramic body armor is made from Alumina, Boron Carbide, Silicon Carbide, and Titanium Diboride. Ceramics can absorb more energy than metal, but they also break more easily. While ceramic body armor can break, it is not fragile like ceramic floor tile. Ceramics are sometimes combined with layers of metal to make a very strong combination sandwich-type armor plate. These are also referred to as steel core. Steel cores add a level of protection and also add weight to the body armor plate, but they won't get you above level III+. Level IV plates are made almost universally from pure ceramic composites. The best unclassified pure ceramic composite is the high-grade boron carbide ceramic, and it is also the most expensive.

If you remember anything from this section on body armor, first, remember to not shoot at each other to test out your body armor. Forget your safety, the body armor is too expensive to shoot at and risk damaging it. Instead, follow the advice written here, do your research, choose wisely, and only test it when you are in a real live shoutout situation. Body Armor is one of those purchases that you hope you will never need, but if you do need it, you will be extremely grateful to have it. Also remember that you get what you pay for, and you always should check the weight, size, protection level, and the material or type of ceramic used to manufacture your body armor.

Illustration 80: I Recommend and A small Army of Drones and Cameras to Help with Security on your Homestead

Drones

Where I live, we have a lot of annoying and sometimes dangerous trespassers on private land. There is public recreation land nearby, and somehow if land isn't fenced, people tend to treat it as public land, and when you confront them, they say something like, "I thought this was open country," or "I'm not hurting anyone, and I've been coming here for years." This type of response has brought out the worst of me in the past, and I am more recently trying to smile when I confront these people,... while standing a half mile away and dive-bombing them with my drone. (joke)

But seriously, it is difficult to get law enforcement to respond to remote areas like where I live, so we are often left to deal with situations on our own. And so, we have the Un-Manned Aerial Vehicle, better known as a drone. There is one scenic area along the public road bordering our land where trespassers enjoy gathering stones from the river to take home for their yard. In the past we have gone down and explained to the people that having "right of way" on a road doesn't mean you can stop and take things home or stop for a picnic or have a romantic rendezvous on private land. This is not only awkward but can also lead to an argument or even mutual threats to call the cops. We have found that it is much less awkward for us to send the drone, which buzzes like a swarm of bees and can hover around the trespassers and their vehicles, even dive-bombing them for good measure (just kidding). This drives people crazy, and they usually leave within 5 or 10 minutes. It's also a good way of saying, "I'm watching you fool!!"

Drones have been around for a relatively short amount of time, but they are here to stay, and their uses are multiplying every day. We have used drones on our ranch not only for trespassers but also to check livestock, plan out and map land improvement projects, track wildfires, scare off predators, and even blow the snow off our solar panels. It has really been a labor saver and a force multiplier.

When purchasing a drone there are several factors to consider, and a few options to keep in mind. Drones come with a huge price range and varying levels of quality. You can basically forget anything under $200 as it will not last long or be very functional. If you are willing to spend close to $1000 or more, then you can really start to experience the full range of functionality. I recommend purchasing only from well-established drone manufacturers, such as DJI. There are many emerging brands within this industry that do not have the experience or reputation to be trustworthy.

Besides manufacturer, it is important to consider the range that you can operate your drone within. The range of a drone is determined by communication method. Bluetooth and Wi-Fi are the typical solutions for flying a drone. These will generally not be particularly useful on a homestead of any size, except for taking pictures of your home. The longest-range commercial drones currently use cellular service to control drones. Just imagine taking a vacation but having a drone ready to fly at your homestead to go check on livestock or check the security of your property. This gets into the realm of fantasy-prepping, but we are after all in the 21st century. While cellular-controlled drones are not very common, there are now adapter boxes that you can purchase so that you can fly your drone from a remote location, even thousands of miles away. The first limitation with cellular drone control is that there is often a lag time in the communication. It is comparable to the delays and glitches that you may experience when calling someone using facetime. If you have a strong signal on both ends, then it may be feasible, but otherwise it may be difficult not to crash. There is also the issue of cellular networks going down in a disaster situation. If this happens, the cellular controls for a drone are rendered useless. In addition, I always like to visually observe the take-off and landing of my drone because of obstacles and to avoid a hard landing. If you plan on using your drone remotely, then you had better have a rock-solid take-off and landing zone.

Ease of take-off and landing, as well as reliability and fairly long-range capability is why I recommend using drones controlled by Wi-Fi signal. In this case, typically at the radio frequency of 2.4 GHz, a drone will travel up to 1.6 km from the operator, as long as there are not significant sources of interference. This Wi-Fi signal does not need functional internet to work, so it still can be used in a grid down situation. I have found that when I fly my drone at far distances, I have to fly at higher altitude to avoid interference. 2.4 GHz is a happy medium where you can get fairly long range, a good signal, and you don't use excessive battery power. It is possible to lower the frequency which will increase range, but this is often in violation of local laws or FCC rules in the U.S., because it may interfere with air traffic control or other users of radio waves. In certain situations, it is advantageous to use a drone that communicates using 5.0 GHz, which is less susceptible to interference. Things like garage door openers and Wi-Fi devices may interfere more easily with a 2.4 GHz drone. A 5.0 GHz drone can transmit more data at faster speeds, but it is limited to 500 meters range between the controller and the drone. There are also a few drones in existence that use 1.2 GHz, and are capable of longer ranges of operation from the operator, up to 10 km or 6 miles! This frequency also has better penetration through trees and even walls. The problem is that in most states you are not legally permitted to use 1.2 GHz without a license. This is because it is frequently in use by commercial aircraft and could interfere with their communications. Another problem with a drone with a 6-mile transmitter to receiver range is that if the drone goes down at long range, you may not be able to find it without a beacon. When shopping for a drone, keep in mind that many vendors advertise the range of the drone as the distance it can fly without recharging the battery. For this reason, make sure that you know the frequency at which the drone operates which will give you the true range from operator to aircraft.

Another consideration when choosing a drone is GPS capability. Many higher-end drones have a GPS feature which will allow the craft to make adjustments when flying in high winds, typically up to 15 miles-per-hour. This means that if you are hovering over a target, the drone will stay in place, even with high winds, because it is maintaining its GPS location, regardless of wind. If your drone does not have GPS, then it should only be flown in very calm wind conditions, because it can be easily blown off course and even lost. My drone has GPS, but can be flown without GPS, in what is called "Atti mode," short for "attitude" mode. This means that the drone will fly at a specific altitude, but not at a set position left or right, forward or back. In Atti Mode, a drone will drift with the wind, and you have to hit the brakes when you want to stop, by flying in the opposite direction. In other words, it is very difficult to fly, and you have to make constant adjustments. It is really best not to even try to fly it in high wind. While flying my drone in the past, I have lost GPS signal in high wind and the drone continued to drift with the wind until I was able to do an emergency landing in a field about 500 meters or 1600 feet from my location. In the case of a true global collapse or world conflict, you may lose GPS signals, or the signals could be blocked by government powers. This is why it is a good idea or contingency to have a drone that can work in both GPS mode and in Atti Mode.

There are a number of emerging technologies that can boost your drone-flying capabilities immensely. One expensive but extremely useful accessory that is available for many high-end drones is a thermal camera. A good thermal camera can distinguish a warm object against cool surroundings often from 2km or 1.25 miles away. This can be used to instantly spot even well-camouflaged trespassers, individuals that are lost, lost livestock, or even to track down a game animal that was shot but then lost. Thermal cameras are one of the most important tools of the U.S. military because it is very difficult to conceal a thermal image. Even smoke and fog do not completely conceal a thermal image.

Drones are a huge force multiplier for your survivalist kit that will take your preparedness to the next level. It is a good idea to wait to purchase a drone until you have acquired other more basic survival items, and you have enough capital to buy a drone with adequate capabilities. You want to make sure that the drone has excellent battery longevity, and that it has adequate range from operator to drone, for your specific needs at your location. This might mean ensuring that the range will allow you to monitor key areas of concern or potential danger areas on your homestead. You also want to understand the frequency that your drone will operate at, so that you understand its range and capabilities. Next, make sure that it has GPS mode, but that it can fly in Atti Mode when required. Finally, make sure that your drone is compatible with other accessories that you might want to purchase in the future, such as a thermal camera. This means of course that the camera can be removed and replaced, or that there is space for an auxiliary camera. If you keep these factors in mind when purchasing your drone, then you will truly have a force multiplier and the first aircraft for your own personal homesteading air force!

Cameras and Early warning Devices

The advent of game and hunting cameras has been a huge help to my homestead security. I use over a dozen game cameras on my property, not only to keep track of the movement of deer, but also to detect unwanted trespassers. A few years ago, during deer archery season, I had been keeping an eye on a stream crossing near one of my favorite deer stands. My game cameras will transmit images back to a home camera that is at my house. One afternoon while checking the home camera, I saw the images from my favorite stream crossing, first a couple of small does, and then of a young man with jeans, a cheap rifle, a big cheesy knife on his belt, a red bandana on his neck, and a goofy tattoo of a deer on his forearm. I guess he was trying to shoot a deer to match his tattoo. He was chasing animals around on my property instead of putting in the time and effort like most deer hunters do by developing their own hunting spot. There is plenty of public land in my area such as the National Forest and so trespassing and poaching on private land is just a super nasty thing to do. Since my high-quality photos showed him clearly chasing deer, I was able to get the game warden to issue a citation both for hunting with a rifle during archery season without a permit, and for trespassing. Later, the offender decided not to pay or to go to court, so he got to spend a little time in jail. For me, it was priceless, and the cameras paid for themselves right then and there.

Any run-of-the-mill game camera can help record not only animals that you would like to hunt for food, but also trespassers, and even criminal activity. A few options that I look for are what kind of batteries they have, if and how they will transmit images, resolution, and type of night vision. First, I prefer the larger D cell batteries as I think they last longer and hold up better to cold weather. Cameras that have small solar panels for charging are a great idea, just be prepared to spend a little more time setting up your solar panel properly.

Some cameras do not transmit images, while others use cellular networks, and a third option uses FM signals to transmit back to a home camera. While a cellular signal can send images to your phone anywhere that you receive phone service, there is generally a monthly charge depending on volume of data. In addition, a cellular signal is obviously dependent on a cell phone tower, which may or may not work in a grid down situation. For this reason, I enjoy having cameras that send images using an FM signal. They do not rely on any external power grid or communication network. Instead, there is a direct radio transmission from the remote cameras to your home camera. The only downfall is that you must check the SD card on your home camera in order to know if an image has been sent. With a cellular transmitted image, you can have an app on your phone that will notify you that your game camera is active. So, there are pros and cons to each.

Illustration 81: A Poacher that I nabbed on my Property with the Use of Image-Transmitting Cameras, "Smile, Big Cheese!"

Virtually all game cameras now come with night vision, but it is highly advised to purchase a game camera that can work in stealth mode. This means that you want it to take a photo without a visible flash that will scare off game animals and warn nighttime trespassers that they are being recorded. Game camera resolution varies from 2 MP to 20 MP, with the higher resolution being better. The only downfall is that a high resolution photo can take a long time to send back to your home camera or through your cell phone network. I have found that a happy medium is to choose a camera that will record photos between 5 MP and 7 MP so that it is still sufficient to ID a trespasser but will not take all day to send the photo back to you. On either type of camera with a decent signal, you should have a photo within 1 to 2 minutes, allowing you to keep an unblinking eye fixed on the security of your homestead.

Chapter 15: Making the Leap, How to afford your Rock n' Roll Survival Lifestyle!!!

My main hesitation in writing this book was my concern that many individuals may see the inevitability of the coming collapse and then end up in debtors' prison because they spent beyond their means to prepare. While the collapse of our current prosperity seems inevitable, the uncertainty of how events may unfold means that you need to prepare for a number of contingencies. One such contingency is the strong possibility that in the United States, our own government may violate our inalienable rights in an effort to avert the coming crisis. Debtors prison, seizure of property, and confiscation of weapons are all very real possibilities. If the collapse does come, you do not want to be in prison when it happens. Here is some advice that will help ensure that you are at your homestead retreat when that time comes.

First, always spend within your means. Prepping is what you do with expendable income. Treat it like a useful hobby and work extra hard to earn extra money for prepping. Our economy, our civilization, and even our planet is like a giant ship that may start to turn in the wrong direction, but it takes a long time to fully turn towards and reach a tipping point. Being truly prepared means being ready for a disaster to happen farther down the road than you expect or for it to unfold slowly. So don't go into debt or use your credit cards to fill your gear locker with expensive gadgets.

If you have a family, please take care of all their needs first. Don't expect your kids to be survivalists. The best way to make them tough and competent is to nurture them with healthy food, a good education, sports, and enjoyable outdoor activity. They should be given challenges that they enjoy and that help them learn. In some of my officer training they taught us that a good leader sets the example and that through competence, confidence, and an optimistic, genuine tone of voice, people do want to follow you. I have found this particularly useful as a parent. Leaders that use condescension and unnecessary scolding will soon find themselves alone. If you want to be a tough guy and live in the dirt, go without food, and without a bath, then you can do that yourself and don't drag some poor kid into it. The whole point of preparedness from a family perspective is to take better care of your loved ones, so think of family homesteading as an adventure, like a fun camping trip, a fulfilling agricultural hobby, and a fitness routine all rolled into one.

Second, never break the law. There are plenty of legal preps that will keep you busy without crossing that line. One of the most common avoidable violations of the law involves firearms. You may believe that you have an unlimited right to own and carry firearms, but the days of the colonial militia have long passed, whether you like it or not. Law enforcement is almost always on your side if you are a good person so don't endanger yourself or them by carrying something that you are not allowed to have or in a way that is dangerous or illegal. Locking guns up properly is not an inconvenience, but being in jail is an actual inconvenience.

Third, pace yourself and set achievable goals in a logical order. Rome was not built in a day, and neither is a homestead. Set up a list of tasks and then break them down into sub-task lists. They may look like this abbreviated example:

1) Establish Off-grid Water Source
    a) Drill well
    b) Install Solar Pump
    c) Install Water Storage Tank
2) Start Garden
    a) Till Soil
    b) Remove Rocks
    c) Add Mulch
    d) Add Irrigation
    e) Plant
3) Build Root Cellar
4) Learn to Can Vegetables
5) Build Security Fence and Driveway Gate

Obviously, you need to expand and fill out this list which, incidentally, can look much like the contents of this book. The point is that a list will help you focus on one item at a time so that you don't get overwhelmed. Long journeys are accomplished one step at a time.

Finally, I have a few suggestions on how you can afford to add preparedness to your lifestyle, but everyone's financial situation is going to be different. One important consideration is that it is much easier to build and develop a sustainable and prepared homestead while you are actually living there. This means that certain types of jobs are more compatible with rural homesteading than others. Recently, remote working and an abundance of IT jobs that can be done remotely have led to more people being able to move far from cities and even from the suburbs into rural America. Even in my remote location, we have many new neighbors that work remotely. This can be an ideal situation in which you can earn an income not only to support yourself financially but also to build important homesteading preps like fences, barns, water wells, greenhouses, etc.

There are also many people who earn decent paychecks working in rural communities. There can be financial and government incentives to teach in underserved communities that are in rural areas as well as perform healthcare jobs in these types of communities. This means that you can earn a living and still have just a short commute to and from your homestead in fairly remote areas. I have one friend that has built a very respectable homestead, with livestock, gardens, and excellent food storage. He is a high school teacher and takes advantage of holidays and summer breaks in order to work on preparedness, which is something that he enjoys and uses as a way to stay in shape.

A third way to finance and afford a homesteading and preparedness lifestyle is to start a business from home. I have yet another neighbor, that has started a very successful business selling spiritual craft items and books from her home, on venues such as etsy. This neighbor and her family have been able to even hire employees to produce their craft items that are sold primarily online and shipped all over the world. They have even built a workshop next to their home in the country, to expand the business. By getting creative, you can build the lifestyle that you want wherever you would like to live.

Finally, my family has created a livestock operation on our farming homestead, that helps us turn our pastures and meadows into profit, which is generally reinvested into our land and farm. We sell primarily live grass-fed beef and high-quality show and breeding stock to include registered Boer goats, Registered Angus cattle, and miniature cattle. We have also occasionally sold timber products, hay that we bale, and even produce. For a time, we sold at a local farmers market, which helps you bring every possible retail dollar back to your operation. As we grew, we began to sell enough volume that wholesale markets and live animal sales became more feasible and easily managed. What I like about selling agricultural products is that if you can produce enough food to sell to others, you can easily produce food for yourself and your family. While it is hard to establish an agricultural business that is profitable, the skills that you learn could very well help your family survive and thrive in meager times or during an economic crisis or even social collapse.

While it may seem strange to speak of crisis and collapse in the same sentence as profit, skills, and family adventure, these are all part of the joys, sorrows, and challenges that we face in life. While we don't choose the times, nor the events that occur in our lifetimes, we do choose how we react to those things. While I have laid out several possible scenarios of what may occur in the near future, the only prediction that is certain, is that we will all find many surprises in this life. What I have attempted to do, is to give you an expanded toolkit to deal with what many of us believe will be very challenging times. One thing that should give you comfort is that your ancestors are survivors. The human race has survived ice ages, droughts, war, and famine. Many individuals did not survive, but those that were willing to adapt, face adversity, and think creatively, and optimistically were the ones that made it through, and they have passed those very same genes and instincts on to you.

Let us not fear change, even if it may bring unexpected challenges. Instead, let us embrace newfound skills, rely on ourselves and our loved ones in a way that builds love and respect for one's self and each other, and let us be prepared in a stoic manner, thinking critically and pragmatically about what lies ahead, and how to not only survive but also to thrive in whatever future that lies ahead.

About the Author: Joshua Morris has a Master's Degree in Engineering from Missouri S&T and taught Environmental Science at Drury University for seven years, including a class on Sustainable Living at his own Homestead and Farm. Joshua is also an expert in Societal Collapse and the Demise of Civilizations with a Bachelor's, Summa Cum Laude, in History and Anthropology from Columbus State University. In the United States Army, Joshua served in the 1st Ranger Battalion, as a Ranger Instructor, an Infantry Officer and Company Commander, and finally as an officer in the Engineer Corps. Highlights of his career include parachuting into Iraq in March of 2003, graduating Ranger School, Sniper School, Pathfinder School, and Jumpmaster School. He is an expert in survival, marksmanship, off-grid construction, and engineering to include renewable and sustainable building techniques. He currently owns and manages Cold Spring Farm, LLC, a renewable-powered and self-sufficient homestead, and renowned livestock operation in the Heart of the Ozark Mountains. He has been recognized twice by the Farmer Veteran Coalition for his military record and subsequent success as a farmer, receiving the Fellowship Award in 2022 and the Kubota Geared to Give program award in 2023. He was also chosen as a guest speaker for the Farmer Veteran Stakeholder Conference in Washington, D.C., in 2023, gave a TEDx talk about the Homestead of the Future at Missouri S&T TEDx in 2019, and was the guest speaker for the Midwest Grazing Conference in 2019, where he showcased his farm's restored "Native Warm Season Grass Prairie." Today, Joshua continues to grow his farm, which has raised production year over year since its inception, and he continues to raise awareness about self-reliance and sustainability in order help individuals deal with turbulent times and be prepared to "Thrive in the Coming Dark Age."

What would it look and feel like during a Global Collapse on your very own survival homestead? This apocalyptic scenario is the setting in my Dystopian novel, '**Saeculum, Book1: Collapse'.** Meet Jacob Moreland, Prepper, Homesteader, and Combat Veteran, as he fights to save his family and farm from a Catastrophic Global and Societal Collapse. Jacob, former Army Ranger, and his beautiful wife Ana, the fierce daughter of a Croatian Sniper, have prepared their family for every contingency. Or have they?? Jacob and Ana are masters of self-reliance and experts of both off grid survival homesteading and self-defense. Their intriguing global connections grant them an inside look at the sinister geopolitical maneuvers behind the calamitous events and a first row seat to observe the seismic forces of this terrifyingly plausible scenario. See how they fend off one disaster after the next as they witness and struggle to thrive on their flourishing homestead in this perfect storm, "Saeculum": Dystopian Global Collapse and Homestead Survival Novel, Book 1.

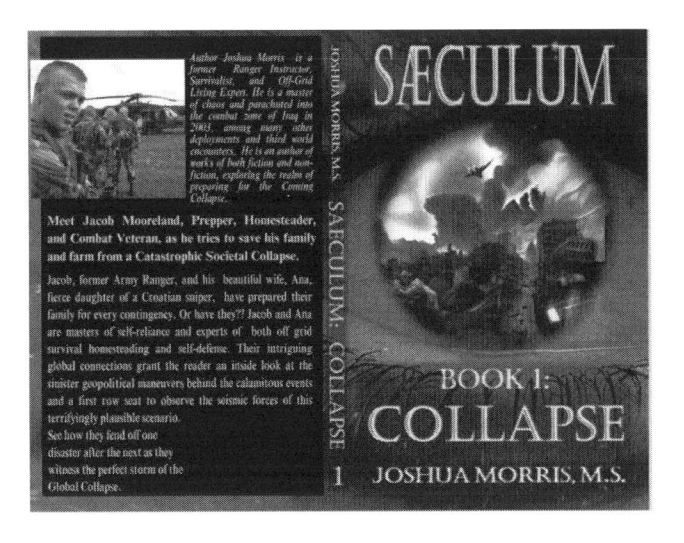

SCAN HERE!

SCAN HERE!
For My Youtube Channel

SCAN HERE!
For My Preparedness
and Homesteading
Facebook Group